Transpositions
Migration, Translation, Music

Contemporary French and Francophone Cultures, 79

Contemporary French and Francophone Cultures

Series Editor

This series aims to provide a forum for new research on modern and contemporary French and francophone cultures and writing. The books published in *Contemporary French and Francophone Cultures* reflect a wide variety of critical practices and theoretical approaches, in harmony with the intellectual, cultural and social developments which have taken place over the past few decades. All manifestations of contemporary French and francophone culture and expression are considered, including literature, cinema, popular culture, theory. The volumes in the series will participate in the wider debate on key aspects of contemporary culture.

Recent titles in the series:

ALISON RICE

Transpositions

Migration, Translation, Music

LIVERPOOL UNIVERSITY PRESS

First published 2021 by
Liverpool University Press
4 Cambridge Street
Liverpool
L69 7ZU

British Library Cataloguing-in-Publication data
A British Library CIP record is available

ISBN 978-1-789-62111-2 cased
ISBN 978-1-789-62112-9 limp

Typeset by Carnegie Book Production, Lancaster
Printed and bound by CPI Group (UK) Ltd, Croydon CR0 4YY

Contents

Figures

Introduction

Tracing Transpositions, Transposing Traces

Alison Rice

> Il y a, entre la parole du poète et le silence
> des transpositions d'empreintes — sur fond d'abîme.
> (Abdelkébir Khatibi, *Vœu de silence*)

> Même le souffle, tu le transposes.
> (Hélène Cixous, "Le Théâtre surpris par les
> marionnettes")

Transpositions. The term is rich with meaning that can be applied to diverse domains. It is a word that can be played with, modified, and ultimately adapted to a variety of settings. In music, to transpose a piece means to rewrite it, or to play it in a key or pitch other than the one in which it was originally written or in which it is usually performed. To transpose a story or incident means to take it out of its usual setting or time and relocate it in another. It is important to note that the verb can also refer to the action of making two things change place; for instance, a transposition on the page can constitute a reversal of the normal order of two letters in a word. Transpositions can therefore upset expectations, whether orthographic or symphonic, and destabilize conventions that are sometimes taken for granted. Something may be lost when a transposition occurs, but there is also much to be gained when a text or a score contains a change in key, a modification in tonality.

This volume takes as its starting point this evocative term in order to engage in a wide-ranging examination of francophone literary, musical, cinematic, theatrical, and artistic creations from the 1990s to the present. All contributors are literary scholars who explore in these pages the interpenetration of various languages and art forms in French-language texts that are influenced by linguistic and cultural factors reflecting other places, notably Mediterranean and European, and that contemplate what these geographical and political designations mean at present, and how they are making an impact on creative work in many forms.

The works under study in this volume exemplify transpositions in various senses, ranging from literary translation to musical innovation to artistic interaction among different genres, particularly with respect to contemporary migrations toward Europe. "Transpositions" serve as a conceptual tool for contemplating how writers, filmmakers, playwrights, composers, and artists are inspired to transpose migratory realities into a different linguistic and cultural context in an effort to make them legible or audible in fresh ways. The works in French that embody such transpositions are often situated beyond the borders of what is customary. They nonetheless communicate a great deal as they incorporate inventive elements that push the limits of formal composition to represent—and speak to—an expanding audience.

Traces of Influence

This volume finds inspiration in a growing critical corpus to which many of its authors have contributed, including the 2018 *Critically Mediterranean: Temporalities, Aesthetics, and Deployments of a Sea in Crisis*, coedited by yasser elhariry and Edwige Tamalet Talbayev, the 2017 book by Talbayev titled *The Transcontinental Maghreb: Francophone Literature across the Mediterranean*, the 2014 study by Claudia Esposito on *The Narrative Mediterranean: Beyond France and the Maghreb* and the 2016 monograph by Hakim Abderrezak, *Ex-Centric Migrations: Europe and the Maghreb in Mediterranean Cinema, Literature, and Music*. The last publication in particular serves as an impetus for reflections in the present volume, not only because of its focus on texts depicting migration, but also because of its examination of creative work in a variety of genres. *Transpositions* likewise explores very different texts in an effort to discern how recent innovations in French reveal that this language is moving in interesting directions that demonstrate newfound influences, many of which are related to migratory movements.

The present volume also examines conceptions of Europe and the Maghreb, paying special attention to connotations of the Mediterranean Sea that owe much to the insights of Iain Chambers in his 2008 publication to which the title of the first part of the book pays homage. A number of the central themes that interweave and echo throughout *Transpositions* are articulated in a powerful passage on language in *Mediterranean Crossings*:

> Language not only travels elsewhere—the French of Assia Djebar, the English of Derek Walcott—but is literally elsewhere. Representation, its languages, codes, and technology, is not only translated and transformed but also resisted, revalued, and rerouted. Obstacles lie in the path of language itself. Music, sounds, and silence, like extraneous linguistic, cultural, and historical matter strewn across the page, announce refusals to adopt a readily recognized representation or to settle within the boundaries of preexisting meaning. Here in the stubborn insistence of the nontranslatable, there in linguistic darkness, emerges the challenge of the incomprehensible, of what remains within and yet resists translation. Words slip away in the excess of language that refuses to mean, that deliberately confuses the desire of self-confirmation with the oblique insistence of an elsewhere that repeats and renews language in a reply to power. (Chambers 2008, 21)

The emphasis placed in this passage on "music, sounds and silence" and their capacity to make meaning in ways that are often difficult to decipher carries resonance for the evocations of music and other art forms that are contemplated in this volume. The intimation at the close of this quotation that repetition is able to acquire significance that may contribute to the renewal of language and its ability to resist both preestablished import and structures of power is crucial to considerations of transpositions in various artistic creations. Language travels in many senses, and literary and artistic developments embrace innovative forms related to language that also exceed it by incorporating other means of expression, "music, sounds, and silence," that are redolent of histories and traditions and that can be modified through movement. Rather than finding anchor in immovable ideas of nation and identity, the writers, artists, filmmakers, and playwrights whose work is under study in *Transpositions* hint in their creations at new, wide-reaching points of reference that bear witness to fluid influences and a plurality of interactions on a variety of levels, many of which are the result of recent transcontinental movements that render impossible any static conception of being—or belonging.

Tracings through *Transpositions*

This volume could be read in a number of ways, as various chapters in different parts of the book contain themes that respond to each other in vibrant tones, and I will suggest different lines of approach in a moment. The groupings that have been created have their own logic, which I will mention first. Movements across the Mediterranean Sea come to the forefront in the first three chapters, each of which focuses on a particular creative work. Madeleine Dobie elucidates in a chapter devoted to the experimental documentary film *Les Messagers* (2014) the changing character of migration as an increasingly non-linear experience that necessitates new forms of representation like this one, situated at a remove from the predictable narratives of the traditional novel or feature film. In order to respect the particular temporality of tentative journeys, *Les Messagers* gives precedence to speech, providing migrants with the opportunity to express themselves in a work that privileges self-representation and respects multilinguality without ignoring the challenge that this linguistic diversity poses to the tasks of translation—and subtitling—in the film, questions that carry weight not just artistically, but also politically and legally. In Dobie's analysis, this documentary film is exemplary of a trend of new, intermedial practices that combine a variety of genres ranging from video and photography to poetry and testimony to music and dance as they navigate among languages to transpose a version of a tenuous reality onto the screen.

The roles of author and subject are transposed in the collaborative textual undertaking that is *Mopaya: récit d'une traverse du Congo à la Suisse* (2010), a work that foregrounds the migratory movements of Gabriel Nganga Nseka, a psychiatric nurse from the Democratic Republic of the Congo who relates his story to the Swiss author Douna Loup. The result is a co-authored text (Loup and Nseka 2010) that highlights the transposition of the protagonist's oral testimony into the literary work, bringing to print a written record that disrupts preestablished notions of authorship, and features a collective approach that gives textual form to an expression of experience that often remains unheard. Kate Averis determines in Chapter 2 that this collaborative publication draws from testimony in ways that give the migrant some control over a personal account that, when converted to print, comprises new francophone migrant writing in a trans-Mediterranean Afro-European context.

Algerian-born author Malika Mokeddem's *La Désirante* (2011) is a novel that grapples with questions of identity and relationality in the Mediterranean, exposing new migrations in this space that are accompanied by minor subjectivities in Edwige Tamalet Talbayev's analysis in Chapter 3. The figure of the African American singer Nina Simone appears in this work of fiction, her voice merging with the movement of the sea and revealing the hybrid cultural forces that come together in this context. The French language significantly serves as a lingua franca in certain exchanges depicted in this work, and this form of expression is affected by different dialects and various vocabularies whose intermingling and interpenetration put into question any dominant versions of the former tongue of imperialism. The resulting textual transpositions constitute what Talbayev terms "transcontinental Maghrebi *francophonies*," expressions that are transformed by the solidarity made possible through the interactions of Mediterranean crossings.

The probing reflections of Abdelfattah Kilito on the possible interpenetration of languages within the literary text are the focus of Jane Hiddleston's insights into *Je parle toutes les langues, mais en arabe* (2013) by this Moroccan writer in Chapter 4. Other languages can be transposed in the written work through translation, which eschews the oft-expected exoticized forms of multilingualism that serve only to bolster the dominant language in which they are composed. Instead of inserting a word or two here or there to appease a certain public, literature is capable of rendering multiple languages in a text that at first appears to belong to a single linguistic tradition. Monolithic, monolingual structures are questioned and ultimately nuanced in Kilito's perspective, whether it is a matter of Europe as an entity—which is not contained or self-same—or untranslatability, which is both a point of contact and a marker of cultural difference. It is crucial to note that transpositions are not only linguistic but also historical in this analysis, as proverbs and figures from different cultures and periods find their way into new work. Ultimately, literature that is not exposed to other languages, in the broadest sense of the term, will wither, for it requires continual translation and transposition in order to thrive.

In an exploration of a textual collaboration between Moroccan writer Abdellatif Laâbi and artist Mahi Binebine, Claudia Esposito suggests that it is in the interstices of form, in the transpositions of mediums, that aesthetic innovation can appropriately address, and perhaps redress, historical wrongs. Chapter 5 demonstrates that *Pourquoi cours-tu après la goutte d'eau?* (2006) constitutes a compelling reworking of an earlier publication by Laâbi of *prosoèmes*—a form between prose and poetry—in an edition that includes images created by Binebine so as to transform the text. This publication is indeed a powerful visual and political statement that probes the dynamic movement between the semiotic systems that it incorporates, pointing toward a plural cultural aesthetic that is part of a long-standing tradition in the Maghreb to seek connections between different art forms and revel in the possibilities that are at once inside and outside language.

The question of visibility—of who has the right to see and who can be seen—that emerges in Esposito's contemplation of the interaction of word and image finds a parallel in Olivia Harrison's consideration of theater's ability to offer a new mode of seeing that which has been removed from the field of visibility in her examination of Mohamed Rouabhi's play *El menfi/L'exilé* (2000) in Chapter 6. This work for the theater is not immediately legible as French or Algerian, in part because it transposes questions of race and nationality—as well as the eponymous question of exile—across diverse yet similar imperial formations, staging encounters between different figures ranging from Palestinians to Native Americans to second-generation Algerians in France. The playwright brings together a range of media—such as film, dance, music, spoken word, and photography—and inserts multiple languages, including French, Arabic, and sign language, into his theatrical creation. This transnational and comparative method employs transposition in a manner that highlights forms of migrant relationality that might otherwise be overlooked because they don't fit neatly into established categories of evaluation.

Transpositions of exile are also at the heart of Olivier Morel's study of artistic and literary reflections by Algerian-born writer Hélène Cixous in Chapter 7. This prolific author has worked with director Ariane Mnouchkine and the Théâtre du Soleil troupe—many of whom are refugees—on collaborative endeavors such as *Le Dernier Caravansérail (Odyssées)*, a 2003 theatrical production that became a film three years later. This creation represents a transposition, not only in its translation of the greatest Mediterranean poem ever written, but also in its embodiment and enactment of meaning through the possibilities of theatrical incarnation and liberation. The filming of this performance constitutes more than a transformation of the theatrical representation into a motion picture, for the camera doesn't hesitate to reveal what is happening behind the scenes, illuminating artifice beneath the magic of make-believe on stage. The action within this play is inseparable from the movement of migrations, and the chapter underscores a similar conception of movement that defines art as that which crosses, in a paradoxical gesture that entails remaining the same and opening up to difference.

Cinematic works that explore education through the lens of the postcolonial classroom exhibit movements across register, genre, and medium. Attentive to the different ways in which adaptation and non-adaptation play out in Abdellatif Kechiche's *L'Esquive* (2005) and Laurent Cantet's *Entre les murs* (2008), Nicholas Harrison reveals in Chapter 8 that the prestige of various works of French literature is relative and subject to change as the educational setting reacts to and reflects shifting cultural values. The transposition of an eighteenth-century play by Marivaux to a twenty-first-century school in the Parisian *banlieue* in Kechiche's film not only adds rich layers of intertextual signification to the cinematic work, but also brings some of the cultural prestige of the canonical playwright to this production. This French literary tradition fades into the background in Cantet's transposition of François Bégaudeau's eponymous novel (2006) to the screen. The film version has abandoned the nineteenth-century play by Alfred de Musset that figures in the book in order to focus on other forms of creative expression—including photography—that prove to be effective pedagogical tools to engage students in a different classroom. Harrison insists on the importance of distinguishing between theatrical and cinematic creations and reality, emphasizing that reactions to plays and films will differ according to individual interpretations of the multiple meanings that each text contains; the educational environment must allow for these divergences, especially when these works inspire students to consider their own identities in relation to the alterities communicated therein.

Two more recent films, Philippe Faucon's *Fatima* (2015) and Fejria Deliba's *D'une pierre deux coups* (2016), demonstrate how a variety of identities are now making their way to the screen and thereby contributing to a transformation of long-standing stereotypical conceptions of the French nation. Vinay Swamy provides insight in Chapter 9 into this phenomenon by evoking the advent of tempering in Western music, which enabled modulations from one key to another to take place without flattening differences of pitch or losing color. This development can be likened to the creation of new cinematic works that reveal a nuanced alternative approach to the tried topic of integration and unveil the complex ways in which immigration is contributing to the creation of rich variations of what it means to be French. Both *Fatima* and *D'une pierre deux coups* participate in this movement that allows for the appreciation of difference within a republican framework. These films permit other languages to emerge as legitimate forms of expression and provide an opportunity for actors and directors with ties to the Maghreb to tell their stories in refreshing ways that skirt traditional forms and elude classification in productive fashion.

The music, speech, and sound effects that contribute to cinematic creations are often overlooked because of preoccupations with the visual aspects of this medium, but Hakim Abderrezak argues in favor of according more attention to sound in studies of film. Indeed, soundtracks constitute crucial components of the filmmaking process that are often manipulated in order to modify meaning and shape the affective impact of a motion picture. Highlighting the aesthetics, ethics, and politics that are caught up in the act of editing and translating sound, Abderrezak focuses in Chapter 10 on the choices that directors make in cinematic representations of clandestine movements across the Mediterranean, homing in on the options adopted by Merzak Allouache in *Harragas* (2009). Transpositions in this analysis refer to sea-crossings that are traversals, in a nautical sense, enacted by vessels that deliberately avoid a straight line, but the term also designates what happens on the screen after editorial work has been performed to insert voiceovers, ambient noise, and other sounds—including silence—that have a considerable impact on the cinematic work. The decision to include both Arabic and French in this film is rife with significance. The film's face-off between languages carries implications that can be traced back to a colonial past that has been transposed into multiple rifts in Algeria in the present, breaches of communication and confidence that have pushed so many to desperate measures to reach northern climes.

The southern shores of Europe, including such locations as Marseilles and Barcelona, make their way into the itineraries of the musicians and writers Edwin Hill evokes in Chapter 11 as contributors to transpositions that take place in their lives and work. The album *Sketches of Spain* (1960), recorded by Miles Davis and Gil Evans, constitutes an early example of black transnationalism in the Mediterranean that resonates with Jean-Claude Izzo's Mediterranean *noir* trilogy, published three decades later. The Jamaican poet Claude McKay, in novels published in the 1920s and 1930s, contributed to the creation of transnational circuits of the Mediterranean, paving the way quite literally for black transnationalism and inserting music into the literary text in ways that explore hybrid possibilities in narrative form. McKay's travels and writings can be considered to be a series of transpositions, capable of transforming Europe in light of diasporic movements that might be seen as precedents to the more recent displacements of migration. The musical transpositions that help to establish the multiple transnational connections that contribute to black Mediterranean thought are not only geographical, but historical as well, recalling centuries-old musical traditions from West Africa that have been transposed over space and time. Cross-media exchanges and jam sessions in various settings might therefore be understood to draw inspiration from strains of the past in order to point toward a more auspicious future.

The three different novels that I examine in Chapter 12 portray movement in written works infused with musical passages that accentuate the migratory experiences of displacement and distress by simultaneously emphasizing loss and continuity. Songs continue to hold profound emotional meaning for individuals, even if they are cut off from the past that these melodies once accompanied. The juxtaposition of *Tropique de la violence* (2016) by Nathacha Appanah, *Celles qui attendent* (2010) by Fatou Diome, and *Faire l'aventure* (2014) by Fabienne Kanor, publications by authors who hail from Mauritius, Senegal, and France respectively, allows for comparisons among different innovative texts. These three works of fiction demonstrate various approaches to the inclusion of multiple languages that reveal how itineraries can affect the French tongue, not only in oral interactions but also in written renditions. These works contemplate voyages across bodies of water that are sometimes Mediterranean, but also located elsewhere, and Appanah's novel most explicitly invites readers to expand their notions of what constitutes Europe by situating this literary creation not in France or an adjacent country on the continent, but rather on the French overseas department of Mayotte in the Indian Ocean. This transposition is met with other transposed modes of literary composition that present with pressing detail the dilemmas faced by individuals who risk their lives by engaging in perilous crossings that were perhaps initially intended to be linear, but that in many cases result in a circling back to the beginning, to a starting over in a repetitive cycle that Madeleine Dobie evokes in this volume's first chapter as an increasingly common condition among migrants who may never reach their final destination. Unforeseen textual developments in new keys are necessary to relate evolving patterns of coping and communicating, leading to new creative works—in a transposed tongue—that are attuned to these circular movements of migration.

Varying the Volume:
Alternate Itineraries Throughout This Text

This collection therefore examines how a variety of elements from other languages and soundscapes are being transposed into French and are effectively *transposing French*. And since transpositions are inherently open to variation, so too is this text receptive to many possible itineraries within the present volume. Those who hope to contemplate definitions and illustrations of the Mediterranean might adopt a line of reading that begins with the first three chapters, especially Chapter 3, then hops to Chapter 7 before proceeding to peruse the final three chapters. Those who wish to focus on film could start with Chapter 1 and its analysis of the documentary *Les Messagers*, then move to Chapter 7 with its examination of the filming of the play *Le Dernier Caravanserail*, before taking in Chapter 8 on *Entre les murs* and *L'Esquive*, followed by Chapter 9 on *Fatima* and *D'une pierre deux coups*, and then Chapter 10 with its focus on Merzak Allouache's *Harragas*. Those who desire to concentrate on theater can turn toward Chapter 6 on Mohamed Rouabhi, Chapter 7 on Hélène Cixous, and Chapter 8 by Nicholas Harrison on the transposition of *Le Jeu de l'amour et du hasard* by Marivaux in a contemporary film. Those who want to examine multilingual practices might begin with Chapter 1 on multilinguality in film, then turn their attention to Chapter 4 on multilingualism in written work, as theorized by Abdelfattah Kilito, and then take a look at the exploration of plurilingual passages in novels in Chapter 12. The work of Moroccan theorist Abdelkébir Khatibi comes into play in Chapters 3, 4, and 5, wherein concepts such as *interlangue* and *intersigne* prove to be productive in contemplating complicated linguistic and semiotic questions that emerge in literature and art. The theorization of the term "minor" takes place in different ways that present another path through this text, including rich developments of the minor in Chapters 3 and 6 that are followed by evocations of minor transnationalism in Chapter 11 that draw from the collective volume of that name whose editors Françoise Lionnet and Shu-mei Shih identified "minor cultures" as the "products of transmigrations and multiple encounters," and emphasized the "relational" aspects that have contributed to their makeup (Lionnet and Shih 2005, 10). And for those who aspire to migrate through considerations of migration, a suggested line of approach would start out with the first three chapters, move on through Chapter 7, and continue the trip with Chapters 10 and 12. Musical and artistic pathways can also be carved out, as can many other thematic and theoretical routes through this collective work that, faithful to its title, is open to transpositions of every sort.

A Grace Note

"Pour sol, la musique" is an affirmative statement in which Hélène Cixous transposes the frequent claim of writers that their territory, or their homeland, is located not in a national assignation, but rather in a linguistic entity. For this author, as for many other artists and poets, neither her country of origin nor her current place of residence determines her identity. Rather than believing she belongs to a single language or literary tradition, she draws from a wealth of inspirations to create indefinable multilingual, multicultural texts in French. This poetic pronouncement from Cixous's written reflections on her theatrical work *Tambours sur la digue* suggests that the earth is a note on the musical scale, and that the writer finds her ground, and her grounding, in music. *Transpositions* seeks to unearth this phenomenon by examining a contemporary corpus in new terms, at once transposing traces and tracing transpositions.

Works Cited

Abderrezak, Hakim. 2016. *Ex-Centric Migrations: Europe and the Maghreb in Mediterranean Cinema, Literature, and Music.* Bloomington: Indiana University Press.

Appanah, Nathacha. 2016. *Tropique de la violence.* Paris: Gallimard.

Chambers, Iain. 2008. *Mediterranean Crossings: The Politics of an Interrupted Modernity.* Durham, NC: Duke University Press.

Cixous, Hélène. 1999. "Le Théâtre surpris par les marionettes." *Tambours sur la digue,* 115–24. Paris: Théâtre du Soleil. https://www.theatre-du-soleil.fr/fr/a-lire/le-theatre-surpris-par-les-marionnettes-4155. Accessed March 29, 2021.

Crouzillat, Hélène, and Lætitia Tura, dir. 2014. *Les Messagers.* France: The Kingdom/Territoires en marge. DVD.

Diome, Fatou. 2013 [2010]. *Celles qui attendent.* Paris: Flammarion.

elhariry, yasser, and Edwige Tamalet Talbayev. 2018. *Critically Mediterranean: Temporalities, Aesthetics, and Deployments of a Sea in Crisis.* New York: Palgrave.

Esposito, Claudia. 2014. *The Narrative Mediterranean: Beyond France and the Maghreb.* Lanham, MD: Lexington Books.

Kanor, Fabienne. 2014. *Faire l'aventure.* Paris: J.C. Lattès.

Khatibi, Abdelkébir. 2002. *Vœu de silence.* Casablanca: Editions Al Manar.

Kilito, Abdelfattah. 2013. *Je parle toutes les langues, mais en arabe.* Arles: Actes Sud.

Lionnet, Françoise, and Shu-mei Shih. 2005. "Thinking Through the Minor, Transnationally." In *Minor Transnationalism*, edited by Lionnet and Shih, 1–23. Durham, NC: Duke University Press.

Loup, Douna, and Gabriel Nganga Nseka. 2010. *Mopaya: récit d'une traversée du Congo à la Suisse.* Paris: L'Harmattan.

Mokeddem, Malika. 2011. *La Désirante.* Paris: Grasset.

Talbayev, Edwige Tamalet. 2017. *The Transcontinental Maghreb: Francophone Literature across the Mediterranean.* New York: Fordham University Press.

PART I

Mediterranean Crossings

CHAPTER ONE

Migration and Representation, from the Bildungsroman to the Testimonial Genre

Madeleine Dobie

In the final frame of *Les Messagers* (2014), a documentary filmed largely in Morocco in which African migrants speak about their journeys and their encounters with Moroccan and Spanish border control agents, one of the witnesses states his conviction that "Nous sommes les messagers de l'époque" (Crouzillat and Tura 2014). Following these words, the screen turns black and we hear the voices of migrants pronouncing the names of loved ones who have died, mostly by drowning in the Mediterranean. If, on a first level, this pronouncement, from which the film takes its title, refers to the testimony that the migrants who appear in the film provide about the harsh conditions experienced by migrants and the deaths occurring daily in the Mediterranean, in a broader sense it suggests that the plight of these migrants has something to tell us about the age in which we are living. Migration is as such understood as a message: an act of communication addressed to the world. *Les Messagers* is one of a growing number of experimental films and texts devoted to the subject of contemporary migrations. Over the last decade, productions in a wide array of genres and forms, including documentaries, docufictions, video installations, and graphic novels, have attempted to render the situations that migrants regularly experience. The proliferation of these alternative genres and media reflects the urgency of their subject. It also stems from concerns about the assumptions and worldview underlying the public discourse of the "migrant crisis"—not least the perception that there is a fundamental and enforceable distinction between "refugees" and "economic migrants." In their experimental forms, these works also respond to the unique linguistic, documentary, and ethical challenges involved in depicting migration in its dominant contemporary forms. Departing from established conventions for representing migration they explore new intermedial practices combining video, photography, poetry, testimony, music, and dance, and navigating among a multiplicity of languages.

Migration, History, and Genre

Migration and diaspora have long been important subjects of francophone literature and film. They are, notably, central to the rich tradition of *beur* and *banlieue* novels and films that flourished in the 1980s and 1990s. These works, which have attracted a wide and varied audience, speak to the dominant patterns of migration of the twentieth century. For several decades, and especially in the postwar period, France heavily recruited industrial and agricultural workers from its colonies, especially those of North Africa. In the mid-1970s, in response to a global recession and rising unemployment, this migration was halted and the borders closed. Ultimately, the families of North Africans who had been working in France were permitted to join them, creating a diaspora of close to a million people with roots in the Maghreb. This history of relocation— essentially one-directional and permanent—has provided the principal framework for thinking about migration to France at the level of the state and the media. The literary and cinematic works that engage with it, works such as Azouz Begag's autobiographically inspired novel, *Le gone du Chaâba* (Begag 1986) or film director Malik Chibane's "urban trilogy," *Hexagone*, *Douce France*, and *Voisin, Voisine* (Chibane 1993, 1995, 2004), explore hybrid French–Maghrebi cultural and linguistic identities and the dynamics of structural racism. Though *beur* and *banlieue* memoirs, novels, and films are diverse in many respects, their dominant form is the Bildungsroman. Many narrate formative journeys across space, language, and social class. Their protagonists travel from Africa to France and from the shantytown or housing project to the middle class and a literary career. Although these works are often and appropriately read as testimonies to multiculturality and the social marginalization that can accompany it, they are also interwoven with the official discourse of "integration," i.e., the elusive goal of being recognized as "fully French." Writers such as Begag have authored powerful accounts of growing up in marginalized communities with parents who spoke little French. By virtue of their own accomplishments, however, they also exemplify the ideals of integration.

Since the closing of the borders of France and other European nations in the mid-1970s, the landscape of migration from Africa to Europe has gradually yet profoundly changed. Much migration from the southern shores of the Mediterranean now occurs outside official channels. As citizenship laws have tightened, so have those governing the apprehension and detention of undocumented migrants. The frequent labeling of migration as "illegal" or "clandestine" expresses a new reality in which migrants have come to be viewed as criminals and subjected to parallel regimes of policing and punishment (Manfredini 2019). The monitoring of migration now extends far beyond the borders of Europe. Under contracts with the European Union, the security forces of several North African nations dispatch migrants to their own southern borders, often in the Sahara Desert.[1] Migration has lost the essentially linear character that it had in the mid-twentieth century. Many migrants today repeat the same journey over and over and the destination they are aiming for might change along the way. Some refer to themselves with resigned humor as *aventuriers*, acknowledging the unpredictability of the roads on which they're embarking. Their travels may stretch over a period of years, becoming a near-permanent condition and mode of identity. The Kenyan writer Shailja Patel speaks of a transition from the Pan-Africanist and anticolonial era of Negritude to that of "Migritude" (Patel 2010).

The concept of Migritude is also an acknowledgment of the rising number of people seeking safer conditions and better opportunities outside their home countries. The UNHCR estimates that there are over 70 million forcibly displaced people in the world, less than half of whom are officially recognized as refugees (UNHCR n.d.). As Stephen Smith has argued with regard to Africa, demographic growth in the global South along with local and global factors such as climate change and political instability mean that this number is highly likely to rise (Smith 2018). Immigrants have all too often been targets of xenophobia and racism, but these forces are particularly acute today, as the rise of anti-immigrant populist parties in many parts of the world illustrates. Perhaps the most chilling development in this regard, however, is the tacit

---

1   The EU's external border agency Frontex also conducts search operations within the territorial limits of several African nations. On these various types of agreements, see Dünnwald 2011.

recognition of migrants as disposable people. The term "undocumented" indeed unintendingly captures the fact that migrants have become, in the words of Seloua Luste Boulbina, "supernumerary" others whose deaths are unrecorded and whose lives count for nothing (Luste Boulbina 2018). The changed realities of migration have, in turn, reshaped the sphere of activism and modes of representation. Whereas in the 1980s and early 1990s, social and political movements such the French organization SOS Racisme focused on citizenship rights and eliminating bias and discrimination, today, activists question the exclusive linkage between rights and citizenship, with some calling for the recognition of mobility as a human right. Thomas Nail, Sandro Mezzadra and Brett Neilsen among other scholars have called for a "kinopolitics" that supplements and challenges nationally and regionally based laws and policies (Nail 2015, Mezzadra and Neilsen 2011).

In this new landscape of migration, xenophobia, and activism, previous literary and cinematic modes of representing migration have lost much of their currency. The Bildungsroman form, for example, seems less appropriate given that the journey from migration to citizenship and some form of integration has become less common than other, less linear circuits. As recent examples show, neither the novel nor the feature film is particularly well suited to portraying the open-ended and unpredictable journeys of today's migrants. For example, these forms tend to efface the slow, repetitive time of migration by compressing it into the bounded temporality of a plotted narrative and to transpose a multilingual reality into a monolingual framework.

In veteran director Merzak Allouache's film *Harragas* (Allouache 2009), a group of young Algerians seeking better opportunities and greater personal and political freedom, try to reach Europe in a small motorboat. The film portrays the despair and boredom that has led many young Maghrebis to take this kind of risk. But the migration story is complicated by the introduction of a "bad guy," who improbably threatens his companions with a gun in the middle of the Mediterranean. Allouache perhaps felt that the sea-crossing alone did not provide enough dramatic interest to sustain a feature-length film. In Boris Lojkine's *Hope* (Lojkine 2014), a woman from Nigeria and a man from Cameroon fall in love as they travel across Africa from the Sahara to the Mediterranean. The film draws effectively on the techniques of realism—for example, by filming on location and casting former migrants in the principal roles—to depict aspects of migration that have received little media coverage in the mainstream media. It draws attention to the dangers and forms of hardship and violence encountered by migrants crossing the Sahel and the Sahara: sites that have received less media coverage than the situation in the Mediterranean. This documentation is, however, combined problematically with the devices of fiction, notably a plot centering on a love story that builds toward a tragic ending. One problematic aspect of the sentimental focus on the two protagonists is that it generates a good migrant/bad migrant dynamic: the lovers are thwarted at every turn by other Africans, with little acknowledgment of the wider political and economic frameworks that incite people to migrate or/and to try to profit from this movement. The realist mode of the film conceals these and other representational choices that reflect an underlying eurocentrism. For example, while Lojkine's decision to organize the film around two people who don't share a common language draws attention to the multilingualism of migration, his choice to focus on the romance between a francophone and an anglophone character erases the presence of other, non-European languages. Had the film depicted, say, two Nigerian partners, they might have spoken to each other in a mix of English and Hausa or Yoruba.

Recent novels about migration raise different though related questions about temporality, narrative structure, and the use of individual stories to represent broader currents of experience. For example, the renowned Moroccan writer Tahar Ben Jelloun's *Partir* sensationalizes migration by focusing disproportionately on sexuality as a motive and as an opportunity for migration (Ben Jelloun 2006). Laila Lalami's debut novel *Hope and Other Dangerous Pursuits* portrays the life situations and hopes of four different Moroccan migrants who cross the Mediterranean in a zodiac (the inflatable motorboats often used by migrants) (Lalami 2005). Unlike *Harragas*, it focuses more on the before and after than on the crossing itself. Though less one-dimensional than Ben Jelloun's novel, it too draws on cultural stereotypes, as the characters veer from Islamic fervor to prostitution. In this narrative-driven work, each character's story takes shape as a subplot, effacing the broader quotidian forces the lead people to uproot themselves at risk of their lives.

The representational choices of these and other recent depictions of Mediterranean migration reflect the conventions associated with mainstream genres as well as the market forces that drive the film and publishing industries, even at the "indie" or "auteur" ends of the spectrum. They also raise some questions about perspective and voice. *Beur* and *banlieue* narratives were in many cases authored by writers or filmmakers drawing retrospectively on their own life experiences or those of their parents. By contrast, current films and novels made about the migration taking place today are almost all the work of people observing these realities from a certain distance. Though some of the novelists who write about migration, e.g., Ben Jelloun, Lalami, or the Senegalese writer Fatou Diome, are themselves migrants, the circumstances of their migration in the 1970s, 1980s, or even 1990s were in many ways different to the experiences of the characters they portray.[2] It seems legitimate to ask how deeply such works are grounded in knowledge of migrants' experiences, and whether they contribute to the pervasive erasure of their perspectives and voices.

The limitations of established genres as vehicles for representing the contemporary experience of migration is one explanation for the proliferation of new and alternative genres and media. The most compelling recent explorations of migration experiment with new, hybrid, and intermedial forms. These include experimental documentaries such as *Les Messagers*, *Qu'ils reposent en révolte* (George 2010), *Babylon* (Chebbi et al. 2012), *Brûle la mer* (Berchache and Nambot 2014) and *La Traversée* (Leuvrey 2013), docufictions such as the Syrian–Italian film *Io sto con la sposa* (Augugliaro et al. 2014), in which a group of migrants and journalists film their progress across the borders of several European nations under the guise of a wedding party, and Swiss–Gabonese writer Bessora's graphic novel *Alpha: d'Abidjan à la Gare du Nord* (Bessora and Barroux 2014), which comes with a mock board game, "Dinghies and Ladas."[3]

I would also include in this grouping avant-garde feature films and novels that challenge the conventions of their mediums. Among these are the Algerian director Tariq Teguia's films *Rome plutôt que vous* (Teguia 2006) and *Gabbla (Inland)* (Teguia 2008), which, while they portray fictional characters and situations, privilege the experience of space and the modalities of representation over storytelling, and the late Algerian writer Hamid Skif's hallucinatory novel, *La géographie du danger* (Skif 2006), which unfolds in the mind of a migrant who has withdrawn from the dangers of the outside world into a small room. *La géographie*

---

2   Diome's novels explore migration in a number of different contexts, some close to her own experience as a student. I am thinking here primarily of *Celles qui attendant* (Diome 2010), in which a group of women await the uncertain return of sons and lovers who have crossed to Spain.

3   *Alpha*'s illustrator, Olivier Barroux, has said that he chose to draw the story in felt-tip pen because he wanted to use tools to which a migrant might have access.

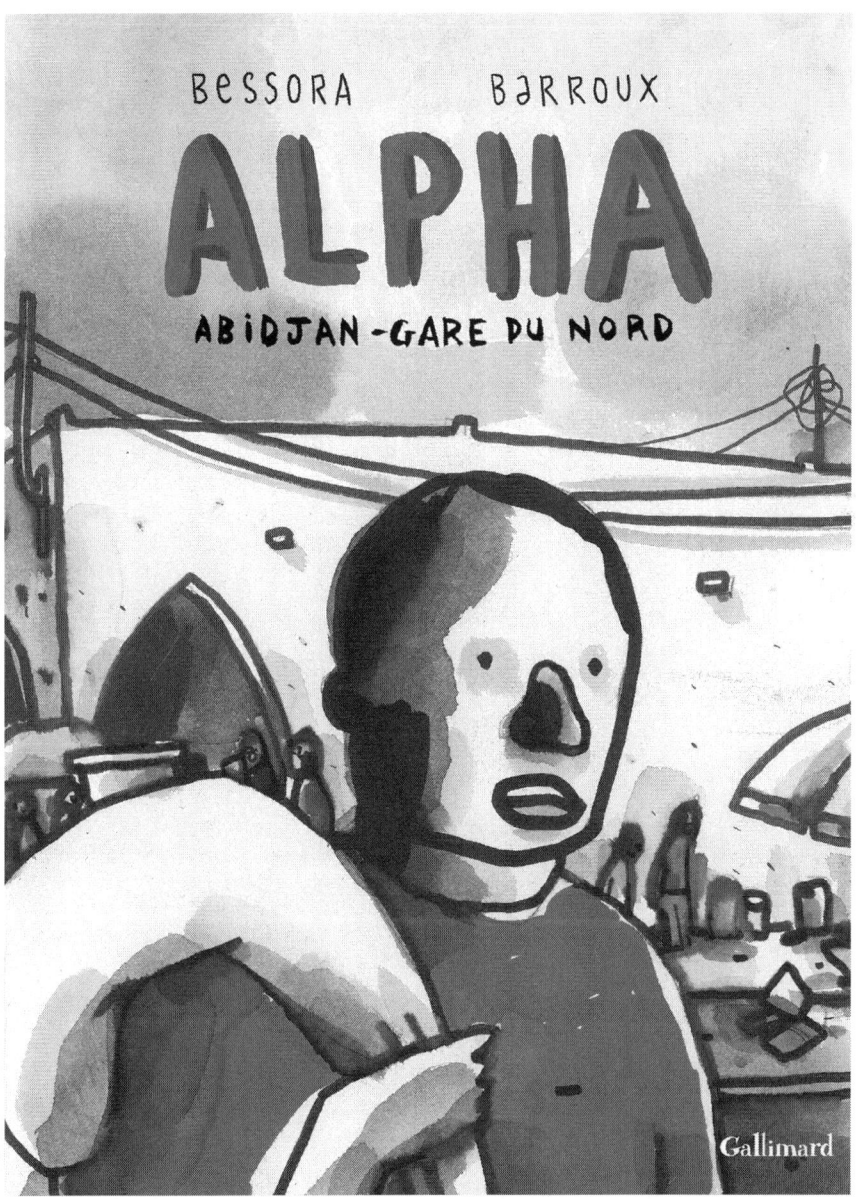

Figure 1.1 Book cover, *Alpha: Abidjan-Gare du Nord*, Bessora 2014.
Courtesy of Editions Gallimard.

du danger has been adapted as a dance performance by choreographer Hamid Ben Mahi (Ben Mahi 2010). Dance has become an important medium for the creative exploration of migration. It also figures in the documentary *Brûle la mer*, and in recent projects such as Marlene Miller and Sandy Silva's *Migration Dance Film* (Miller and Silva 2016), a collection of eight short dance films exploring the meanings of migration in different contexts. Perhaps this is because, more than any other medium, dance apprehends bodies moving through space, and the interplay of mobility and constraint.

Though extremely diverse, these works reflect a set of shared priorities and strategies. These include: breaking with narrative and visual conventions to render the unpredictable character of contemporary migration and as a gesture of rupture with social and political regimes that dictate what can be said and heard—for example by exploring alternatives to structured and plotted narratives; attending closely to the lived experience of time and space, and demonstrating concern with the perspectives from which stories are told and heard. Below, I focus on two interconnected features of many recent representations of migration in which these different concerns converge: the privileging of testimony as a narrative mode and the emphasis placed on multilinguality and translation.

Migration and Testimony

Testimony about circum-Mediterranean migration is gathered and presented in a variety of forms in recent art projects. In *Qu'ils reposent en révolte* (George 2010) filmmaker Sylvain George carries a handheld camera around Calais, the site of the notorious "Jungle" camps, filming urban landscapes and speaking with migrants about their experience. In his later film, *Paris est une fête* (George 2017), on the other hand, he accompanies a single teenaged migrant living on the streets of Paris, viewing the city from the alternative, mobile, and embattled perspective of an undocumented migrant. Both films create a strong sense of place, and contrast the interiority expressed through testimony to the migrants' relegation to exterior spaces. Italian director Gianfranco Rosi's acclaimed film *Fuocoammare* (Rosi 2016), filmed on the island of Lampedusa, also observes the encounter between local lifestyles and global migrations. Though the film is not based primarily on testimony, a sequence in the middle of the film invites us to think about migration itself as a form of testimony. When a group of Christian migrants who have been rescued at sea gather for an improvised ceremony, a man from Nigeria proclaims "This is my testimony," then proceeds to recount why he and his companions left Nigeria and what kinds of pain and loss they experienced on their journey. In his account, the evangelical practice of bearing witness before God merges with a secular tradition of addressing the human community.

The proliferation of testimonial approaches to migration can be traced to several different factors. Testimony foregrounds the unique subject position of the speaker. As the case of testimony given in a court of law exemplifies, no one else can speak in the place of a witness. To bear witness to an event is to do something other than giving an historical report. It entails evoking what happened in all of its material detail and affective dimensions. Testimony establishes a connection between a speaker and a listener or audience and may, by extension, have political or legal repercussions. In the words of Shoshana Felman:

> To testify—before a court of law or before the court of history and of the future ... is more than simply to report a fact or an event or to relate what has been lived, recorded, and remembered. Memory is conjured ... essentially in order to address another, to impress upon a listener, to appeal to a community. (Felman 1992, 204)[4]

This address to a community, along with the potential for material consequences, is in turn a reason for the cultural prestige of testimony. To bear witness to an event is to acknowledge its moral gravity.

The prestige of testimony is hard to disentangle from its association with the memory and commemoration of the Holocaust. Several of the most widely known and admired works about the Holocaust, for example Elie Wiesel's *La nuit* (Wiesel 1958), Charlotte Delbo's Auschwitz trilogy (Delbo 1970), Marcel Ophuls's documentary *Le chagrin et la pitié* (Ophuls 1969) and, above all, Claude Lanzmann's *Shoah* (Lanzmann 1985), privilege testimony over third-person narrative and archival footage. The critical literature on these and other works has, in turn, provided a rich set of reflections on the moral and aesthetic qualities of testimony. Both Annette Wiewiorka and Shoshana Felman have dubbed the post-Holocaust era the "Age of the Witness" or "Ère du témoin," suggesting that testimony gained importance as a response to a

---

4   This observation appears in a chapter devoted to Lanzmann's Shoah in which Felman discusses, among other cases, the Eichman trial of 1961.

"crisis of witnessing" in which the evidence of crimes was systematically erased (Felman 1992, 206, Wiewiorka 1998). A parallel argument could be made with respect to migration, which has occurred largely outside the public gaze, and with little public effort to record or commemorate the toll of suffering and death.

Recent public debates have contrasted the cultural prominence of Holocaust memory in countries such as the United States and France to the lower visibility of other traumatic episodes in the past, notably slavery and colonial violence. Responding to these conversations about enduring eurocentrism, a number of scholars have highlighted connections between the persecution of Jews during the Holocaust and racism and genocide in colonial context, and argued that memory has at times circulated "multi-directionally" between European and colonial contexts.[5] Current engagement with the humanitarian disaster of migration adds another element to these connections. The turn to testimony in this context evokes Holocaust memory, indirectly conveying recognition that the deaths of migrants are not "accidental," but rather the symptoms of a new kind of warfare and the transnational violation of human rights.[6] At the same time, the association between migration and the Holocaust recalls the forced displacements of the Second World War and the global refugee crisis that took shape in its wake.[7] But there are also differences between these two contexts of testimony. Whereas testimonies relating to the Holocaust were, in the majority of cases, collected and made public long after the events the witnesses describe, those about migration bear on situations that are still unfolding. They call as such, not only for a moral response, or in a few cases for legal sanctions or reparations, but also for urgent political and economic interventions.

In the francophone context, the use of testimony to explore the history and transgenerational legacies of migration was inaugurated by Yamina Benguigui's ground-breaking documentary, *Mémoires d'immigrés, l'héritage maghrébin* (1997). Benguigui conferred dignity on immigrants,

5   On multidirectional memory see Rothberg 2009, Rothberg, Sanyal, and Silberman 2010 and Sanyal 2015.

6   The language of warfare runs through several recent works about migration. The first part of Sylvain George's film about migrants in Calais (George 2010), for example, is entitled "Figures de guerre" and several the witnesses interviewed in *Les Messagers* speak of "war" and "destruction," characterizing their efforts to scale the border wall at Melilla as "assaults" and "attacks."

7   On memory and human mobility see Erll 2011.

long an invisible or scapegoated figure in French society, by recording a collection of oral histories. Divided into three parts titled "Les pères," "Les mères," and "Les enfants," the film depicts people who have migrated from the Maghreb to France looking back on the experience of migration, racism, and marginalization, and reflecting on the intergenerational struggle for integration and recognition. This testimonial practice is, however, quite different from more recent examples in the sense that while *Mémoires d'immigrés* records the pain of exile and the humiliations of racism, it is oriented, like Holocaust testimony, toward the preservation of memory and its transmission to future generations rather than, as in the recent works that I examine below, toward the exposure of an ongoing situation. The testimonies that appear in Benguigui's film complement established historical narratives about migration, as the film's three-part organization illustrates. By contrast, in works produced in and since the 2000s, testimony is presented more open-endedly and as an incitement to historical reflection.

Witnesses to a Disappearance

Filmed on the Moroccan Mediterranean coast in and around the Spanish enclave of Melilla and in the Tunisian port of Sousse, *Les Messagers* juxtaposes witnesses speaking about their experiences with panning shots of the landscape that from time to time freeze abruptly into stills, a visually disorienting cinematography that blurs the separation of past, present, and future. The film's primary subject is the pervasive social and political erasure of migrants' deaths as reflected in the scarcity of public records and the disappearance of their remains. The filmmakers visit sites where migrants have passed but where few traces of their passage remain, and interview witnesses who occupy different positions in relation to this disappearance. The film includes testimony from migrants who have witnessed the deaths of companions and loved ones, fishermen who recall seeing dead bodies in the water and wondering who these people were, and a parish priest who presides over a churchyard in which migrants' bodies are buried, for the most part anonymously. In different ways, and with different degrees of concern, these speakers confirm that people are disappearing, yet no one is keeping track.

Les Messagers has affinities with documentaries about the Holocaust such as *Shoah* and Alain Resnais's *Nuit et brouillard*. Like these works, it refrains from showing images of violence or human remains, electing

Figure 1.2 Still from *Les Messagers*, Hélène Crouzillat & Laetitia Tura, 2014.
Courtesy of Laetitia Tura and Kingdom Films.

instead to make indirect visual allusions to histories of violence and suffering. This is in part a moral choice, grounded in respect for privacy and dignity, but it also reflects these films' shared concern with the erasure of evidence and the disappearance of the traces of death. In *Les Messagers*, as in *Shoah*, much is made of the contrast between tranquil and sometimes beautiful landscapes and the wrenching stories told by the witnesses. In lieu of graphic images of death, *Les Messagers* presents visual metaphors. When a frame freezes into a still, we don't always know what we're looking at. A mound of earth might indicate a burial place, a bundle of fisherman's netting suggests a shroud, but nothing confirms these interpretations. Viewers are guided to look beyond the visible for traces of the invisible or evidence that has been erased.

The testimony of the migrants is a necessary complement to the film's emphasis on the erasure of traces. In the absence of records and physical evidence, they alone can bear witness to the lives that have been lost and the circumstances in which these deaths occurred. But although

Figure 1.3 Still from *Les Messagers*, Hélène Crouzillat & Laetitia Tura, 2014.
Courtesy of Laetitia Tura and Kingdom Films.

testimony necessarily bears on things that have happened in the past, the onscreen presence of these relatively young witnesses reminds us that the events they describe are continuing to occur and calls for a response that is oriented to the present and future.

Defamiliarizing Testimony

How can testimony, which, especially in legal contexts, denotes direct empirical knowledge of events, coexist with imaginative and abstract approaches to a phenomenon? This has been a central question for works of literature and film that incorporate testimony, and it is examined anew in recent works about migration. In *Brûle la mer*, a collaboration between Maki Berchache, a Tunisian who migrated to France in the uncertain aftermath of the 2011 revolution, and a filmmaker/activist, Nathalie Nambot, the representation of migration shifts between empirical detail provided through oral testimony and a figurative approach to what it means to encounter and traverse borders. A major theme of the film

Figure 1.4 Screen shot, *Brûle la mer*, 2014.
Courtesy of Maki Berchache & Nathalie Nambot.

is the question of freedom: what it means and how it is experienced. Though the filmmakers acknowledge the poverty and oppression that lead people to cross borders at great personal risk, they also connect migration to revolution and self-emancipation, effectively embracing a form of kinopolitics (Nail 2015, Mezzadra and Neilsen 2011). The film is described by Jean-Pierre Rhem as "un essai sur la liberté ou plutôt de liberté: une tentative d'évasion réelle et fictive auquel la fabrication d'un film participe, prenant part de ce processus d'émancipation: brûle la mer, les frontières, les lois, les papiers" (Rhem n.d.). It participates formally in the acts of insurrection and evasion that it evokes by juxtaposing image, voice, music, and poetry in an open-ended structure.

Since testimony is often highly personal, it can create a false sense of familiarity with a witness, what they have experienced, and the broader circumstances of their life. This propensity is exacerbated in filmed testimony, where facial expressions and emotional responses are shown in close-up. Testimony-based documentaries have sometimes drawn criticism for exploiting witnesses' emotional responses to elicit empathy. *Brûle la mer* draws attention to the fine line between attending to a speaker's unique perspective and deriving a superficial sense of knowing them and understanding their lives. For much of the film, voices are disconnected from bodies; we hear migrants telling their stories, but instead of their faces, we see places in Paris or Tunisia that bear a thematic relation to what is being said. In a long sequence in the middle of the film, Berchache is filmed talking about his life in Tunisia and what he has experienced in France. Though we see him speaking, he looks stiffly past the camera as though he were reading a written text and without making eye contact. Though the film as a whole has an intimate feel—in several scenes we see Berchache interacting informally with friends and family members—he describes the circumstances of his migration almost without affect. This alternation between the deeply personal and the impersonal serves as a reminder that witnessing is always solicited, framed, and edited.

Testimony and Translation

As this example illustrates, oral testimony foregrounds the human voice: what is said is interwoven with the speaker's tone and the cadence of their speech. In a case such as migration, which is inherently multilingual, the language in which the speaker communicates, the presence of a foreign accent, or the need for translation are also integral to testimony. The multilinguality of migration poses challenges to representation; one of the limitations of the novel form, for example, is its fundamental monolingualism. Though novels can evoke the presence of multiple languages or try to imitate a foreign accent (Begag's *Le gone du Chaâba* is a good example), there is almost always a primary language of expression. Films capture multilingualism more easily than literature, but nonetheless have to make choices with respect to translation and subtitling. How multilinguality and translation are reflected has been a central concern of a few recent films about migration. For example, in *Babylon*, filmed in 2011 in the Choucha refugee camp on the Libyan–Tunisian border, nothing at all is translated. The migrants gathered in the camp are shown speaking many different languages, as signaled by the film's Arabic title *Babel* [بابل], but there are no subtitles or elucidations. In this case, the filmmaker Youssef Chebbi's decision not to include translations reflects a wider orientation toward what might be called opacity. Rather than trying to explain what is happening in the camp, *Babylon* leaves viewers feeling conscious of all that we don't know about the migrants gathered in the camp. As the critic Nicolas Féodoroff observes, Chebbi's purpose in visiting Choucha seems to have been less to "cover" the "migrant crisis" that followed the Arab Spring than to "discover" what the people there were going through (Féodoroff n.d.).

A different choice with regard to language is made in *Les Messagers*, in which most of the witnesses speak in French, albeit with different accents and levels of ease; a few speak in Spanish or Arabic, with subtitles appearing at the bottom of the screen. The encounter of these different languages is for the most part naturalized, but in a few punctuating sequences, the force of words and the effects of translation are underscored.[8] The filmmakers don't appear in the film, nor do we hear their questions, with one brief exception. In the course of an interview in which the chief of the Spanish coastguard in Melilla is giving a technocratic description of the spectacular border wall that separates Melilla, which is part of Spain and thus the European Union, from Morocco and the rest of Africa, one of the filmmakers, Lætitia Tura, interrupts him to ask for a clarification. The officer has just explained that the wall was constructed to be an effective barrier but not to do harm to the migrants. He uses the words "non lesivo," which roughly translates to "not detrimental" or "not damaging." Tura repeats these words, asking him what "non lesivo" means. Without registering the possible irony in her question, he clarifies that the wall doesn't physically harm the migrants. In the French subtitles, the term used to render "non lesivo" is "non prejudiciable"—an awkward and legalistic translation that stands out from the rest of the text, drawing attention to the veiled character of official language as well as to the approximative nature of translation.

This exchange reveals much about Spanish and EU policy toward undocumented migrants from Africa, which is to prevent them from entering European territory where they can apply for asylum. To avoid this outcome, the Spanish authorities try not to intervene directly in incidents occurring near Melilla, Ceuta, or the Straits of Gibraltar, and

---

8 A further comparison could be made here to *Shoah*, in which contrasting memories of events are interwoven with the multiplicity of languages—German, Polish, Yiddish, Hebrew, English—spoken by the witnesses: "The incommensurability between different testimonial stances, and the heterogeneous multiplicity of different cognitive positions of seeing and not seeing is amplified and duplicated in the film by the multiplicity of languages in which testimonies are delivered," as Felman explains (Felman 1992, 204).

Figure 1.5 Still from *Les Messagers*, Hélène Crouzillat & Laetitia Tura, 2014. Courtesy of Laetitia Tura and Kingdom Films.

instead delegate to their Moroccan counterparts the responsibility of apprehending, detaining and, where necessary, rescuing migrants. What this means in practice is that they often stand by, waiting for the Moroccan police or coastguard to respond. As the migrants interviewed in the film explain, the Moroccan authorities often fail to intervene in a timely fashion or, in the worst-case scenario, they respond with violence. Several witnesses recount incidents in which either the inaction or the action of the Moroccan coastguard led to the death of a migrant. These stories often register the complicity of the Spanish authorities, whose policy of doing nothing "harmful" effectively put the migrants in harm's way.

The selection and range of meaning of a word is explored to different effect in the final sequence of the film—the interview with the migrant who says "nous sommes les messagers de l'époque." After sharing several harrowing experiences, this man searches for the right word to describe the lack of dignity afforded to migrants and, in the event of their death, their remains. He alights on the word "chosification," noting that he has looked it up to confirm the meaning. Reaching for a heavy French dictionary, he reads the definition aloud. Strikingly, the dictionary links *chosification* to *colonization*. Though the man doesn't comment on this association, the linkage speaks volumes. A man denied entry to France consults a French dictionary, seeking legitimation in a language that he speaks as a result of the colonial occupation of his country … This speaker's characterization of migrants as the "messengers of our age" also, of course, calls for interpretation. He means, presumably, that they are symptomatic figures of deepening global inequalities, war, environmental catastrophe and—as the linkage of colonization and objectification suggests—the toxic afterlives of colonial domination. Their journeys send a message to the world about the deep-seated structural factors underlying what is all too often labeled as a punctual "crisis."

Whereas *Les Messagers* portrays migrants attempting or waiting to cross from the Maghreb to Europe, *Brûle la mer* straddles the Mediterranean, including sequences in both France and Tunisia and exploring the experience of migrants who have arrived in France as well as a migrant who, disillusioned with Europe, has chosen to return to Tunisia. As the scene shifts between France and Tunisia, so the language of communication moves from French to Tunisian Arabic and back. These languages are juxtaposed, yet not symmetrical. Berchache speaks for the most part in French, and explains that he learned to speak the language because he worked in the tourism industry. He is one of several Tunisians who speak French in the film; by contrast, no French person speaks Arabic. This asymmetry connects one of the major themes of the film: the question of hospitality to foreigners. Berchache observes that when he worked in the hospitality industry in southern Tunisia, his role was to make French guests feel welcome [*accueillir*] and indeed he and his coworkers were instructed to welcome people with a smile and to make them feel at home. Regular visitors to Tunisia called him when they arrived, asking him to take them on excursions. But though they gave him their phone numbers, when he got to Paris and tried to call them, they weren't interested in seeing him. This pervasive lack of hospitality is contrasted with the solidarity nurtured in political protest movements. Berchache speaks of his "apprentissage de la lutte" [apprenticeship in political protest], and we see him speaking at a demonstration protesting France's lack of support for Tunisian migrants when compared with its official statements of solidarity with the Tunisian uprising.

In the last sequence of the film, Berchache and a friend are filmed sitting on a hill overlooking an urban neighborhood, with their backs to the camera. We hear them speaking together in standard Arabic, distinct from the Tunisian dialect used at other moments. Berchache's friend, a Palestinian, says that before coming to France he had never met anyone from Tunisia or Maghreb. They agree that while they share a language and a culture, they never met other Arabic speakers because they couldn't obtain visas to travel abroad. The Palestinian observes that "Maybe we could only have met in France," highlighting the political geography that favors south–north over south–south travel and exchanges.[9]

In a number of post-2000 works, the harsh realities of migration are represented through the medium of testimony. Drawing on but also renewing and transposing the tradition of Holocaust literature and film, these works herald a new "age of the witness," if not an "age of the messenger," conferring moral significance on the experience of migrants. By foregrounding the speech and self-representation of migrants they resist the pervasive effacement of people who have few political rights and who are often forced to remain on the social margins in order to avoid detection. In representing the multilinguality of migration, they invite recognition of the challenges—and opportunities—that linguistic diversity poses to communication and representation in the political, legal, and artistic senses of the term.

Works Cited

Film & Media
Allouache, Merzak, dir. 2009. *Harragas*. Algeria and France: Librisfilms Baya Films and France 2 Cinéma. DVD.
Augugliaro, Antonio, Gabriele Del Grande, and Khaled Soliman Al-Nassiry, dir. 2014. *Io sto con la sposa*. Italy: Gina Films. DVD.
Ben Mahi, Hamid, choreog. 2010. *La géographie du danger*. France: Compagnie Hors-Série. Filmed dance performance. YouTube: https://www.youtube.com/watch?v=DKL_Lz7WOYI. Accessed January 19, 2020.
Berchache, Maki, and Nathalie Nambot, dir. 2014. *Brûle la mer*. France: Films de L'Atalante. 16 mm & Super 8 mm. https://vimeo.com/149435922. Accessed January 19, 2020.

9 During their exchange, the occupation of the West Bank and the limitations imposed on Palestinians' freedom of movement are both compared with and contrasted to the limitations confronted by working-class Tunisians. Whereas Berchache expresses his desire for the freedom to travel and see other places, his friend underscores the crucial place that the native land occupies in Palestinians' political imagination and hopes for the future.

Benguigui, Yamina, dir. 1997. *Mémoires d'immigrés, l'héritage maghrébin*. France: Bandits films & Canal +.

Chebbi, Ismaël, Youssef Chebbi, and Ala Eddine Slim, dir. 2012. *Babylon*. Tunisia: Exit Productions. Vimeo. https://vimeo.com/63152235. Accessed January 19, 2020.

Chibane, Malik, dir. 1993. *Hexagone*, 1995. *Douce France*. 2004. *Voisins, Voisines*. France: Alhambra Films. DVD.

Crouzillat, Hélène, and Lætitia Tura, dir. 2014. *Les Messagers*. France: The Kingdom/Territoires en marge. DVD.

Féodoroff, Nicolas. n.d. *Film-documentaire.fr*. http://www.film-documentaire. fr/4DACTION/w_fiche_film/36716_1. Accessed January 19, 2020.

George, Sylvain, dir. 2010. *Qu'ils reposent en révolte*. France: Noir Production. DVD.

——. 2017. *Paris est une fête*. France: Noir Production. DVD.

Lanzmann, Claude, dir. 1985. *Shoah*. France, United Kingdom: British Broadcasting Company, Historia, Les Films Aleph. DVD.

Leuvrey, Elisabeth, dir. 2013. *La Traversée*. France: Alice Films, Artline Films, Les Écrans du Large. DVD.

Lojkine, Boris, dir. 2014. *Hope*. France: Zadig Films. DVD.

Miller, Marlene, dir., and Sandy Silva, choreog. 2016. *Migration Dance Project*. https://vimeo.com/185881794. Accessed January 19, 2020.

Ophuls, Macel, dir. 1969. *Le chagrin et la pitié*. Switzerland and Germany: Télévision rencontre, Norddeutscher Rundfunk (NDR). DVD.

Rhem, Jean-Pierre. n.d. *Film-documentaire.fr*. http://www.film-documentaire. fr/4DACTION/w_fiche_film/42157_1. Accessed January 19, 2020.

Rosi, Gianfranco, dir. 2016. *Fuocoammare*. Italy: Stemal Entertainment. DVD.

Teguia, Tariq, dir. 2006. *Rome plutôt que vous*. Algeria and France: Neffa Films. DVD.

——, dir. 2008. *Gabbla*. Algeria and France: Neffa Films.

UNHCR, "Figures at a Glance." n.d. https://www.unhcr.org/figures-at-a-glance.html. Accessed January 19, 2020.

Print

Begag, Azouz. 1986. *Le gone du Chaâba*. Paris: Seuil.

Ben Jelloun, Tahar. 2006. *Partir*. Paris: Gallimard.

Bessora, and Olivier Barroux. 2014. *Alpha: Abidjan—Gare du Nord*. Paris: Gallimard.

Delbo, Charlotte. 1970. *Auschwitz et après*. Paris: Minuit.

Diome, Fatou. 2010. *Celles qui attendant*. Paris: Flammarion.

Dünnwald, Stephan. 2011. "On Migration and Security: Europe managing migration from Sub-Saharan Africa." *Cadernos de Estudos Africanos* 22: 103–28.

Erll, Astrid. 2011. "Travelling Memory." *Parallax* 17 (4): 4–18.

Felman, Shoshana. 1992. *Testimony: Crises of Witnessing in Literature, Psychoanalysis, and History*. New York: Routledge.

Lalami, Laila. 2005. *Hope and Other Dangerous Pursuits*. Chapel Hill: Algonquin Books.

Luste Boulbina, Seloua. 2018. "The Factory of Supernumeraries."

Manfredini, Tommaso. 2019. "The Multilingual Grammar of Illegalization: Law, Aesthetics, and Translation in the Central Mediterranean." PhD diss. Columbia University.

Mezzadra, Sandro, and Brett Neilson. 2011. "Borderscapes of Differential Inclusion: Subjectivity and Struggles on the Thresholds of Justice's Excess." In *The Borders of Justice*, edited by Étienne Balibar, Sandro Mezzadra, and Ranabir Saaddar, 181–203. Philadelphia: Temple University Press.

Nail, Thomas. 2015. *The Figure of the Migrant*. Stanford, CA: Stanford University Press.

Patel, Shailja. 2010. *Migritude*. New York: Kaya Press.

Rothberg, Michael. 2009. *Multidirectional Memory: Remembering the Holocaust in the Age of Decolonization*. Stanford, CA: Stanford University Press.

Rothberg, Michael, Debarati Sanyal, and Maxim Silberman, eds. 2010. "Noeuds de mémoire: Multidirectional Memory in Postwar French and Francophone Culture." *Yale French Studies* 118–19.

Sanyal, Debarati. 2015. *Memory and Complicity: Migrations of Holocaust Remembrance*. New York: Fordham University Press.

Skif, Hamid. 2006. *La géographie du danger*. Paris: Naive.

Smith, Stephen. 2018. *La ruée vers l'Europe: La jeune Afrique en route pour le Vieux Continent*. Paris: Grasset.

Wiesel, Élie. 1958. *La Nuit*. Paris: Minuit.

Wiewiorka, Annette. 1998. *L'ère du témoin*. Paris: Plon.

CHAPTER TWO

Transposé et pourtant juste

Collaboration and Transposition in New Francophone Migrant Writing

Kate Averis

Collaboration

At the end of the twentieth century, Jean Déjeux noted the tendency of francophone Maghrebi women's writing of exile and migration to be dominated by a focus on the author's personal experience of displacement, an experience most frequently related in the autobiographical or autofictional mode (Déjeux 1994). Déjeux's claim still holds true for women's writing of displacement and mobility in the wider Euro-Mediterranean sphere at the beginning of the twenty-first century (Averis and Hollis-Touré 2016). Such narratives have tended to relate the relatively privileged and singular experiences of authors with access to cultural if not material capital (for example, in the seminal works of Assia Djebar and Leïla Sebbar, and more recently, in those of Malika Mokeddem, Leïla Marouane, and Zahia Rahmani originating in the North African region, and, for example, by Fatou Diome, Kim Thúy, and Chahdortt Djavann in the wider *francosphère*). Emphasizing a solitary, individual experience of transnational mobility—frequently born of a sense of isolation or alienation that is seen to preexist displacement (Averis 2014)—by a speaking subject with extraordinary access to the means for relating her experience, these literary accounts, however, fail to reflect more collective contemporary experiences of those fleeing conflict, economic deprivation, the effects of climate change, or other overwhelming circumstances. Displacement is, of course, often a collective experience, whether experienced alongside family members, acquaintances, or strangers, and particularly when it is the result of collectively experienced events such as those listed above. Yet dominant practices of the production, circulation, and reception of literary texts means that they privilege an understanding of literature as a singularly individualistic activity, where the experience of displacement is most often expressed in individualistic terms.

This chapter focuses on a recent iteration of francophone women's writing of migration that departs from this historical, individualistic focus to examine an innovatively collaborative approach to writing migration, thereby contributing not only to the discussion of more varied literary expressions of migration but also to expanding the existing scope of analyses of the genre. The innovations and scope of a collaborative approach are exemplified in particularly productive ways in the relatively recent publication of *Mopaya: récit d'une traversée du Congo à la Suisse* (2010), which breaks with the paradigm of the single-authored autobiographical or autofictional mode that has been seen to dominate the discursive representation of migration and has resulted in the literary inscription of a limited range of migratory experiences. As its subtitle suggests, *Mopaya: récit d'une traversée du Congo à la Suisse* recounts the trans-Mediterranean journey of its subject from the center of the African continent to the heart of Western Europe. Co-authored by a Swiss writer resident in France, Douna Loup, and Gabriel Nganga Nseka, a psychiatric nurse from the Democratic Republic of Congo and a resident of Geneva, this multi-voiced literary narrative provides an example of recent experimentation in modes of authorship that allow for the transposition of a wider range of experiences of migration into the French-language literary canon, while also transposing the roles of the author and subject of narratives of migration. It thus constitutes a significant and innovative contribution to new francophone migrant writing in a twenty-first-century trans-Mediterranean, Afro-European context.

Collaborative production and expression are perhaps more readily associated with performative visual and sonorous modes of cultural expression, such as music, cinema, theatre, or dance, and have been adopted to a significantly lesser degree in forms of written, literary expression, where, in spite of twentieth-century post-structuralist efforts (Barthes 1967), the figure of the author continues to reign supreme. Despite recent experimental collaborative attempts,[1] the novel has

---

1   One notable example being the aborted "A Million Penguins" experiment in joint authoring run by De Montfort University with Penguin Books (Mason and

persistently remained the special preserve of the individual writer, and consequently, a proponent of a unifying individual perspective, even where a diffracted subjective perspective is employed as an explicit narrative strategy. This might explain the preference for visual narrative forms of cultural expression in the effort to communicate experiences of migration that lie beyond those of its *auteur*, such as, for example, the hybrid documentary film *Fuocoammare*, directed by the Eritrean-born Italian director Gianfranco Rosi (2016), which tells the story of refugees who seek (and some who fail, with tragic consequences) to make safe passage across the Mediterranean to Lampedusa.

In the francophone tradition, comics and graphic novels have been particularly effective at articulating migratory experiences in the first person by migrants and refugees who may not have access to the means of production and systems of publication of literary texts. If collaborative writing is faced with difficult negotiations of space (including geographical, cultural, ethnic, gendered, and social space), current publishing trends suggest that these divides are more readily negotiated in textual-visual media than in narrative prose texts. Mohamed Arejdal and Cédric Liano's *Amazigh: itinéraire d'hommes libres* (2014) is a pertinent example of such a tendency as it apportions the tasks of writing the text, drawing the images, organizing the narrative, and ensuring publication between the Moroccan artist and illustrator, Arejdal, and the French *bande dessinée* author, Liano, in a collaboration that is structured around Arejdal's first-hand (visual) expression of his own experience of making the dangerous, clandestine crossing from Morocco to the Canary Islands.

The Paris-based *bande dessinée* collective "Dessins sans papiers" similarly demonstrates the potential for untold stories of migration to emerge as the result of bringing together refugee storytellers with the space and means to create and disseminate their stories. This

Thomas 2008), which aimed to write a collaborative novel open to anyone willing to participate in its writing, created on the same software used by Wikipedia. The project "seeded" a first line and invited contributions over a five-week period, and while the "wikinovel" created excitement in the social media community, it didn't exactly create a readable novel or attain anything like a readership, and the project effectively evolved from a literary to a social experiment. Loup and Nganga Nseka's collaborative writing demonstrates entirely contrasting social interactions to those modeled by the "Million Penguins" experiment as the basis for successful experimental, collaborative writing in the form of an intimate, empathetic cooperative relationship with clearly defined roles.

collaborative effort has led to the publication of four albums so far, among which *Le Voyage de Hafiz El Sudani* by Hafiz Adem (2017) and *Le Journal de Mickey Le Vieux* by Mohamed Ndepe Tahar (2018), while collaborations between professional writers and *bande dessinée* authors (such as Yasmine Bouagga and Lisa Mandel's *Les Nouvelles de la jungle* [2017], which relates a range of experiences from Calais's now-dismantled refugee and migrant camp) conform more closely to a sociological or ethnographic mode of compiling and recounting others' stories of migration.

Mopaya is thus somewhat of an outlier among its literary peers, relating an individual experience of migration that is reflective of a wider phenomenon through a collaborative approach that has been more readily embraced in the francophone tradition in the textual-visual literary space of comics and graphic novels. By contrast, in anglophone writing two particularly significant recent literary collaborations in prose stand out for the challenge they pose to the institutional silencing of stories of migration in contexts of heightened and calculated hostility toward migrants, a defiant telling, which is enabled through literary collaboration that also involves translation. In an important recent instance of such a collaboration—in this case between an incarcerated refugee and journalist, and two academic translators and scholars—*No Friend but the Mountains* (2018) gives an autobiographical account of Kurdish Iranian Behrouz Boochani's journey from Indonesia to Christmas Island, and his eventual incarceration in a detention camp on Manus Island, from where he painstakingly wrote his account in instalments on a mobile phone that were received, compiled, and initially translated from Farsi into English by Moones Mansoubi, and then edited by Omid Tofighian who also completed the translation and secured the book's publication.

In a further instance of a significantly innovative if not co-authored collaboration, Valeria Luiselli's recent publications relate the experiences of undocumented, unaccompanied Central American migrant children at the federal immigration court of New York City, resulting in texts that are inherently multivoiced. Not only does Luiselli translate these children's experiences of moving through the geographic and symbolic contact zones of Central and North America for juridical purposes in her role as Spanish–English translator to the court, she also transposed them for interlocutors beyond the court setting when she published *Los niños perdidos* in 2016. An extended version of an earlier English-language publication in Freeman's magazine, *Los niños perdidos* is, in itself, both a translation and a transposition of the oral accounts of the children, many of whom speak Spanish in addition to primary, indigenous languages. In her subsequent 2017 publication, the book-length *Tell Me How It Ends* (with the title tellingly modified from the "lost children" of the 2016 Spanish version), Luiselli offers the children's testimonies in English translation, thus completing the writerly triptych, which exceeds a merely linguistic operation of transcription and translation by also transferring these stories across languages and registers to carry these children's words to diverse readers and interlocutors in a range of new environments.

Following on from this brief overview of these examples of recent literary collaborations, produced in hotspots of political hostility toward migrants and migration at the borders of Europe, Australia, and the US, where the stakes of storytelling and claiming authorship are high, the present analysis adopts Lorraine York's (2002) definition of collaborative writing as that which is self-consciously so, and characterized by "any overt co-authorship or co-signature of a work of art" (4) excluding collaborations published under a singular composite name or pseudonym. Drawing on Barthes's assertion that "a text's unity lies not in its origin but in its destination," whereby the reader is the space in which the citational fabric of the text comes together and meaning is produced (Barthes 1977 [1967], 148), the present analysis similarly highlights the importance of the reader's role in reading the collaborative text as precisely that: a collaborative, co-authored literary work produced cooperatively by individual authors. Thus, the reading of literary collaboration undertaken here relies both on Barthes's "birth of the reader" and on Foucault's "author-function" (1977 [1969]) in its assumption of the importance of the reader's attention to the individual authors of the text—or at least, of the reader's construction of said authors. As such, "collaborative" literary writing is also distinguished here from "collective" literary writing due to the different author and reader functions at work in these distinct endeavors, insofar as collective writing is commonly published under the name of the writing collective, relying on precisely the opposite of readerly attention to or construction of the authors, in that it is dependent on anonymized, collectivized authorship in its reception. Such an effacing of identity may be a risky undertaking for female, migrant, racialized, indigenous, third-world, or otherwise subaltern or minority writers who undertake writing collaborations, for whom drawing attention to the author figures behind their overt co-authorship may be a deliberate strategy of redress or politicization.

In her 2002 study, in which she outlines her definition of collaborative writing, York is careful to stipulate that the (primarily late-twentieth-century anglophone Canadian) women's collaborative writing that constitutes its object of analysis is far from being a post-structuralist or postmodern phenomenon. York details the rich history of women's collaborative writing and its particular strength in the nineteenth century, "a time when yet another watershed in authorship experimentation coincided with a higher level of opportunity and access for women writers" (York 2002, 8). Imogen Long too highlights the importance of women's writerly collaboration for twentieth-century French feminist writing, where "the concept of co-authorship is indicative of the ethos of cooperation and collectivity of second-wave feminism" (Long 2013, 34). Two of the authors studied in Long's book, the sisters Benoîte and Flora Groult, published some of the earliest and now most iconic instances of "four-handed" writing in the twentieth-century French feminist tradition (Groult and Groult 1962, 1965, 1967), thereby consolidating a tradition of women's collaborative writing in French to which Douna Loup contributes in the twenty-first century, while also modifying it in important ways. By contrast with the work of York and Long, the present analysis examines an instance of a female author's collaboration not with another female writer, but with a male author in Loup and Nganga Nseka's *Mopaya*, where Loup diverges from an established tradition of women's literary collaboration to undertake the collaborative writing project with a male co-author. While joint female–male publications are certainly not unprecedented in the canon of literature in French, this twenty-first-century iteration of the tradition does not derive from the exploitation of existing gender hierarchies to enable women's access to publication, as seen, for example, in the joint publications of George Sand and Jules Sandeau, and Colette and Willy in the nineteenth and early twentieth centuries. It is more closely related to Long's "ethos of cooperation and collectivity," driven as much by feminist egalitarianism as by transnational solidarity, which seeks to expand existing literary spaces, to accommodate a wider ranges of voices within them, and to reach new audiences.

If, as York emphasizes, women's literary collaborations "harbour various ideological potentials, some more hierarchical, some more liberatory and subversive" as well as positing "difficult negotiations of space (both of the page and of geographical spaces)" (York 2002, 4; 7), this is also true of literary collaborations that span a wider range of spaces and distances, not only literary and geographical, but also of gender, class, ethnicity, and age, for example. Thus, as well as adopting a critical framework of collaborative, and particularly women's collaborative writing, the present analysis also draws on the body of theoretical work surrounding testimonial narrative, which relies on the very separation and bridging of these spaces for both its production and the realization of its ethical imperatives. A particularly rich theoretical vein has been developed, in particular, in Latin American studies of *testimonio*, which shows that testimonial narratives have emerged wherever subaltern or minority storytellers have historically lacked access to the means to tell and disseminate their own stories, from Palestine to Angola and from Vietnam to Bolivia, to the minorities at the centers of the world's major metropolitan cities. As John Beverley has observed, *testimonio*, or testimonial narrative, relies on the existence of a hierarchical imbalance between narrator and interlocutor, and between narrator and reader (Beverley 1987, 13), as seen in *Me llamo Rigoberta y así me nació la conciencia* [*I, Rigoberta Menchú: An Indian Woman in Guatemala*], published by Rigoberta Menchú and Elizabeth Burgos Debray in 1985, a widely studied exponent of women's collaborative writing as well as a key example of testimonial narrative. The present analysis of *Mopaya* is informed by the insights of Beverley (1987, 1989) in relation to its narrative form, its account of its own production and its author and reader functions, while also diverging from them in important ways, as will be discussed.

Mopaya

Mopaya tells the story of its subject, Gabriel,[2] who leaves Kinshasa in what was then Zaire and is now the Democratic Republic of Congo, at the age of 22, and eventually makes it to Geneva after a long and circuitous journey by air and overland via Angola, Belgium, and France.[3]

---

2   "Gabriel" is hereafter used throughout to refer to the subject of *Mopaya*, while "Nganga Nseka" is used to refer to its co-author.

3   The text gives an account of Gabriel's journey from the Democratic Republic of Congo to Angola, Belgium, France, and finally Switzerland. Initially passing through Angola on his way to Brussels, he discovers in Luanda a lawless and dangerous place, racked by civil war and poverty, where as a foreigner who does not speak Portuguese, he is immediately an object of suspicion and subject to enforced recruitment in the Angolan civil war. He suffers a setback in Luanda, his journey held up for almost a year, after a police raid during which all his savings are extracted

Gabriel's story is recreated at a temporal and geographical distance
from the events recounted, in a narrative present in Geneva, where
he has reached the age of 40. Despite an absence of explicit temporal
markers, a number of historical and cultural references in the text—to
the Mobutu regime which forms the backdrop to his years in Zaire, the
civil war in Angola which threatens his passage through the country,
and Ayrton Senna's fourth Belgian Grand Prix victory which coincides
with his arrival in Europe—permit the reader to situate Gabriel's arrival
in Europe in 1991, and the time of writing in 2009 (one year prior to the
text's publication).

Divided into six unnumbered sections, each in turn prefaced by
a Burmese, Indian, French, American, Ethiopian, and Arab proverb
translated into French, *Mopaya*'s structure might be likened to that
of a musical composition that progresses through six movements that
shift back and forth in time, modulating in tempo and tone, to recount:
(1) Gabriel's departure from Zaire and journey to Europe; (2) his
childhood in the village where he was born; (3) his arrival in Europe;
(4) his adolescence and highschool in Kinshasa; (5) his asylum request in
Switzerland; and (6) its refusal. The sixth and final section also provides
a translation of the Lingala term of the text's title, offered by Gabriel in
response to the question posed to him—"Comment vous dites *étranger*

from him by way of extortion by the police officers in exchange for avoiding arrest
and deportation, forced recruitment in the civil war, or an even worse fate that might
be arbitrarily meted out to him by the police officers. After eventually obtaining a
fake passport, a visa to travel to Europe "et du liquide encore pour passer les
frontières" (11), his journey continues by air to Brussels, and then by train to Paris,
and eventually Geneva, passing through numerous Belgian, French, and Swiss cities
on the way. The bureaucratic torsions of the asylum process in Switzerland lead him
to become an expert in negotiating the asylum application process, just as he became
"un as de l'administration. Un surdoué en visa" in response to the system's demands
in Angola (27). Having discovered that the true account of his precipitous departure
from Kinshasa fails to satisfy the criteria for acquiring refugee status, and lacking
the necessary supporting scars, photos of torture, or other proof of persecution, he
hires "un coach chargé de [lui] concocter une histoire plus vrai que nature," and
endeavors to fulfill the image of the 'requérant d'asyle parfait' (76) that is demanded
of him in order to "pass": "[il se plie] aux usages, si c'est ça qu'ils attendent en
Suisse" (77). In Switzerland he discovers that, in contrast to Angola where he had to
"[m]ontrer que tu n'es pas ce que tu es, que tu n'es pas dans le besoin le plus absolu
de tout" (27), he must instead "rempailler de mensonges" the story of his "fuite
trop hasardeuse, mettre du tonus dans le scénario" (77) in order to meet European
bureaucratic expectations of suffering.

ou *exilé* dans votre langue de là-bas?" (107, original emphasis)—by the director of a theater production in Zurich in which he is invited to participate, essentially playing himself in the role of the "mopaya." Appearing in French in this linguistically multilayered text, the question is originally posed by the theater director in Swiss German, the language in which the play is eventually performed and one of the languages that Gabriel has applied himself to learning after being transferred from one *centre d'enregistrement des requérants d'asile* to another, first in Basel, then Chiasso, and finally Zurich, demonstrating not only Gabriel's high level of linguistic competence but also the rich linguistic texture of the otherwise francophone text.

Within each of these six sections, the text employs a complex, split narration with frequent shifts in narrative voice. It opens with a second-person narration in which an unidentified narrator addresses the text's subject: "Tu es un peu triste de laisser derrière toi, ton pays, ta famille, ton emploi, tes amis, tes élèves. Mais tu ne penses qu'à une chose. Te mettre à l'abri" (11). The narration returns to the second-person "tu" in the unnumbered third section, shifting to the third person in interim sections that recount the subject's past, referring to "l'enfant" and "le petit homme de quinze ans" in the unnumbered second and fourth sections. The tone of intimacy of the informal "tu" conveys a close relationship of careful listening and empathy between the narrator and the subject, while the external perspective expressed by the unnamed third person reflects the adult subject's distance from the young boy's experiences. While these are related at a distance—that is temporal and spatial for the subject, and experiential for the narrator—they are nevertheless fully situated in a family, community, and national context, allowing the work of fictional empathy to take place in these third-person narrative passages that most closely resemble novelistic discourse. In the unnumbered fifth section, the narrative voice shifts once again, this time to the second-person "vous" to recount the subject's tribulations as an asylum seeker in Switzerland, while also performing the manipulation of the more formal pronoun's presumed tone of respect to strike a scathing tone of distance and othering. The text's subject is identified only in the sixth and final section in a first-person affirmation of identity that is expressed in reported speech in his most recently adopted language: *"Ich bin Gabriel"* (109, original emphasis). Reverting to the third person in this section in which Gabriel both meets his future wife and is refused asylum, the narration at this point alternates between "l'Africain" and "Gabriel" to refer, respectively, to the persona whom audiences see perform in the play, and to the man to whom Renata proposes marriage.

This complex, shifting narration is punctuated at regular intervals throughout all six sections by 20 brief numbered passages narrated in the first person by the subject, interjections that are further distinguished from the primary narration by the use of italics. In these brief, intermittent passages in italics, the subject describes aspects of his day-to-day life in Geneva at the time of writing. He refers, for instance, to his job as a psychiatric nurse, to caring for his young daughter, to the break-up of the relationship with her mother and to other, more recent relationships, to his first return to Africa (not to the Democratic Republic of the Congo, but to Senegal), and notably, to the emergence of the text at hand, as well as to the dreams and memories that are the emotional and psychological cargo of the past. These intermittent passages also eventually provide an account of the circumstances of his (hitherto unexplained) departure from Kinshasa: after excelling at high school albeit without graduating due to the reigning corruption where "*les bonnes notes, ça s'achète*" et "*les baccalauréats subventionnés, ça se fait à la pelle*" (84, original emphasis), he is employed as a language teacher and private tutor by "*l'homme d'action qui provoque [s]on départ précipité de Kinshasa*" (78, original emphasis). The latter's characterization, in Gabriel's words in his first-person account, as "*un métis noir américain*" avec "*une gueule de gosse de riche*" et des "*allures de garçon gâté et capricieux*" who at 20 took up residence in Zaire and a life "*sans loi et sans limite*" (78–79, original emphasis) in cahoots with members of Kinshasa's military and political elite, points to the economic and social privileges enjoyed by those with advantageous local and global connections to which Gabriel himself can lay no claim, and to which his lack of access in fact determines his flight to Europe. Gabriel suddenly flees Zaire, at a moment's notice, with a fake passport and a visa for Angola, when his employer frames him as an accomplice in his ivory-trafficking racket, effectively pronouncing a death sentence for "*un Zaïrois des bas quartiers, issu d'une famille d'inconnus et non mobutiste*" (94, original emphasis) in a description of himself that reinforces the gulf of inequality of opportunity between him and his employer, "*né à New York dans une famille aisée*" (79, original emphasis), and now member of a wealthy, corrupt local elite. The twentieth and last of these italicized passages in the first person concludes *Mopaya*'s sixth and final section as well as the text itself, in which Gabriel envisages summoning the courage to one day return to the village of his birth with his daughter to place a tombstone on the burial plot of his father, who has died in his absence.

Both of these narrative strands—the shifting, second- and third-person narration, and Gabriel's first-person interjections—are in the present tense. Both the intimate ('tu') and the performatively formal ('vous') second-person narrative passages are articulated in an eternal present that reinforces the dead waiting time—"du temps vide" (20)—that characterizes Gabriel's trajectory: "Il ne vous est demandé qu'une seule chose, attendre. Et en attendant, votre vie est une parenthèse, une vie sous hypothèque, une vie dans l'attente de l'enveloppe jaune en provenance de Berne qui vous annoncera la décision finale. Cela peut arriver demain, dans deux mois, dans trois ans" (106). The eternal present of waiting is also reiterated in Gabriel's first-person interjections, which evoke his sense of powerlessness to be able to influence his present and proceed with his goals and projects as he waits for Swiss immigration officials to process his application for asylum: "*Je suis pris dans le flot des jours*" (94, original emphasis).

While the text's narrative style communicates the solitude and despair arising from Gabriel's experience of the asylum process, it also reflects the traumatic impact of his precipitous departure from Zaire and of the resulting rupture with his family and community, in ways that encompass and exceed the narration's already discussed temporal and subjective leaps. Gabriel's first-person narrative interjections at the time of writing relay a distance and certain degree of resolution of past trauma insofar as he describes activities (i.e., creating a home, forming a family, undertaking employment) that are generally understood as constituting indicators of settled living. Yet their consistently reflective tone conveys unresolved fractures, as seen, for example, in the expression of his hope to summon the courage one day to visit his father's burial plot. Furthermore, and perhaps more tellingly, the primary narration (at least in the sense that it occupies the most textual space) initially adopts a syncopated, truncated syntax in a series of enunciative statements that are typographically separated on the page, punctuated only by the rare, short paragraph, and that are devoid of any analysis or reflection. The narrative style of the "primary" narration as well as its *mise en page* become less fragmented and increasingly fluid as the text progresses, and most notably, as the text's subject describes his discovery and increasing contact with autobiographical writing. Reading and writing are thematized in *Mopaya*, a theme whose appearance in the text coincides with Gabriel's arrival in Europe, where written culture is typically highly valorized, as illustrated by his observation of the number of people reading on the train, which prompts him to pick up a newspaper that is left behind by a passenger when she disembarks. In fact, the theme of reading and writing serves to introduce an explanation of the genesis of the text at hand when Gabriel declares a need to apply narrative order to his existence while lamenting that he lacks the wherewithal to do so:

> *Ma vie ressemble à un puzzle éclaté. Il faut mettre de l'ordre dans tout cela. ... Cette idée m'est venue lorsque j'ai découvert les récits autobiographiques. ... En les lisant, toute mon histoire est remontée vers moi ... Mais je ne sais par quel bout commencer, je scrute désespérément l'apparition d'un signe, d'un îlot auquel me raccrocher pour commencer à dérouler le fil de mon existence.* (32, original emphasis)

While the above claim appears to anticipate an explanation of the circumstances of the text's production, this only ever remains a partial explanation as the conditions of its production are never fully and explicitly accounted for. What this claim does do, however, is conform to testimonial narrative's need for an ethnic or class other in order to ensure its existence: *Mopaya* too relies for its existence on the differential relationship between the narrator of the oral testimony that lies at its origin and the oral testimony's interlocutor, transcriber, and compiler to fulfill the fundamental conditions for its production: to elicit the narrative, to give it textual form, and to see it to publication and distribution (Beverley 1989, 18).

However, *Mopaya*'s paratextual apparatus does not include the preface—a paratext typically associated with the testimonial narrative (Vera León 1992)—which might give the subject's interlocutor's account of the circumstances in which the oral testimony was gathered and arranged into a written text. Such prefaces are often provided in the interests of transparency, yet they may equally have the inadvertent effect of hijacking the subject's story or even, ironically, clouding the degree of the interlocutor's own role in shaping it, as seen in the much-discussed case of Burgos Debray's preface to *Me llamo Rigoberta*, referred to above (Sommer 1992). What *Mopaya* does include is a "postface biographique" that provides details not of the interlocutor's role in creating the text but of the subject's trajectory subsequent to its publication. As well as giving a brief overview of his education in Kinzadi, the village of his birth, and then in the capital, Congo-Kinshasa, and describing his professional qualifications and employment in Geneva, the *postface* reassures the reader that: "Arrivé en Suisse comme requérant d'asile, il obtient son permis de séjour par mariage, avant la fin de sa procédure" (115). No such biographical information is given for Nganga Nseka's co-author, Loup. *Mopaya* thus displaces the focus from testimonial narrative's typical emphasis on the text's conditions and mode of production to a singular focus on the subject, while also providing some relief from the hopelessness and despair of the narrative conclusion. That the text itself refuses any satisfying narrative resolution, which is instead provided by its *postface*, suggests its inclusion is less the choice of Nganga Nseka than that of the publisher, perhaps in anticipation of readers' desire for reassurance regarding the fate of its subject.

If certain aspects of *Mopaya*'s paratextual apparatus appear to lie beyond the control of Nganga Nseka, the genesis of the text itself appears to lie entirely within his authority. Rather than explicitly accounting for its production within the text, Gabriel merely refers to *"ma récente décision de commencer un travail autobiographique,"* which is already under way in the form of *"une série d'entretiens enregistrés qui servent de matériau de base à la personne chargée de la rédaction"* (35, original emphasis), in a fleeting metatextual account that emphasizes *his* decision to undertake the project and his recruitment of someone to undertake the task of its composition. Neither his interlocutor nor the organization and transcription of the interviews is described in the text, beyond brief reference to their existence, such that it remains entirely focused on the experience of the migrant subject, whose verbal outpouring is described as a salutary, if not life-saving, exercise:

> *J'ai déjà livré des heures de paroles à l'enregistrement et je ne suis pas encore tari, mon passé est encore gorgé d'images et de ressentis dont j'aimerais parler. Je ne sais pas pourquoi j'ai tant besoin de poser ainsi ma vie noir sur blanc, mais je sens que cela me permet de voir plus clair dans les dessins entremêlés de mon existence.* (68, original emphasis)

Thus *Mopaya* resolutely remains Gabriel's story, and not the story of their collaboration: while the text is the result of a collaboration, it is not a story of collaboration.

The paratextual apparatus that couches the main text of *Mopaya* thus reinforces the singular focus on the migrant subject already established by the text's structure and the voicing of the narration by insisting on Nganga Nseka's authorship and relegating Loup's role to that of a scribe, spokeperson, and interpreter-translator. In the "Remerciements," Nganga Nseka thanks "Douna qui a accepté d'être une plume, une parte-parole, une traductrice, une interprète dans la réalisation de ce projet" and dedicates the text "à mes filles, Miomey et Soaniry" in a series of textual gestures that can be performed only by a text's author. In this way, *Mopaya* forfeits testimonial narrative's traditional "erasure of the function, and thus also the textual presence, of the 'author'" (Beverley 1989, 17–18), instead insisting on the individuality and authority of the author-figure, and perhaps camouflaging what Antonio Vera León sees as the interpretative, organizational, and "corrective" intervention of the interlocutor (Vera León 1992, 192).

Mopaya therefore presents a number of significant coincidences as well as divergences from the testimonial narrative as it has been theorized in the twentieth-century Latin American tradition, thereby renovating the genre in a twenty-first-century Afro-European context. Despite Vera León's warning that the inscription of the oral testimony, rather than performing a democratizing operation on cultural expression in fact reaffirms the monoculture of writing (Vera León 1992, 196), *Mopaya*'s borrowings from both collaborative and testimonial methodologies enable the transposition of a singular story of migration into the French-language literary text while also transposing the roles of author, narrator, and subject, as discussed in the next and final section.

Transposition

In keeping with the generic characteristics of *testimonio*, *Mopaya* is not a work of fiction and much less a novel, as indicated by a subtitle that presents it as a *récit*, thus foregrounding the text's origins in orality. In this way, it negotiates a course between the ethical imperatives of a genre that poses "a challenge to the loss of the authority of orality in the context of processes of cultural modernization that privilege literacy and literature as norms of expression" (Beverley 1989, 17) while also staking a claim to its status as a written literary text and the migrant author's rightful place to his role as such. *Mopaya* thus effectively transposes an individual experience of a widely shared contemporary historical phenomenon—flight across the Mediterranean to seek safe haven in Europe—into literary narrative, and in doing so recovers for its migrant author some degree of control over his own life trajectory—albeit retrospectively and in narrative form— that was seen to evade him in the powerlessness he expressed during his displacement and first years in Europe. More than a mere transcription of Nganga Nseka's experience into a testimonial-documentary mode, *Mopaya* constitutes a literary reworking of an experience of migration that departs from the testimonial-documentary imperative of testimonial narrative by its adoption of fictional, poetic language and through its very narrative structure, which disrupts teleological chronological progression and coherent subjective development, evincing an aesthetic as well as an expressive drive.

If *Mopaya* transposes into literary narrative a first-hand account of migration of the kind that is typically inaudible in the francophone literary canon, it also recalibrates the role and position of the reader. In contrast with other literary forms, most notably the novel or autobiography, which can generally be said to reflect, confirm, or authorize the reader's world view, the collaborative testimonial narrative implies an experiential gap between subject and (most) readers, for whom the text implies an ethics of reading that will lead to a destabilizing, or at least a questioning, of their world view. For readers who do not share a comparable experience to that of Nganga Nseka, Doris Sommer reminds us that we are "intellectually and ethically inept" in the face of such experience and that the only appropriate and responsible way to read such a text is with a distance that is similar to respect, in a reading that resists the longing to force the unfamiliar experience onto a familiar frame of reference (Sommer 1992, 139–41). *Mopaya* is less an invitation to identify, or even to empathize with its subject, than to practice the simultaneously close and distant listening modeled by Loup which enables Nganga Nseka's story to emerge, on its own terms, in a borrowed tongue, traced by a borrowed hand.

Herself a migrant, as a Swiss woman living in France and who has lived for a time in Madagascar, Loup appears less interested in exploring her personal experiences of migration as a relatively privileged white European woman than in contributing to the creation of a literary space able to accommodate more widespread contemporary experiences of migration. Collaboration is, indeed, a characteristic methodological approach in Loup's literary writing, and also features in the production of her subsequent book publication, *Les Lignes de ta paume* (2012), based on her recorded interviews with the 85-year-old French-Swiss artist Linda Naeff.[4] Employing many of the same narrative devices that have been described in operation in *Mopaya*, such as a split, multi-voiced narration, oscillation between past and present as it shifts between the first, second and third person, and the incorporation of references to the

---

4 For an analysis of the collaborative narrative ethics in this text, see Averis (2021).

interviews that lie at its origin, Loup nevertheless appears as the sole author on the cover of the more recent text. Of note is the significant difference in the two textual subjects' access to self-expression: despite being acquired in late life, Linda Naeff already had an outlet and audience through her painting and sculpture, and the text is a further means of expression: *"je peins déjà, je sculpte, alors j'aimerais que tu écrives pour moi"*; *"je veux que tu écrives ma vie"* (Loup 2012, 15, original emphasis). It is also pertinent to recall that Gabriel's path to self-representation is initially performative—when he plays himself in a theater production in Zurich—before it is literary: in both cases, it is collaboration with others that enables the emergence of the "mopaya" subject, yet it is only in the literary representation that he assumes authorship.

In transcribing, composing, and collaborating on the publication of her co-author's story, Douna Loup effectively breaks new ground in women's writing of migration in French, and with Nganga Nseka, they together transform francophone migrant writing while also transposing the roles of author, narrator, subject, and reader within this tradition. In demonstrating an ethics of empathy and a practice of careful listening, Loup enacts a self-effacement in her co-authored text that reflects Sommer's "defense of difference" (1992, 141). That Loup's efforts are effective is suggested by Gabriel's claim to be taken aback by the effect of seeing his story transformed into another's words, thereby also incorporating into the written text a commentary on the process and impact, if not the conditions, of the text's production in a kind of feedback loop that operates between the oral testimony and the written text:

> *C'est étonnant de lire ma propre histoire dans des mots qui ne sont plus le miens. Cela me permet un recul inhabituel. Je peux aborder les phases tourmentées de ma vie avec un calme étrange. Je découvre au travers des pages de la poésie, là où je ne trouvais en moi que des plaintes. Tout semble transposé et pourtant cela reste juste.* (68, original emphasis)

The transposition of his story through its narrative organization and articulation in written form indicate, rather than a purely cooperative endeavor, a collaboration in which Loup and Nganga Nseka are, as York puts it, "differently engaged" (York 2002, 5). In the overt co-signature of *Mopaya*, its focus on the migrant subject's experience, and the self-effacement of his interlocutor's voice and role, its co-authors expand the current limits of migrant writing to contribute to a new poetics and ethics of writing migration in the Euro-Mediterranean literary space.

Works Cited

Adem, Hafiz. 2017. *Le Voyage de Hafiz El Sudani*. Paris: Atelier SP / Collectif Dessins sans papiers.

Arejdal, Mohamed, and Cédric Liano. 2014. *Amazigh: itinéraire d'hommes libres*. Paris: Steinkis.

Averis, Kate. 2014. *Exile and Nomadism in French and Hispanic Women's Writing*. Oxford: Legenda.

——. 2021. "The Boundaries of the Imagination: Writing Female Old Age from the Perspective of Youth." In *Trangression(s) in Twenty-First-Century Women's Writing in French*, edited by Kate Averis, Eglė Kačkutė and Catherine Mao, 182–97. Leiden: Brill-Rodopi.

Averis, Kate, and Isabel Hollis-Touré, eds. 2016. *Exiles, Travellers and Vagabonds: Rethinking Mobility in Francophone Women's Writing*. Cardiff: University of Wales Press.

Barthes, Roland. 1977 [1967]. "The Death of the Author." In *Image Music Text*, edited and translated by Stephen Heath, 142–48. London: Fontana Press.

Beverley, John. 1987. "Anatomía del testimonio." *Revista de crítica literaria latinoamericana* 13 (25): 7–16.

——. 1989. "The Margin at the Center: On *Testimonio* (Testimonial Narrative)." *Modern Fiction Studies* 35 (1): 11–28.

Boochani, Behrouz. 2018. *No Friend but the Mountains: Writing from Manus Prison*. Translated by Omid Tofighian. Sydney, Picador.

Bouagga, Yasmine, and Lisa Mandel. 2017. *Les Nouvelles de la jungle*. Bruxelles: Casterman.

Déjeux, Jean. 1994. *La Littérature féminine de langue française au Maghreb*. Paris: Karthala.

Foucault, Michel. 1977 [1969]. "What is an author?" In *Language, Counter-Memory, Practice*, edited by Donald F. Bouchard, translated by Donald F. Bouchard and Sherry Simon, 113–38. Ithaca, NY: Cornell University Press.

Groult, Benoîte, and Flora Groult. 1962. *Journal à quatre mains*. Paris: Denoël.

——. 1965. *Le feminin pluriel*. Paris: Denoël.

——. 1967. *Il était deux fois*. Paris: Denoël.

Long, Imogen. 2013. *Women Intellectuals in Post-68 France*. Basingstoke: Palgrave Macmillan.

Loup, Douna. 2012. *Les Lignes de ta paume*. Paris: Mercure.

Loup, Douna, and Gabriel Nganga Nseka. 2010. *Mopaya: récit d'une traversée du Congo à la Suisse*. Paris: L'Harmattan.

Luiselli, Valeria. 2016. *Los niños perdidos: un ensayo en cuarenta preguntas*. Mexico City: Sexto Piso.

———. 2017. *Tell Me How It Ends: An Essay in Forty Questions*. London: 4th Estate.

Mason, Bruce, and Sue Thomas. 2008. "A Million Penguins Research Report." Leicester: Institute of Creative Technologies, De Montfort University. http://www.ioct.dmu.ac.uk/documents/amillionpenguinsreport.pdf. Accessed May 20, 2018.

Menchú, Rigoberta, and Elizabeth Burgos Debray. 1985. *Me llamo Rigoberta y así me nació la conciencia*. México: Siglo XX. [*I, Rigoberta Menchú: An Indian Woman in Guatemala*. 1984. Translated by Ann Wright. London: Verso.]

Ndepe Tahar, Mohamed. 2018. *Le Journal de Mickey Le Vieux*. Paris: Atelier SP / Collectif Dessins sans papiers.

Rosi, Gianfranco. 2016. *Fuocoammare*. New York: Kino Lorber.

Sommer, Doris. 1992. "Sin secretos." In *La voz del otro: testimonio, subalternidad y verdad narrativa*, edited by John Beverley, special issue of *Revista de crítica latinoamericana* 18 (36): 137–55.

Vera León, Antonio. 1992. "Hacer hablar: la transcripción testimonial." *La voz del otro: testimonio, subalternidad y verdad narrativa*, special issue of *Revista de crítica latinoamericana* 18 (36): 185–203.

York, Lorraine. 2002. *Rethinking Women's Collaborative Writing: Power, Difference, Property*. Toronto: University of Toronto Press.

CHAPTER THREE

Accidental Form, Mediterranean Transpositions, and New *Francophonies* in Malika Mokeddem's *La Désirante*

Edwige Tamalet Talbayev

[M]oi, j'étais venue au monde exilée. De sorte que je ne saurai jamais si l'arrachement tient du handicap ou du salut.

(Malika Mokeddem, *La Désirante*)

In their article "The concept of minority for the study of culture," Timothy Laurie and Rimi Khan (Laurie and Khan 2017, 1–2) use extended musical metaphor to illuminate the dialectic of power, dread, and desire, keeping the major and minor in fecund tension. The usual symbolic dichotomy between the two scales, they argue, overlaps with gendered social relations and, in its classical instantiation (they cite Viennese symphony), follows a predetermined path eventuating in the overpowering of the feminized minor by the major for the delight and relief of enthralled audiences. In their own words: "Even in gorgeous compositions woven through with natural minor (or Aeolian) lyricisms, listeners expect that wobbly minor refrains—melancholic, unsettled, anxious—will segue into steady major statements … The minor is never opposed to the major as such; rather, the minor is a thing to be dominated, and listeners are taught to enjoy this domination" (1–2). As the authors make clear in their final conceptualization of the issue, posing the question in musical terms boils down to anchoring musical appreciation—and the dialectics of power that underpins it—in desire: "what do listeners want from the minor, if not a return to the major?" (2).

Though this pronouncement may seem at first sight to bear little resemblance to the internal movement of Malika Mokeddem's 2011 novel *La Désirante*, I would like to suggest that it, in fact, powerfully intersects with the narrative's *primum mobile*—desire, the novel's eponymous, central concept, which surges in the wake of loss and trauma (of one's family, of one's land) as a desire for "crossings," here to be understood in their rich polysemy as physical movement but also, and crucially, as cultural and linguistic syncretism on a world-encompassing scale. This chapter poses the following question: how may the Mediterranean as method propose a novel critical idiom colored by the specific material history of the sea to bear on current-day reflections on interculturality? With such an interrogation in mind, this argument probes the contours of the new *francophonies* induced by Mediterranean crossings in a migratory context in *La Désirante*. In an effort to undo the "statut ingrat de l'intruse, doublement étrangère" (Mokeddem 2011, 80), the exiled Algerian narrator's nautical peregrinations affirm her minor position against the two monoliths of French and Algerian cultures, two actualized, reified structures of national consciousness oblivious to the multiple nuances and modulations of the myriad identities that their form encloses. "[B]ercé … par les blues de la Méditerranée" (32), the novel operates a "mise en récit" of identity that follows the ebb and flow of the maritime space here recalibrated as a tabula rasa on which the post-traumatic subject can project and transpose her wounded identity. By drawing on Catherine Malabou's *Ontologie de l'accident* and Kaja Silverman's work on an "ethics of desire," I study the ramifications of this Mediterranean transposition of identity originally figured on the minor mode by probing the rich tension set up by Mokeddem between ontological exile, Mediterranean deterritorialization, and the subject's relation to (and inscription in) "tout un monde" (234). I conclude that the transcontinental[1] Maghrebi *francophonies* featured in the novel crystallize not as an exercise in minorization, but rather as an effort to work through a pervasive

---

1   I define the "transcontinental Maghreb" as "the transnational deployment of the former North African colonies of Morocco, Algeria, and Tunisia within the millennia-old relation that has materially and culturally bound the region to a variety of sites throughout the broader Mediterranean" (Talbayev 2017, 3).

sense of post-traumatic melancholia through the reclaiming of a fully agential, interactive form of subjectivity attuned to a planetary plane of relationality. In this respect, it provides a compelling corrective to the putative reincorporation of the minor into the major that Laurie and Khan propose.

Couched in terms of an enigma, *La Désirante* relates the search for a disappeared sailor, Léo, across the Mediterranean. The novel can be approached as a continuation of the trope of liberating Mediterranean *cabotage* inaugurated in *N'Zid* ten years earlier. A similar plotline (a woman on a quest sailing around the Mediterranean, a disappearance, a personal investigation into the incident but also into the depths and recesses of the female protagonist's identity palimpsest, a searing look at Algerian postcolonial politics) and a parallel narrative technique (*La Désirante* also alternates between chapters in the second and third person) both point to a continuation of the same reflection on the power of mobility on the Mediterranean and of the types of fractures and pressure points that this focus reveals.[2] The female protagonist, Shamsa, has fled an unwelcoming Algeria at the height of the Black Decade to find solace in a new life with Léo on the French Mediterranean coast, a life punctuated by months-long bouts of sailing across the (in)hospitable waters of the contemporary Mediterranean. When Léo disappears without warning, Shamsa's painfully constructed life of normalcy comes tumbling down under the accumulated weight of compounded traumas experienced in Algeria—her abandonment by her mother on the first day of her life in the deep Algerian desert but also the cataclysmic violence that tore Algeria apart during the 1990s. Faced with the resurgence of unresolved trauma, Shamsa's Mediterranean search for Léo paves the way for an in-depth consideration of her own identity quest in an effort to resist dissolution in a world order marked by extremism and violence: "Je vacille sous le choc. Soudain, j'ai le sentiment d'être de nouveau là-bas sous les bombes. Ma tête explose. ... 'Je n'en peux plus des tragédies.' ... [elles] me rappellent à ce que j'ai déjà vécu. Ce que j'ai fui" (17).

In an earlier argument, I identified a "Mediterranean nomadism" at work in Malika Mokeddem's novelistic corpus (Talbayev 2017, chapter 3). At an angle to received accounts of her well-known trope

---

2 Significant differences exist, however, notably in the treatment of the female figure. For instance, in *N'Zid,* Nora is the one lost at sea without recollection of the past, while, here, it is Shamsa who is undertaking the search.

of "desert nomadism," this sea-inspired form of mobility operates beyond the framework of exile and of the cultures brought in contact by colonialism. Mediated through the crossing of the sea, Mediterranean nomadism purveys new transnational social affiliations in the wake of violence—in the case of Mokeddem's novels, the devastating brutality that engulfed Algeria during the Black Decade. I argued that texts such as *N'Zid* engender a transcontinental deployment of Maghrebi subjectivities across the sea that function as a working through of past trauma born of marginalization from a monolithic national body: "At the core of working through, the ethical necessity of haunting—preserving alterity within the self through the melancholic incorporation of other repressed voices—looms large, shifting the weight of trauma from the purely individual to the collective" (135).[3] Yet, in *N'Zid*, this Mediterranean, melancholic approach to diversity works on the national level as it "mediates the nomadic subject's reinsertion into a revised national collective attentive to its intrinsic heterogeneity" (32). I want to suggest that, though the post-traumatic process afoot in *N'Zid* persists throughout *La Désirante*, Mokeddem's later novel reworks the imperative of moving beyond trauma on a planetary scale, indexing any form of reterritorialization of identity to a concurrent movement of global deployment.

Accidental Form

Anne Emmanuelle Berger locates the source of the subject's identification with a national community in the use of a common mother tongue. Through a shared linguistic code imbued with the enduring memory of one's own past in the maternal bosom, a "symbolic wedding … with [one's] fellow nationals" is performed, prompting the subject's continuous shuttling between the intimate world of family relations—the realm of the endogamic—and the exterior sphere of national affiliations and exogamic alliances (Berger 2002, 65). Through the use of a layered, palimpsestic form of (dialectical) Arabic, a foundational overlap between family and community is enacted in which

---

3   Significantly, and quite presciently in the context of this argument, Mokeddem couches this in terms of an "accident vital de mémoire" (Mokeddem 2008, 38) in *Je dois tout à ton oubli*, an intercalary narrative bringing her triptych on dispossession and rememoration to full completion.

the subject's strong attachment to the collective order originates. As self and other remain coterminous, the subject's turn to the other is reconfigured as a return to the self. Or, to dub Berger, the turn to the outside world morphs into a return home through a different kind of collective affiliation—"another home, the home with the other: the *home*land" (65).

Language politics in *La Désirante* runs counter to this commingling of endogamic and exogamic impulse as Arabic functions first, if paradoxically, as a vector of deterritorialization. The protagonist's name, Shamsa, derived from *al-shams*, the sun, deviates the strict semantics of luminosity and searing violence into a minor, feminine morphological desinence. Rather than the powerful, unyielding *shams*, Shamsa conjures the more ambiguous *soleil noir* of an inherited, lingering melancholia. She owes her "déshérence" to her exclusion from the incandescent order of the tribe, the kinship forged in fire and blood, the one whose eclipse has left its indelible mark on her: "Le soleil avant la lumière … Plutôt Shamsa que Shamse, oui, Soleil et au féminin, n'en déplaise à tout ce qui a motivé qu'elle soit expédiée aux antipodes de ses origines un jour noir de vent de sable. Un jour de soleil exilé" (58–59). Whether an exiled sun or "la fille du soleil," in her father-in-law's tender ascription, her solar deployment is one of bereavement and excommunication: "Il m'a toujours appelée ainsi, la fille du soleil. Cela me convient. Son enthousiasme répudie la part ténébreuse, indissociablement liée à l'aveuglante lumière algérienne. Je n'y entends qu'une manière élégante de désigner une fille sans famille" (14).

This structure of exclusion from the tribe gives rise to a productive sense of non-belonging. The narrative unfolds along a deviated trajectory, swerving away from any patriarchal ordering principle toward a minor position—here a feminized one in an echo of what Abdelkébir Khatibi has dubbed "la marge des marges: le féminin" (Khatibi 2008, 10). Obviating any clear-cut sense of origins, this drifting semantic applies to the many flights punctuating Shamsa's life—out of the desert against her volition as a one-day-old baby, but also her journey out of Algeria at the height of violence, as well as her many escapes away from Léo in the early days of her relationship when "dépendance affective" (80) was anathema to her. Perpetual motion without destination, Shamsa's original itinerary bears the mark of endless wandering and re-routings. Echoing Gilles Deleuze and Félix Guattari's "lines of flights," these sequential escapes deploy identity along multifold ruptures, denying any deep-reaching sense of reterritorialization.

The post-traumatic fragmentation they induce lies at the core of Catherine Malabou's concept of an "ontological refugee" (Malabou 2012, 24). Malabou demonstrates how, under the onslaught of trauma, the self seeks refuge in a "void of subjectivity," a "distancing" (24), which relegates her to a solipsistic position on the margins of existence. Rejected from the community, but also in exile from her own ontological integrity—here a stable, unified sense of being—a split subject inhabits the space of the interval, where the self "is being other to the self" (11). In this form of intrinsic alterity, others have no remanence. At an absolute remove from the world, the wounded subject is ever withdrawn into herself. In contexts in which a physical flight out of traumatic circumstances proves impossible, this dual form of self-exile—exile of the self from the environment but also exile of the self from itself—secures a sheltered space where identity may be suspended and reconfigured in dissociation from the world. According to Malabou, this metamorphosis is devastating, the product of a "[d]estructive plasticity" (11), in which resilience implies durably renouncing any claim to connectivity: "the flight identity forged by destructive plasticity flees itself first and foremost; it knows no salvation or redemption and is there for no one, especially not for the self" (12). Disappeared from themselves and from others alike, these forsaken subjects inhabit a realm of ruins where identity lies disassembled, prey to unfathomable emptiness: "Existing, in these cases ... amounts to experiencing a lack of exteriority, which is as much an absence of interiority, hence the impossible flight, the on the spot transformation" (14).

La Désirante teems with such examples of "identitarian abandonment" (14). Teetering between the two poles of Malabou's dialectic of flight and transformation, the Algerian subjects populating Mokeddem's fictive universe exemplify various degrees and combinations of *étrangeté*. Shamsa's life is a variation on the theme of desertion: "J'avais été abandonnée à ma naissance dans une Algérie violente" (31). Be it as all-engulfing void or a diffracted sense of self (broken *psyche* as both mirror, in the etymological sense of the word, and psyche), Algeria presides over the novel as a principle of annihilation— the traditional ogress of folk tales, only in this case one insatiably feasting on her hapless children. Setting the self in perpetual motion, this original disappearance is that of the Algerian land itself, its mise en abyme of self-dispossession: "Heureux ce premier jour où j'ai quitté cette terre *exilée en elle-même*" (95, emphasis added). Shamsa's traumatic disenchantment and subsequent withdrawal coalesces around the deafening absence of an ordering principle. Standing at empty coordinates, Algeria triggers off a dynamic of endless flight (Shamsa experiences "deux années et demie d'errance à travers la France," 52). This logic of *déplacement* (Shamsa is said to be "déplacée" [29], thrown off course) shares significant ground with the process of spectralization that progressively takes hold of the novel: "Je ne me sentais plus de corps. Plus de peau. Plus de cœur" (84). Shamsa's wandering through the desert town of her birth elicits a sense of disembodiment as she morphs into a ghost haunting back the place haunting her: "j'avais la sensation d'être un fantôme errant dans un village qui n'existe pas" (94). This mise en abyme of virtuality relegates Algeria—and all who anchor themselves in her—to the realm of the unrealized, or even the unrealizable: "C'était ça l'image de mes origines, un mirage. Juste un mirage" (95). Algeria's ontological vacuity spreads its diaphanous hue onto any sense of origin. As self-destruction reigns supreme, notions of belonging are displaced toward exclusion and extraneity to the self: "Je partais pour ne pas disparaître à mon tour comme disparaissait mon passé" (101).

Shamsa's distanciation from Algeria finds its material expression in the sterile "empathie" imbuing her journalistic investigation of the Algerian carnage, the culmination of the country's long-standing *déshérence*. A mere ploy to deflect attention from her own traumas ("à enquêter sur autrui, j'occultais ma propre histoire," 70), her work seeks refuge in distance and objectivity: "cette obstination féroce [d]es faits, uniquement les faits, la vérité" (69), a position that feeds into the logic of self-exile brought about by trauma. This disfigurement of the self bears the imprimatur of the fragmentation affecting the Algerian *matres dolorosae* mourning the loss of their relatives. The grieving bodies of the victims' female relatives fall prey to floating immateriality: "ces visages ravagés" (18), "[d]es visages sans corps. Tous confondus en une masse de calamités et d'obsessions" (29). Likewise, Léo haunts the text in the shape of several dozens of dematerialized portraits, all of which eventually blend into a vortex: his "visage démultiplié" (28) finds echo in Shamsa's "mine défaite" (29) only to better establish the corrosive influence of loss. This disintegration rehearses the self-mutilation of Algeria: "l'Algérie défigurée par la masse des foulards, des œillères" (18), and prolongs the orphaning it induces. Significantly, this emptiness takes root in the desert: "Avant toi, j'étais déserte" (103), what survives before the fertile encounter with otherness: "C'était cette différence qui m'accueillait … Notre rencontre m'a rendue désirante" (102–03).

Mediterranean Transpositions

Mokeddem's dialectic of female desire, the primum mobile of Shamsa's mobility, appears as a powerful force far exceeding the limits imposed by a normative social order premised on the eradication of its margins. Thriving at the limit of the symbolic, Shamsa's peregrinations concurrently reveal and undercut the ties binding together the familial (that from which she has been excluded) and the political (that in which she cannot find her place). Shamsa allows her protean, unspecified desire to drive her personal quest. The embodiment of feminine desire's transgressive potential, her itinerary reshuffles the order of the symbolic on multiple scales and redefines subjectivity in terms of autonomy (in a fashion resonant with Jean-Luc Nancy's *singularité*) but also of vulnerability and exposure. Shamsa's first dealings with the Mediterranean from her emplacement on the shore divulge this vulnerability. The sea first figures a "grand espace," the pendant of Shamsa's native desert. An expanse free of any extraneous presence, it offers a temporary reprieve from real world relationships: "courir vers la Méditerranée. Pour faire le vide. Le miroir des eaux chassait mes hantises … éprouver la solitude dans le murmure de la mer" (62). It is a dematerialized space, a virtual expanse bereft of actuality. Through contemplation, the subject can eschew relationships to others. An extension of her impenetrability, her "solitude" rejoices in what she envisions as her absolute difference, her fundamental incommensurability to social forms. The Mediterranean becomes a blank surface upon which her irreducible opacity is sealed.

It is only through navigation across the Mediterranean that Shamsa can reclaim her power to impact the world. Her regular crossings alongside Léo take the shape of a rehabilitation; it is a praxis for how to navigate the unknown: "Léo … soufflait régulièrement dans la corne de brume afin de signaler notre présence. Fascinée, je regardais sa silhouette se brouiller, s'effacer par intermittences" (21). From "intermittences" to long-lasting agency ("Je pars seule sur tes traces," 15), Shamsa learns how to exist in the eyes of others without fleeing or defaulting. Fully inhabiting the world, she learns to negotiate a place for herself. Léo's boat *Vent de Sable* becomes a cradle: "avoir enfin trouvé ma place dans ce berceau flottant entre deux rives. Une coque de plastique pour des amours bercées par les blues de la Méditerranée" (32). The Mediterranean "blues," here to be taken in their visual *and* aural reverberations, stand in for a mode of relationality imbued with fluidity and renewal. In Iain Chambers's words, "Music is here [in the Mediterranean] a form of becoming that puts to the test not only what might have been as much as what might be ... thinking the Mediterranean in the incomplete terms of a composition in progress makes it critically dissonant with respect to fixed representations" (Chambers 2012, 57; my translation throughout). Through mobility, the Mediterranean affords acuity of vision. The sharpness gained from the maritime journey purveys insight, undoing barren melancholia: "Je ... me laisse captiver par le ruissellement des lumières à fleur d'eau ... Cette acuité recouvrée est ma première victoire sur la tristesse" (12).

This liquid light, a diluted form of the searing light of Algerian extremism, radiates warmth and mediation. Taming the brute force of the flashes of trauma besetting the wounded psyche, its diffraction resemantizes the trope of post-traumatic demultiplication woven through the narrative. The pervasive motif of the eye (`*ayn* in Arabic, one semantic resonance of Aïn Dakhla, her birth town) or, rather, *ocularism*, ties in to the most extreme forms of fragmentation: "A force de chercher à en sonder les abîmes, je n'étais plus qu'un œil effaré. Un œil avide qui captait, disséquait, scrutait les différences. Une violence muette s'imprimait sur ma rétine jusqu'à me décérébrer" (84). Shamsa's becoming-*oeil* is a product of Algeria's blinding violence, "la part ténébreuse, indissociablement liée à l'aveuglante lumière algérienne ... je tombe dans son œil noir. Sans fond" (14, 18). From the bottom of this abyss, a distorted vision of the country surges. In contrast, Shamsa's newfound, Mediterranean-inspired clarity of vision weaves a searing critique of the Maghreb she has left behind: "Dans l'exil ... , la Méditerranée m'est devenue une sorte de loupe braquée sur le Sud" (213). Her critical scrutiny delivers a blistering indictment of the rampant corruption reigning supreme on the Mediterranean's southern shore—what could be dubbed a form of *monocularism* by the powers that be: "ceux-ci [les officiers] ne fermaient jamais que l'œil de la légalité, l'autre restant braqué sur le volume des denrées illicites en transit dont dépendaient leurs gains frauduleux" (227). In contrast, mediation through the Mediterranean affords a unique dual vantage point into a relational modernity whereby northern and southern shores evolve in tandem on either side of the sea's reflecting surface: both are home to "'réseaux dormants'" (52) (disenfranchised youths in the south, decaying boats in the north), whose reintegration into a more tolerant national construct may foster productive change. The promise of a better future surges from the effort to come to terms with a traumatic past, not by denying its enduring resonance but rather by elaborating within the remains of this past a "politics of mourning that might be active rather than reactive, prescient rather than nostalgic, abundant rather than lacking, social rather than solipsistic, militant rather than reactionary" (Eng and Kazanjian 2003, 1). In the context of Mokeddem's novel, coming to grips with the remanence of trauma implies questioning the kind of social practice that a process of transposition aiming to reactivate the Mediterranean's long-standing congregating function may devise.

Against any Renan-inspired concept of community formation—namely his proposition that nation building relies on oblivion—Chambers insists:

> [t]he musical maps of a *minor* modernity and Mediterranean designate an archive that is concurrently a vault, the threshold of oblivion and amnesia, and also the manifest foundation of a *tombeau*, an enduring blues: an emptying out of space in the present *so that the past may be left free to interpellate the future*." (Chambers 2012, 51, emphasis added)

Musical imagery courses through the text. The panacea against violence, navigation effects a transposition of Shamsa's minor position of solipsism: the sea voyage "est rythmé par une polyphonie fortissimo: le boucan de l'hélice qui va crescendo avec le volume de l'onde déplacée" (Mokeddem 2011, 116–17). The elemental violence troubling the purported polyphony renders the intense strain of the quest for Léo, the difficulty of a pursuit that will bring Shamsa right back to the desert and the source (ʿayn) of her trauma. In a superimposition between the two "grands espaces" governing the score of her life, the sea comes to channel the desert, with beach sand and dune sand commingling in auditory continuity, earning Shamsa her "revanche" (218) against the desert: "J'écoute la mer, j'entends le vent de sable" (218), a formula echoing as a leitmotiv throughout the novel's coda. Dislodging the shuffling chronology of self-repeating trauma ("je ne suis plus condamnée à la perte à perpétuité" [218]), the novel inaugurates the extrapolation of the self and a natural movement toward alterity: "mon désir vital de compter pour quelqu'un. Quelqu'un d'autre pour une autre rive. Un étranger, forcément" (217). Shamsa's itinerary is rife with the echo of the past, as it is only through its acceptance that forward movement can occur: "cette fois, ma fugue est le contraire du bannissement et du renoncement" (231–32). Inaugurating yet another meaning of the term "fugue,"[4] the musical metaphor privileges the contrapuntal as well as

---

4   For a thorough discussion of the polysemy of the term with regards to literary writing, see Rice 2006, 233.

imitative transposition. Emulating Léo, Shamsa learns a new form of being in the world that concurs with what Kaja Silverman has named a "release … from the paralysis of being into the mobility of becoming" in all its interactive resonance (Silverman 2000, 67).

Through her imitation of Léo's maritime praxis, Shamsa gains individual agency through an initiatory, single-handed, maiden voyage: "ma première traversée seule" (33). Though the journey starts as a solitary undertaking ("La côte à peine disparue, je ne suis pas mécontente de voir mon portable afficher 'sans réseau'" [35]), the tutelary presence of the polyphony constructed through the lovers' peregrinations excavates other "networks." Through this mirroring, the Mediterranean transposition of Shamsa's minor position impels forms of solidarity with other subjects also imbued with "solitude,"[5] stretching the limits of her "exercise in narcissistic solipsism" to accommodate its "extension in ever new directions of [her] capacity to care" (Silverman 2000, 62). This is what Silverman calls an "ethics of desire—an ethics grounded in a passion for symbolization, in a delight in the manifold and ever new forms that the past can assume" (62). This ethics of desire lies at the core of the onomastics underlying the text: in Shamsa's words, "ton bateau file plus vite que le vent. Je l'aurais volontiers renommé: *La Désirante*. Je me sens bien" (Mokeddem 2011, 230–01), enacting a perfect overlap with the novel's titular quality.[6] This resurgence of past bonds, beckoning across time and space, resurrects another class of "déracinés" (81)—a "horde d'expatriés sans tribu, de solitudes déplacées, livrées à la même précarité" (81). Through cross-Mediterranean displacement, a common condition of exile plants the seeds of solidarity in Shamsa's mind. A substitute for the "aride quête de parenté" idiosyncratic to the "majorité érigée en normalité" (113), her identification with the "Nord-Africains errant … Ces solitudes juxtaposées" (150–51) lifts the veil on the proximity of both subject positions: it is only sheer luck that has afforded Shamsa a fate different from that of the "errants de la misère" (110).

Yet this common destitution still falls short of constructing a long-term, robust community. Only in the lasting time of the transcontinental Mediterranean does the novel locate a truly *desirable* social

5   Interestingly, Léo is presented as the one who has led Shamsa out of the "labyrinthe de la solitude" (83).

6   This desire is imbued with a clear Sufi resonance, which would deserve more analysis than I am able to provide here. See for example Shamsa's statement: "Je suis entrée dans la transe. Je fais corps avec *Vent de Sable*" (230).

order. This ideal is presented in the novel through the idyllic, exoticized space of the Kerkennah Islands off the Tunisian Coast, "un petit bout de désert en pleine mer" (203). The evocation of the rudimentariness of the fishermen's equipment or their timeless techniques points to an aesthetic construction evocative of an eternal Mediterranean: "loin, très, très loin dans le temps" (205). The figure of Jamila, the mother of her friend Nabil whose intervention will prove conclusive in solving Léo's disappearance, incarnates the presence in the world and mindfulness to others that the islands symbolize. A liminal space deactivating the threat intrinsic to desertic spaces, the Kerkennah Islands stand for long-awaited harmony, as well as a concept of Mediterranean measure owing much to Albert Camus. The islands lie outside the logic of Western humanitarianism: "[Jamila] ne tolérait qu'on portât sur elle un regard compatissant" (206). Against voyeuristic, objectifying sympathy for the various forms of violence and exploitation perpetrated on North African subjects, the relationship that morphs between the Western(ized) lovers and the Tunisian woman is one resting on mutual respect and affinity. At cross-purposes with venality and self-interest, hospitality and support prevail as modes of interaction between "altruiste[s]" (207). When the pair repay Jamila's hospitality by defraying the cost of her house renovations, Shamsa denies any charity, invoking instead an advance on future assistance of another sort. Only this time-tested exchange of favors, the currency of Mokeddem's idealized eternal Mediterranean, can make the debt bearable. Mutual assistance materializes as an "élan" (207), the cement of this alternative form of affiliative kinship.

The ideal of peace and harmony epitomized by the islands cuts across any rigid conceptions of Maghrebi identity, and it is no surprise that Shamsa's conception should revitalize a "Berber" cultural substrate inclusive of its Jewish, Christian, and even animist margins in a foretelling "métissage" (131).[7] The "unisson" (223) born of her fusional relationship with Léo extends out into the world, and its polyphony reflects the Mediterranean's usefulness as a "dispositif à faire de la civilisation" (Khatibi 1997, 86). Significantly, the last journey to Léo veers closer to reterritorialization: "Depuis Reggio, je navigue au plus près des côtes pour garder le contact avec les réseaux téléphoniques … Je n'ai jamais autant discuté, en mer, avec ceux restés à terre" (233–35). This informal

---

7   Yet the notion itself is not devoid of discriminatory blind spots: thus, narrow-minded Algerians are dubbed "moricauds … ancrés ailleurs, dans d'autres valeurs" (217), a turn-of-phrase congruent with disturbing racialized discourse.

network of like-minded Mediterraneans stretches from Cephalonia, to Southern Italy, Northern Tunisia, and, of course, Southern France. The French Mediterranean coastline is also where Nina Simone, who embarked on her own identity quest between continents, came to rest. Her voice expresses "la clameur de tout un monde en devenir" (234), an ever-fluid, relational whole extending beyond geographic and political confines, a world both attuned to the past and dedicated to moving beyond its multiple traumas: "Qui ne renonce pas à fouiller les failles et les fragilités, à questionner les humains, à forcer l'oubli" (234). The community that it shapes shares in the imperative of forgiveness and compromise, though not oblivion (the text enjoins to "puiser aux sources vives des toujours," 234). This process is generative of a new Mediterranean, intersubjective plasticity unfolding along the vast networks of *entraide* that maritime mobility has activated.

New *Francophonies*

This Mediterranean configuration articulates a new form of expression inclusive of this enduring diversity. Thus, under the surface of the French through which the novel is scripted, a Mediterranean lingua franca transpires. An early episode of plurilingual interaction sheds crucial light on the economy of language use in the novel. As Shamsa and Léo's father meet with the Italian police in Reggio to go over possible scenarios explaining Léo's disappearance, a subtle undertow comes to distort the signifying surface of the French language in which the narrative is couched. The reader learns early on in the text that the main investigator, "le *carabiniere* Lorenzo" (17), speaks French with "un fort accent italien" (17), insufflating through his intonation an element of foreignness into the common language. Both reinforcing the dominance of French as a potential lingua franca of the Mediterranean and also disjointing it through its foreign inflection, Lorenzo's distorted diction paves the way for a reconsideration of the symbolic and political power of French. The conversation shapes up along the lines of an interrogation as both Shamsa and Léo's father Régis are investigated first as suspects in the kidnapping. In an effort to rule them out, various lines of inquiry are pursued, some incriminating Léo himself, others Shamsa. Yet it is the supposition that a former lover of the woman—by which Lorenzo seems to imply an Algerian—might have exacted a jealous revenge on Léo that is dismissed most forcefully by the pair, sparking a surge of violence in Régis. Reviving the most hackneyed stereotypes of Othello-like ruthlessness and perfidy, Lorenzo's line of questioning provokes "consternation" and "sidération" (47). This unexpected mention of irreconcilable cultural differences between the northern and southern shores of the Sea drives the three characters to a dramatic dead end: "Régis ... lâche ma main, s'arc-boute, prêt à sauter sur Lorenzo" (47).

This reaction obviates any possible form of dialogue and mediation on both ends as Lorenzo's aide "se prépare à intervenir" (47). The scene seems to be set for untamed violence to erupt. Yet against all expectations, the climactic tension suddenly eases, giving way to dialogue and negotiation among all the actors. The shift from one of the most emphatically Orientalist clichés against North African men to a Mediterranean language of mediation is striking. What the novel suggests, in fact very soon after this melodramatic crescendo, is that Lorenzo's provocation stems more from an epistemological problem than ontological incompatibility between Northern and Southern Mediterranean subjects. The main issue at stake is Lorenzo's inability to distance himself from his disciplinary role as a representative of a European police force to consider the full complexity of Shamsa's identity. His initial persona is first, if not foremost, that of an investigator, and for that reason his engagement with the potential suspect needs to follow the letter of European policing methodologies. This inflexibility provides a paradigmatic example of the dangers of a literalist adherence to "over-determined protocols of encounter" that forestall any possibility of deviation or "performativity" (Rosello 2005). Only when Lorenzo recognizes the heuristic potential of undetermined, impromptu intellectual interaction can the confrontation mellow into regenerative dialogue. Deflecting the potential scuffle, the protagonists' shared desire for understanding makes room for differences and presuppositions to be explained away and for common ground to be identified: "D'un geste apaisant, Lorenzo admet qu'il n'ignore pas combien tous ces poncifs, avec lesquels il vient de nous charger, peuvent nous paraître inopportuns voire agressifs. C'est son devoir de creuser dans toutes les directions" (Mokeddem 2011, 47). Through empathy and openness to the other, Lorenzo ("il s'inquiète"; "[a]vec plus d'égards ... [il] finit par nous confirmer," [47]) and Shamsa (who filters Lorenzo's voice through free indirect speech) come to an understanding. Breaking apart any binary epistemological framework, their genuine interaction reveals the intrinsic fictitiousness of all ready-made cultural reading grids.

It is this chapter's argument that the new model of *Francophonie* that the novel propounds follows the logic inaugurated by this shift from dichotomous, rigid descriptions of identity to compromise and collaboration. The episode concludes with the signing of the "déposition" drafted by Lorenzo's aide, possibly in French, though the language of the document is never quite ascertained. Significantly, the episode is said to take place in the *"caserna dei carabinieri,"* an expression couched in Italian in the text. Yet, through naturalized suspension of disbelief, the writing (and acceptance) of the deposition is carried out in a mutually understandable, albeit undesignated, language. Here the Mediterranean functions as a cipher for a spirit of rationality and dialogue; it is what allows the deposition to come into being. In ratifying the signed deposition, the protagonists establish a shared Mediterranean idiom unmoored from the sterile, exclusive grammar of the European Union's disciplining discourse, whose influence over the premises of Lorenzo's investigation had come close to endangering the collaboration.[8] Other moments similarly thematize the undoing of entrenched prejudices and dichotomous models of interaction through the critique of long-established protocols and the acknowledgment of their implicit bias. Thus, as Shamsa and Lorenzo discuss his network of collaborators across the Mediterranean, the Italian policeman quips, "Nous avons l'habitude de nous rendre mutuellement service en bonne entente" (221). Shamsa is prompt to point out the opportunism underlying the expression of Mediterranean mutuality which Lorenzo mobilizes: "Vous voulez dire que vous travaillez donnant-donnant. A la police tunisienne le gang des Nord-Africains et pour vous, le témoin principal? (221). Lorenzo's response—"Lorenzo s'est esclaffé de bon cœur et j'ai senti toute la tension de la journée s'évanouir" (221)— demonstrates both his willingness to accept criticism and the forgiveness necessary for community building. Instead of defending the corps that he embodies, Lorenzo draws nearer to Shamsa's ironical stance and accepts her critical insight, while his peal of laughter blurs the dividing line between the two. As she settles in their interactive collaboration, Shamsa experiences a similar form of displacement when, abandoning

---

8 I am here referring to Dominic Thomas's point that "when one investigates the vocabulary employed by officials, the language of conventions, treaties and pacts, a new grammar of migration comes into evidence whose referentiality, signifying power and linguistic coding highlight forms of intolerance" (Thomas 2013, 172).

her stance of radical exteriority and difference, she inches closer to the strictures of Lorenzo's own official position. As she prepares to take over the final investigative episode through direct interrogation, she morphs into a police collaborator and learns to accept the limitations that this new affiliation imposes: "[tu es] quelqu'un qu'ils savent de mèche avec toute la flicaille de la Méditerranée" (216).

This fluid motion colors the epistemological foundation of language as it is empirically enacted in the novel. Dominant discursive forms, including those still subjected to dichotomous logics, such as stereotypes, are disassembled. In contrast, new, incongruous relationships between disparate semantic elements are formed. Antithesis is absorbed as part and parcel of the fluid semantics in a move unsettling any leaning toward essentialism.[9] Symbolic networks are reinvented, and new de-hierarchized forms of ordering between concepts fostered. As their subject positions intersect, the two partners uncover common ground from which to approach one another and create a mixed form of language. During his early interactions with Shamsa, Lorenzo read her Algerian origins within a racialized, Orientalist order that marked female identity with the stigma of gender oppression. Nevertheless, during their last encounter, Lorenzo brings Shamsa sunflowers, in a meaningful symbolic gesture, and addresses the Arabic resonance of her name: "Tous les soleils pour Shamsa. Je fais des progrès en arabe, n'est-ce pas?" (233). A far cry from the Orientalist clichés saturating their early encounter, Lorenzo's cross-linguistic offering re-anchors Shamsa in the orbit of the tutelary sun and restores her to a heritage that is here perceived in its singular density rather than as the object of an essentialist reading. The cross-linguistic polysemy of the Arabic word *shams* is here detached from the opacity of Arabic and incorporated into a common language incarnated in familiar objects and gestures: in this case, the sunflowers with which Lorenzo gratifies her in a gesture of friendship.

This shared Mediterranean idiom is transcribed into French in the text. It is in French that the dialogue with the Italian investigator unfolds, in French that the incident report is presented as a tool through which to erode any rendering of identity and culture from a dominant viewpoint. This decentered French, the common language between the Algerian refugee and the Italian *carabinieri*, undermines

---

9   For instance, one of the key revelations of the investigation comes from the owner of a boat named *Le Malvenu*: "Le propriétaire de *Malvenu* est arrivé à point nommé" (169).

their dichotomous positions. In this respect, it brings to mind the hapful colorations of Khatibi's *interlangue*, a space where "le tout-autre veille sur la force poétique" (Khatibi 1987, 205). Revealing language as *tout-autre* within itself, linguistic performance reverberates as a bilingual or interlingual process where the interpenetration between same and other shines through: "Dans chaque mot: d'autres mots; dans chaque langue: le séjour d'autres langues" (205). This language striates French, insufflates new life into it. It uncovers intermingling, cross-pollinating idioms at work beneath its surface, its movement corroding the visible and invisible vestiges of colonial inducement. A new linguistic space is revealed where dialects intersect, vocabularies collide, and discourses interpenetrate to perforate colonial regimes of signification. They reveal permeable, fluctuating strands that query dominant visions of French as the arrow-like language of imperialism. In Gilles Deleuze and Félix Guattari's ascription, this idiom

> remains a mixture, a schizophrenic mélange, a Harlequin costume in which very different functions of language and distinct centers of power are played out … all the degrees of territoriality and relative deterritori-alization will be played out … along creative lines of escape which, no matter how slowly, no matter how cautiously, can now form an absolute deterritorialization. (Deleuze and Guattari 1986, 26)

Enacting a diffracted politics of language, Mokeddem's text foregrounds a series of semantic, geographic, and cross-linguistic movements to open up the French language to the ferment of the historic Mediterranean idiom that the novel reconstructs. As the distinctive grammar of exclusive values loses its stronghold, a new form of *Francophonie* emerges that feeds from the wellspring of cross-Mediterranean contact and interaction. The investigative language of the search for Léo, a language inflected with multiple encounters along the Mediterranean coast, naturalizes this Mediterranean form of expression—a common idiom that all parties share in their fight against political extremism. In Jane Hiddleston's words, "All languages are open to flux and ambiguity, creating diverse specific idioms at different moments in time … absorbing new nuances and inviting new associations [… they are] part of a dynamic network of relations" (Hiddleston 2005, 85–86). Hiddleston's frame of reference is Jean-Luc Nancy's concept of singularity which, once brought to bear on language formation, highlights the "'articulat[ion of]' particular idioms while displaying the traces of their contact with other linguistic influences" (85).

The novel indicates that it is through the process of negotiating differences and moving beyond past stereotypical views—that is, through the recognition and cultivation of each party's singularity—that true collaboration can germinate. The same intimation extends to the sphere of family ties: whereas Shamsa originally experienced Léo's family as an intrusion, she finally accepts her mother-in-law's attempts at reinserting her into the order of another tribe: "Elle ponctue ses questions, ses recommandations en répétant 'ma fille' avec une telle douceur que j'ai appris à accepter cette appellation, à composer avec son étrangeté" (235). This *apprentissage* stands as a paragon for all quests, all flights born of an uprooting dynamic. Through this dual perspective, a fully fledged *binocularism* brings the subjects ever closer together in a stark refutation of the venal monocularism of those afflicted with self-interest and corruption. It is this multifocality that marks out new Mediterranean migrations and the transpositions of minor subjectivities that they induce.

Mokeddem hinges her relational hybrid cultural model around the titular figure of Nina Simone. The African American soul singer emerges, appropriately enough, through the wafting of her voice, which is said to blend with the ebb and flow of the sea. Piercing the eternal rumbling of the waves, her melancholy cry, "Who am I?" (234), carries within it the universal song of the nomadic soul adrift in the world. As Shamsa suggests, it is less the woman herself than her mobility that has worked to disseminate her song. Her perpetual search across continents, the magnetism that Africa as the original continent has exerted on her life, her ultimate decision to settle down in a third space along the Mediterranean shore—all of Simone's life choices conspire to create the persona of a "nomade géante" capable of harnessing the power of a truly global form of consciousness awash in the world around it: "Ni plainte ni pleur, mais la clameur de *tout un monde* en devenir qui s'élève au-dessus des mers, des terres, des frontières" (234, emphasis added).

In the "tout un monde" formula, shared echoes of Édouard Glissant's *tout-monde* surface, tying the novel's model of nomadism to a fluid relationality:

> analogy is at the heart of Glissant's theory of Tout-monde, understood now as an epistemological program, a mode of inquiry that seeks to get a better sense of the meaning of objects, events, people, and communities by emphasizing their participation in the larger webs of relation that link them to analogous phenomena elsewhere in the world. (Prieto 2010, 116)

Following the logic of Glissant's *tout-monde*, binocularism may also be perceived as the dual paradigm that considers subjects in their singularity while concurrently replacing them in this larger, global context. In the swell of back-and-forth modulations, in a break from rigid major tones, working through multiple modulations and dissonances, the melodic line reaches a final resolution. Reterritorialized in the humus of her new life—in a decentered plane rid of stifling dichotomies, both mindful of its planetary reach and attentive not to mediate any universalizing impulse in the process—Shamsa lays claim to "tout un monde." A non-totalizing world. A world left in suspension through the use of the indefinite article. One cadence among many.

Works Cited

Berger, Anne Emmanuelle. 2002. *Algeria in Others' Languages.* Ithaca: Cornell University Press.

Chambers, Iain. 2012. *Mediterraneo Blues: Musiche, malinconia postcoloniale, pensieri marittimi.* Translated by Sara Marinelli. Torino: Bollati Boringhieri.

Deleuze, Gilles, and Félix Guattari. 1986. *Kafka: Towards a Minor Literature.* Translated by Dana Polan. Minneapolis: University of Minnesota Press.

Eng, David, and David Kazanjian (eds.). 2003. *Loss: The Politics of Mourning.* Berkeley: University of California Press.

Hiddleston, Jane. 2005. *Reinventing Community: Identity and Difference in Late Twentieth-Century Philosophy and Literature in French.* Abingdon: Legenda.

Khatibi, Abdelkébir. 1987. *Figures de l'étranger dans la littérature française.* Paris: Denoël.

——. 1997. "Paradigmes de civilisation." In *L'Œuvre de … Abdelkébir Khatibi,* 69–87. Rabat: Marsam.

——. 2008. "Pensée-Autre." In *Œuvres de Abdelkébir Khatibi III, Essais,* 9–27. Paris: Éditions de la Différence.

Laurie, Timothy, and Rimi Khan. 2017. "The Concept of Minority for the Study of Culture." *Continuum: Journal of Media and Cultural Studies* 31, no.1: 1–12.

Malabou, Catherine. 2012. *Ontology of the Accident: An Essay on Destructive Plasticity.* Translated by Carolyn Shread. Cambridge: Polity.

Mokeddem, Malika. 2001. *N'Zid.* Paris: Seuil.

——. 2008. *Je dois tout à ton oubli.* Paris: Grasset.

——. 2011. *La Désirante.* Paris: Grasset.

Prieto, Eric. 2010. "Edouard Glissant, *Littérature-monde*, and *Tout-Monde*." *small axe* 14 (3): 111–20.

Rice, Alison. 2006. *Time Signatures: Contextualizing Contemporary Francophone Autobiographical Writing from the Maghreb*. Lanham, MD: Lexington.

Rosello, Mireille. 2005. *France and the Maghreb: Performative Encounters*. Gainesville: University of Florida Press.

Silverman, Kaja. 2000. *World Spectators*. Stanford: Stanford University Press.

Talbayev, Edwige Tamalet. 2017. *The Transcontinental Maghreb: Francophone Literature across the Mediterranean*. New York: Fordham University Press.

Thomas, Dominic. 2013. *France and Africa: Postcolonial Cultures, Migrations, and Racism*. Indianapolis: Indiana University Press.

PART II

Multilingual Aesthetics and Poetics

CHAPTER FOUR

Abdelfattah Kilito

Writing beyond Monolingualism and Multilingualism

Jane Hiddleston

Multilingualism, and a resistance to the idea that language is defined by and confined to national or ethnic borders, has recently been the object of a good deal of critical attention. Yasemin Yildiz, for example, comprehensively punctures the myth of monolingualism in *Beyond the Mother Tongue: The Postmonolingual Condition*, published in 2012, where she traces the growth of the monolingual paradigm in eighteenth-century Europe as a way of structuring modern social life, as well as showing how the notion of the "mother tongue" relatively recently comes to dictate the construction of origin and identity. David Gramling's *The Invention of Monolingualism*, published in 2016, moreover, goes on to trace the continuity between, on the one hand, monolingualism and modernity in the eighteenth century, and, on the other, the promotion of only certain, acceptable forms of multilingualism in the current "linguacene" defined by the global market. Insisting that monolingualism is a "myth" in the sense that Roland Barthes attributes to it, that it is an ideological construction that presents itself as "innocent" or "inherent," he argues that "monolingualism has experienced an asymptotic spike in impact and innovation since the 1990s and has become the organizing fulcrum for a new era of human history, the linguacene" (Gramling 2016, 93). And this "linguacene," he explains, names a society where the global market drives either monolingualism or the demand for only smooth and rapid forms of translation. Both Yildiz and Gramling insist, in response to the "linguacene," on the artificiality of the opposition between monolingualism and multilingualism, arguing that a conception of multilingualism that rests on the assumption that languages should be kept separate perpetuates cultural segregation and isolationism. Indeed, according to Robert Young, "in promoting multilingualism, we are upholding and confirming monolingualism, the idea that people speak separate, classifiable, and classified single languages, each of which by definition is marked by a border that ensures unity, like the boundary of a nation" (Young 2016, 1,209).

Literary writing, however, can be a site for exploring how creative and aesthetic experimentation can dramatize transfer and movement between what are traditionally conceived as distinct linguistic systems. This chapter will explore some passages in the work of the Moroccan thinker and writer Abdelfattah Kilito to flesh out how literature can both perform and conceptualize the interaction and mutual interpenetration between languages in dynamic ways. In Kilito's thinking, literary texts can import or "transpose" traces of other languages by drawing on translations of other works, bringing multiple idioms into their own linguistic framework through their processes of recreation and writing. This reflection nevertheless takes place against the background of a recent swathe of publications on both "world literature" and bilingual or "translingual" writing, from which I contend that the subtleties of Kilito's thinking remain distinct.[1] In the face of recent interest in transnational and "world literatures," both Robert Young and David Gramling have identified the pitfalls of the conception of language underpinning some of these critical discourses. Young argues that despite the apparent celebration of global consciousness, world literature in fact "look[s] for literatures written in identifiable languages and then organiz[es] each language and its literature in relation to nationality, region, or cultural origin" (Young 2016, 1,209). In his more detailed analysis of "world literarity," Gramling notes how "foreignizing" translation and the use of local idiom in the world literary arena actually reinforces the idea that literatures represent particular, determinate territories and introduces them in ways palatable to publishers and readers in a global market still dominated by English. According to Gramling, a form of

---

1   See for example Doris Sommer's *Bilingual Aesthetics: A New Sentimental Education* (Durham and London: Duke University Press, 2004); Steven G. Kellman, *The Translingual Imagination* (Lincoln: University of Nebraska Press, 2000); Maria Lauret, *Wanderwords: Language Migration in American Literature* (London: Bloomsbury, 2014); Isabelle de Courtivron (ed.), *Lives in Translation: Bilingual Writers on Identity and Creativity* (Basingstoke: Palgrave Macmillan, 2003).

"soft multilingualism" "sanctions certain kinds of translatedness at the expense of others" (Gramling 2016, 25), so that despite an apparent opening up to global linguistic diversity, languages are still conceived as set, framed entities and only either exoticized or easily absorbed specific forms of multilingualism are welcomed or approved.

The critics mentioned above suggest that we need an understanding of literary multilingualism that would manage to avoid simply propping up the hegemony of the dominant language and celebrating what is seen as the exoticism associated with inserted foreign terms. This conception would resist the implication that languages for the most part operate in isolation and that any corruption of one language by another is anomalous, to be either fetishized or dismissed as incorrect usage. Critics such as Stefan Helgesson and Francesca Orsini have, in response to the flattening effects of globalizing culture, offered perceptive insight into various forms of plurilingualism and to the creative use of vernaculars in what they still term "world literature." Helgesson's volume, coedited with Annika Morte Alling and Yvonne Lindqvist, *World Literatures: Exploring the Cosmopolitan-Vernacular Exchange* (2018), makes a highly promising start in challenging the anglophone canon that dominates debates around "world literature" and insisting on the notion of the dynamic "cosmopolitan–vernacular exchange" as an organizing principle. Francesca Orsini's concept of "multilingual locals and significant geographies" helpfully critiques the universalizing sweep of "world literature" by proposing alternative geographical models for the dynamic linguistic exchange at work both within and between communities (2015). In the francophone arena, yasser elhariry (2017) has written eloquently about the "pacifist invasions" of the "post-francophone" lyric in order to highlight the rich presence of Arabic in the poetry of francophone writers such as Habib Tengour, Abdelwahab Meddeb, and Salah Stétié. Finally, Alison Rice has also shown how francophone North African writers such as Assia Djebar and Abdelkébir Khatibi both use a wide-ranging lexicon within their written French, but also conceptualize their integration of traces of other languages using metaphors of musicality: translations, transpositions, phonemes, and rhythms of other linguistic systems often imperceptibly interweave themselves into the structures of their prose (2006).

Kilito's work is clearly indebted to that of Khatibi, who is perhaps better known than Kilito, above all for his *Maghreb pluriel* (1983), which undertakes nothing less than the decolonization of North African thought and culture. Most pertinent here is Khatibi's suggestion for a "pensée en langues," a mode of thinking that would overturn the atavistic binaries structuring colonial discourse as well as what he perceives as a form of Islamic theocracy in the Maghreb, in order to privilege a more dynamic and liberating form of cultural porosity. Khatibi's "pensée en langues" calls for "une mondialisation des codes, des systèmes et des constellations de signes qui circulent dans le monde et au-dessus de lui," as if to embrace a global network of cultural connectivity energized by the movement of codes and signs between linguistic systems (Khatibi 1983, 60). The present chapter takes Khatibi's "pensée en langues" as a trigger for a reading of Abdelfattah Kilito's at once philosophical and playful discussion of language and multilingualism in *Je parle toutes les langues, mais en arabe*, published in 2013, to try to come up with a theoretical conception of the form and significance of linguistic border crossing in literature. Kilito's thinking helps us to conceptualize, through a subtle reflection on reading as well as on a series of close engagements with particular texts, the movement of languages within literature so as to offer a deeper insight into the processes of translation and linguistic "transposition" in literary works. Rather than debating the relative usefulness of the various "lingualisms" (bilingualism, multilingualism, plurilingualism, polylingualism, or heterolingualism) now infiltrating critical discourse, his thinking serves to undermine such categories in favor of a more fluid conception of the exchange of languages as they circulate through literary texts.

Moreover, Kilito is one of the few Maghrebian writers who writes extensively in both French and Arabic, and whose writing is deeply immersed in and reflective of literary and philosophical traditions on both sides of the Mediterranean. While highly conscious of the difficulties of the translation process, Kilito works actively in both languages and is constantly attentive both to their mutual communication and to the inevitable friction of their encounter. While Emily Apter in her *Against World Literature* (2013) somewhat reductively reads his earlier *Tu ne parleras pas ma langue* (published in 2008) as a defense of monolingualism, then, I argue that the affirmation "je parle toutes les langues, mais en arabe" is a highly provocative rebuttal to the apparent opposition between monolingualism and multilingualism in that it boldly affirms that the speaker is both monolingual and multilingual at the same time. Kilito claims that he speaks not only several but all languages, and yet he also paradoxically speaks them only as they are somehow translated into his own native Arabic. The assertion of multilingualism in the first part of the sentence appears to negate itself in the second, in the speaker's retention of Arabic as his dominant language of expression. The sentence requires a new conception of language usage in order to make sense, and works as a highly provocative starting point for a reflection on the forms of translation and transposition that render present multiple languages within speech or writing apparently belonging to a single system.

This double-edged statement is reflective of Kilito's complex and ludic thinking, and in the text's more detailed elaboration two complementary strands capture the tension he suggests we need to accommodate in thinking about relations between languages. First, in the chapter "La Guetteuse," where he explains the statement in the book's title, Kilito explores popular preconceptions about our relationships with the languages we speak, and argues that, "on ne se libère pas de sa langue familiale, familière" (Kilito 2013, 34). Even when we speak a foreign language, he suggests, the native language makes its appearance through our accent, our use of construction, perhaps even our facial expression, so that, "quels que soient les mots étrangers que je profère, mon arabe demeure audible, marque indélébile" (Kilito 2013, 34). Here, then, Kilito seems to retain a strong concept of linguistic identity. Our use of another language will always, it seems, be found to originate in the habits of our first language, and its traces in our usage of any other language connote an originary identity or experience—our "langue familiale," the language Kilito apparently associates here with our nurture. The examples of Agatha Christie's Hercule Poirot, and Amélie Nothomb's Japanese-speaking heroine in *Stupeur et tremblements* (1999) are taken to bear out these tendencies. In the case of the detective Poirot, the character knows that his heavy inflection of English with a French vocabulary, syntax, and accent makes him seem more authentic and less suspicious to his English interlocutors. In Nothomb's work, conversely, the heroine's skilful mastery of Japanese when working for a company in Japan is witnessed by her boss with profound unease, as he tells her that the delegates with whom she works, "ont été troublés, la classification à laquelle ils étaient habitués a été profondément perturbée" (Nothomb 1999, 39). Intriguingly, however, while the insistence in Kilito's text on the importance of the "langue familiale" seems to be that of the author himself, in the discussion of Christie and Nothomb, there is a wry sense that characters' demands for secure linguistic parameters and for stable linguistic identities are somewhat shortsighted. The apparent assertion of linguistic identity underpinning Kilito's adherence to his mother tongue may, then, turn out to be more complicated than it first appears.

Kilito's interest in the friction between languages, and in their association with identity, however, is one he also developed in *Tu ne parleras pas ma langue*. In "Défense de parler ma langue," he examines the sense of discomfort we can feel toward foreigners speaking our language —both badly and well, as if the first upsets our attachment to linguistic purity and the second disconcerts the assumed relationship between language and identity. The work more broadly, moreover, explores instances of mistranslation or of incompatibility as languages rub up against one another. Kilito reflects, for example, on the task of presenting the *Séances* of Hamadhânî (968–1008) to a French public, and the leap he has to make in translating the dates in the work from the Islamic calendar to the Gregorian calendar. He also cites the story of Averroes, who set out to translate Aristotle but who was familiar only with Arabic poetry and had no knowledge of the theatrical genres of tragedy and comedy. The conclusion comments on the flawed translations of these terms as "panégyrique" and "satire" respectively by the Christian philosopher Mattâ ibn Yûnus, and argues both that the mistake hindered Arabs from setting out to discover more about Greek culture, and prevented Europeans from reaching their Renaissance earlier by imitating the Arabs. Kilito suggests at the same time, however, that one could imagine that Mattâ ibn Yûnus actually saved Arabs from the "grave danger qui les menaçait," since a better translation might also have compelled them to devote themselves to the study of Greek culture, to imitate and reproduce it rather than preserving a sense of the uniqueness of their own culture (Kilito 2008, 106). Mistranslation, then, and the failure of a smooth cultural transfer could be construed either as a hindrance to, or as a bringer of, creativity. Kilito playfully also intimates that untranslatability is both a point of contact and a significant marker of cultural difference; it is both the result of proper attention to linguistic differences, and something that should not be taken to signify cultural segregation. Languages both signal to one another and conflict, as Kilito argues, "le rapport entre elles n'est pas bâti sur une coexistence pacifique, c'est au contraire un rapport d'attraction, d'opposition et de querelle" (Kilito 2008, 31–32).

To return to *Je parle toutes les langues*, Kilito's reference to Kafka in the title hints at the double-sidedness of his reflection here too, while also betraying an increased uneasiness with notions of linguistic identity and purity. The quotation is a rewriting of a statement he finds in one of Kafka's notebooks evoking a singer from Prague and the expressive movements that accompany her music: "voyez-vous, je parle toutes les langues, mais en Yiddish" (Kilito 2013, 34).[2] The comment is quickly referenced before Kilito moves on to discuss Maghrebian writing. Yet if the quotation is retained for its apparent affirmation of Yiddish language and identity, it is perhaps significant that in the original journal, Kafka cites this artist precisely because he suggests she communicates something more dynamic and compelling than most of those who represent Jewish theater. Kafka's own use of language at the same time constitutes a highly complex dramatization of linguistic mobility, as will Kilito's theory. Deleuze and Guattari's discussion of Kafka's languages in *Pour une littérature mineure* (1986) demonstrates his challenging theory of linguistic deterritorialization, and though Kilito does not refer explicitly to Deleuze and Guattari, this more hybridized vision of language is also borne out by some of the literary reflections that occupy *Je parle toutes les langues, mais en arabe*.

In *Pour une littérature mineure*, then, Kafka is held up as an apt example of a writer of "minor literature" as a result of his multilingualism and his "deterritorialization" of German (the "major" language). Deleuze and Guattari show how Kafka's "tetralinguistic" model of writing operates between four languages: the vernacular, the vehicular, the referential, and the mythic. For Prague Jews, Deleuze, and Guattari note, both Czech and Yiddish are forms of vernacular, with German as the "vehicular" and "referential" language, and traces of Hebrew signal the presence of the "mythic." And Yiddish, for Kafka, is also, as the quotation from the singer suggests, not a signifier of linguistic territoriality but, in Deleuze and Guattari's words, "a nomadic movement of deterritorialization that reworks German language" (Deleuze and Guattari 1986, 25). In addition, however, it is not only the use of idioms from other languages that deterritorializes the major language, but the stretching of its syntax and its testing of the limits of sense. To be a minor writer in this way is not just to insert borrowings from a minor language into prose in a major language, but to undermine the very notions of linguistic homeliness and mastery. Kafka's fragment "The Great Swimmer," for example, narrates the eponymous swimmer's return to her homeland from the Olympic Games, to be greeted by jubilant crowds, even though she claims she cannot in fact swim and is

---

2 The comment comes from Kafka's *Récits, Romans, Journaux*, ed. Brigitte Vergne-Cain et Gérard Rudent (Paris: Librairie Générale Française, 2000) p. 290.

not at home. Deleuze and Guattari argue that this dramatizes Kafka's vision of linguistic defamiliarization:

> To be a sort of stranger *within* his own language; this is the situation of Kafka's Great Swimmer. Even when it is unique, a language remains a mixture, a schizophrenic mélange, a Harlequin costume in which very different functions of language and distinct centers of power are played out, blurring what can be said and what can't be said; one function will be played off against the other, all the degrees of territoriality and relative deterritorialization will be played out (Deleuze and Guattari 1986, 26).

Most importantly, then, there is in *Pour une littérature mineure* a clear abandonment of the association between language, identity, and homeliness, and a foregrounding not of what Kilito called a "langue familiale, familière," but of linguistic defamiliarization in various forms. Read in the light of Deleuze and Guattari's reading of Kafka, Kilito's affirmation that "je parle toutes les langues, mais en arabe" may also be construed to contain something of Kafka's linguistic expansiveness, and to refer not only to the traces of an originary Arabic language in his usage of other languages, but perhaps also to his awareness of the ways in which a language, even for the ostensibly monolingual speaker, is stretched and hybridized as speakers constantly bring in all kinds of influences from other languages as well as blurring and extending linguistic functions.

When he switches from discussing oral language to written language in the above-mentioned chapter, "La Guetteuse," Kilito's argument becomes still more nuanced. He suggests at the outset that linguistic identity is apparently less prominent in written form, though he almost immediately adds that the dissimulation of any foreign element in the Maghrebian writer's written French is seen by many to be neither possible nor desirable, as the under-layer of Arabic or Berber should necessarily make itself felt. Indeed, this resurgence seems to be what readers want, as his reference to the uneasy reception of Driss Chraïbi's *Un ami viendra vous voir* demonstrates: French readers were disappointed because they "semblent attendre d'un auteur d'un nom 'exotique' qu'il les … dépayse" (Kilito 2013, 35), while Moroccans questioned whether Chraïbi could count as one of them if he wrote in French on subjects construed to be more bound up with bourgeois consumerism than with postcolonial Morocco.[3]

---

3   Chraïbi's *Un ami viendra vous voir* was published by Denoël in 1967, but was vilified by critics because it explores a woman's psychological unraveling without reference to cultural background.

In citing these reactions to Chraïbi, Kilito uncovers readers' struggle to conceptualize the dissociation between the use of language and the author's assumed cultural identity. On the one hand, the French expected a certain intermingling between French and Arabic, but the implication here is that this is the result of a sort of exoticist desire, complicit, perhaps, with what Gramling called "soft multilingualism," and tinged with problematic expectations of some kind of linguistic representativity (Chraïbi should "represent" Moroccans by inserting their idioms into his French). This observation in turn makes the reader uneasy with Kilito's earlier apparent desire to preserve a notion of linguistic authenticity: the French response to Chraïbi suggests that this supposed authenticity can be fetishized and commodified. At the same time, however, the Moroccans' objection to Chraïbi's excessive mastery of French language and culture implies not only that they want to preserve the trace of an originary linguistic authenticity (in Arabic), but also that the relinquishment of this originary authenticity ends up propping up the hegemony of French. The Moroccan writer's crossing over to embrace the French language is seen both to occlude what the Moroccan critic would have assumed to be his original Arabic linguistic identity, and to shore up what is conceived as a standardized and hegemonic French. Either way, Kilito suggests, although writers such as Chraïbi may deliberately be exploring the ways in which literature resists territorialization and identitarianism, readers find it difficult to release literary texts from determinate ethnic and cultural categories in ways that would do justice to that kind of writing. This discussion shows how readers cling to a notion of monolingualism (the Maghrebian writer seems to write in monolingual French, but ought to stage a confrontation between two monolingualisms—Arabic and French). Kilito's reflections on a whole range of writers in the rest of the study help to show that another model may be more appropriate.

Kilito's overarching argument in the text is that literature needs exposure to other languages in order to sustain itself. Indeed, it is brought into being by this continual process of translation and transposition of the idioms of existing works. At the end of the nineteenth century, Kilito notes, Arabic literature was lacking in energy, and it was the rise of translation that gave it new life by bringing contact and dialogue with other cultures: "elle a aussi contribué au rajeunissement de la langue littéraire, qui a connu une évolution considérable, précisément parce qu'à l'arrière-plan de ce qui s'écrit, on perçoit une langue européenne" (Kilito 2013, 28). Later in the work, he observes that the modern Arabic novel really only flourished when it took it upon itself to describe Europe, and though this could be construed to dramatize the oppressive power of colonial cultural assimilation, Kilito also suggests that it serves to reveal how Europe is also not bordered and self-same: "l'Europe, en dehors de son espace géographique, gît depuis la fin du XIXe siècle au cœur même des capitales arabes" (Kilito 2013, 67). Examples of novels by Muwaylihî and Shidyâq refer to and display processes of translation between Arabic and European languages, but they also write across linguistic borders by making comparisons between, for example, ancient Egypt and modern Paris, or by including proverbs and figures from different cultures during different periods. These are all modes of "transposition," as traces of different cultures are rewritten into new Arabic work.

Later chapters of *Je parle toutes les langues, mais en arabe* reference a wide range of great writers, all of whom again exhibit their multilingualism not just by juxtaposing distinct linguistic systems but by inventing a language that itself emerges out of multiple previous translations. Commenting on Cervantes's playful affirmation that his novel is built out of the work of the Arabic historian Sidi Ahmed Benengeli, for example, Kilito observes, "le *Quichotte* se présente comme la version espagnole d'un texte arabe, un simulacre donc, l'envers du manuscrit original" (Kilito 2013, 79). A series of commentaries on the linguistic dynamism of recent Maghrebian writers, including Khatibi, El Maleh, Meddeb, Berrada, and Sefrioui, finishes, moreover, with the provocative observation that the question of which language a writer writes in only makes sense if it is complemented with another: "en quelle langue lisez-vous?" (Kilito 2013, 140). Sefrioui's *La Boîte à merveilles*, Kilito contends, is ostensibly written in French but on some level, it is also written in Arabic, as the narrator translates the Arabic-speaking world in which he grew up. Yet although this means that the non-Arabic speaking reader will miss some of the nuances at work in the text's idiom, Kilito is quick to argue that, "la lecture du non-bilingue, quoique limitée, n'est pas fausse pour autant, elle est tout simplement différente" (Kilito 2013, 140). The interpretation made by readers who do not speak all the writer's languages will be different from that of a reader who does, but this is not so much a lack, as a further instance of a text's linguistic movement. The reader too will recreate the text in his or her own language, and if he or she ostensibly only speaks one language, she will also nevertheless be put into contact with traces of another language and recreate it in her own in a way that also bears out the assertion of Kilito's title.

Kilito's vision of writing beyond monolingualism and multilingualism in *Je parle toutes les langues, mais en arabe* can be linked with two broader reflections on literary writing and reading found elsewhere in his work, on which there will be space to pause just briefly here. The first of these is the idea of the writer or intellectual as a porter, as if the writer carries and transposes into his art the baggage of everything he has read, which necessarily feeds into and shapes his creation. The examples cited in *Je parle toutes les langues, mais en arabe*—Cervantes, the modern Arabic novel, the Maghrebian novel in French—all bear traces of this baggage, as the texts weave images, idioms, and references from the various cultures that the writer has brushed up against and from which he borrows. Kilito first links the intellectual and the porter in the playful narrative *Dites-moi le songe*, published in 2010, which reflects broadly on the ways in which the *Thousand and One Nights* is constantly reimagined and recreated by our inevitably partial, situated, culturally inflected readings of it. The figure of the porter crops up in a passage where the narrator (a professor, possibly based on Kilito himself) laments the need he feels to hoard works of Arabic literature when visiting America, as if to retain the memory of that culture as he travels. This literary burden, however, is apparently experienced as a hindrance; he wishes he had the ability to reinvent himself through his travels, like Sindbad the Sailor, but instead, "j'étais plutôt Sindbad de la Terre, misérable portefaix ployant sous le poids d'une tradition en net déphasage avec le monde moderne" (Kilito 2010, 22). Sindbad the Porter is the double, the poorer mirror image of the sailor, weighed down by other people's loads, and the comparison here suggests that the intellectual's attachment to a cultural heritage could be a hindrance to his discovery of the new.

In a more recent essay, moreover, Kilito also compares the intellectual Edward Said to a porter, always carrying a large number of possessions with him when he travels, as if terrified of forgetting his memories of his past self. In both extracts, however, while Kilito on the surface seems to be stressing the oppressive onus carried by the intellectual as porter, at the same time this carrying of one culture into another is precisely a way to resist the rigid segregation of languages and cultures. The task of the writer or intellectual is indeed partly, as Marina Warner argues (2014) in her reading of Kilito as a "story bearer," to transport and transmit literatures to new readers, and Sindbad the Porter will in turn carry the sailor's stories and reinvent them for new recipients. In addition, as the intellectual or writer travels to a new culture, he does not move from one monolingualism to another; he might acquire a new language and culture but carries the existing one within it, just as the maxim "je parle toutes les langues, mais en arabe" suggests. Kilito summarizes Said's position in the following terms:

> The secret of his writing is perhaps in this statement: "I began to think and write contrapuntally, using the disparate halves of my experience, as an Arab and as an American, to work with and also against each other" ([Said 2000], p. 562). Bridging the gap: laying a bridge which makes the language a translation; the identity a movement between two legacies and two cultures, and the intellectual a porter striving to link one shore to another.[4]

Kilito's portrait of Said here again offers a way to theorize writing beyond monolingualism and multilingualism. Just as a translation "carries over" meaning from one language to another, the intellectual as porter carries one language, and one culture, into another. Kilito cites Said's comment in *Reflections on Exile* on the way in which each sentence he spoke in English was echoed internally by its translation into Arabic, and stresses, moreover, this movement between languages as a continued process: Said heard spoken Arabic when speaking English (and vice versa), but only discovered Arabic literature later in life.[5] Like that of Kilito, moreover, Said's writing was not exactly bilingual: it only rarely mixed languages by bringing identifiable and explicable Arabic terms into English. Rather, Kilito suggests, it always bore the memory of Arabic within it at the same time as Said developed that memory through his continued discovery of Arab literature, which in turn shaped his intellectual and personal writing.

The second set of reflections on which I want to pause here relates not to writing but to reading. Kilito's *Dites-moi le songe* artfully plays on the question cited above, "en quelle langue lisez-vous?," in a way that can also contribute to our understanding of literature operating beyond monolingualism and multilingualism. Much of *Dites-moi le songe* explores the various ways in which we read the *Thousand and One Nights*—always partially, with different cultural expectations, with varying agendas, and by establishing any number of connections

---

4   See   http://journeyofideasacross.hkw.de/between-places-al-muthanna-and-undermining-dichotomies/abdelfattah-kilito.html, accessed April 2, 2021.

5   Said writes, "every time I speak an English sentence, I find myself echoing it in Arabic, and vice versa" (2000), p. 557.

with other materials we might have read. The four narratives of Kilito's volume are all in some way focused on notions of forgery and treachery in our reading processes, as we continually translate the works we encounter into different contexts and create new meanings from them. In the second story in the collection, for example, "La Seconde folie de Shahriar," a doctoral student named Ismael Kamlo presents a version of the *Nights* in which the King Shahriar asks his scribes to write down Schéhérazade's stories, even if they did not hear them, a tale that his examiners find unconvincing, and that causes the narrator to reflect: "ne peut-on guère parler des *Nuits* sans tricher, déformer et trahir?" (Kilito 2010, 59). The incident intimates both that the scribes might reinvent the stories even if they have not properly absorbed them, and that the academics are happy to pass judgment on Kamlo's thesis without having read it in full. The title *Dites-moi le songe* also highlights this process of invention, as Kilito's narrator goes on to explain. It refers on the one hand to King Nabuchodonosor [*sic*] from the Book of Daniel in the Old Testament, who, troubled by fearful dreams, demands his advisors, seers, and soothsayers to interpret the visions for him, even though they do not know their content. On the other hand, Kilito also links Nabuchodonosor's impossible request with a scene from the *Nights*, where the Caliph Haroun Al-Rashid is moved both to laughter and to tears by the book he is reading, and exhorts the Vizir Jaafar to explain to him why this should be so, even though Jaafar knows neither the book nor the author that provoked this reaction. Like Schéhérazade, moreover, and like Shahriar's scribes, Nabuchodonosor's advisors and the Vizir Jaafar are in this way compelled to give their reading and narrate their story not by referring back to any original material but by using their imagination.

As critic Bénédicte Letellier has shown, these stories, like Schéhérazade's own fantastic inventions, which she spins without being able to refer back to the library fleetingly mentioned in the frame tale, depict a vision of reading as retelling, as imaginative recreation. And in turn, Kilito suggests that no one ever really reads the full compendium of the *Nights*; rather, his characters find ways to reinvent parts of it, transforming it in the process, as Letellier asserts, "quelle que soit la version des *Nuits*, c'est toujours la fiction qui explique et justifie le livre matériel."[6] These provocative references, and indeed many of the episodes of *Dites-moi le songe*, in this way seem also to ask, "*en quelle*

6 See Letellier 2014.

langue lisez-vous?"; they show how a narrative is recreated by the receiver's imagination as if in a process of translation. This translation offers a further means for a text to cross borders between languages, not just by juxtaposing cultural idioms but by triggering this continual process of reinvention in each new reader's idiolect. The reading process too transports texts across linguistic and cultural borders, as each new reading provides the work with new structures, new images, new terms. Although monolingualism and multilingualism are not the ostensible focus of Kilito's reflection in *Dites-moi le songe*, then, his conception here of the association between reading and invention contributes to the notion of linguistic transfer and expansion found in *Je parle toutes les langues, mais en arabe*. If reading across languages is less overtly theorized in this narrative of reading as reinvention, moreover, this is also because Kilito's understanding of literary translation reaches beyond the model of a confrontation between two monolingual systems to involve forms of transposition within a linguistic system, or between idiolects as well as between languages.

The references Kilito makes to a range of other works, such as those mentioned above, are also themselves ample evidence for his interweaving of languages, as he translates traces of different heritages in his own reading and again in his creative writing. The title's blending of a reference to the *Nights* with a scene from the Bible is emblematic of his interspersing of European with Arabic cultures. The narrative of "L'Equation du Chinois," for example, is another story interwoven with that of Ismael Kamlo, and stems from a reference to a scene in Roland Barthes's *Fragments d'un discours amoureux* (1977). The scene describes how a mandarin is asked by the courtesan, he loves to wait for three years outside her window. At the end of the allotted period, he picks up his stool and leaves. Kilito's own story is an intricate rewriting of Barthes's scene, as the narrator traces the story of the previous occupant of his apartment and the young man's (possibly Kamlo's) relationship with Ada, whom he observes and with whom he converses (about the *Nights*, as well as about Ibn Battuta) through the window from his stool. There will not be space to explore the various levels on which the story operates here, but in his typical literary playfulness, Kilito weaves his tale out of a whole web of references: not only to Barthes and to the *Nights*, but with a nod also to Flaubert, as the stool around which the action circulates recalls the bench upon which Mme Arnoux is sitting the first time Frédéric sees her in *L'Education sentimentale*, and her "banc Frédéric" at the end (Flaubert 2001 [1869]). The figure of the bench or stool reflects in ludic ways on the relationship between textuality (the character's literary imagination) and materiality, but is also worth noting here as it shows precisely how the narrative weaves together images, words, and figures from literary intertexts of various different origins. The narrator's puzzling "escabeau" contains within it the traces of Barthes's and Flaubert's love stories at the same time as it announces its origins in a Chinese folktale, and the enigmatic affairs in these texts help to develop and inflect our reading of the curious relationship evoked in Kilito's tale. The mysteriousness of the lover's departure, moreover, is at the same time provocative in its dramatization of the open-endedness of such textual moments and of the active part the reader must play in making sense of the story.

Kilito's texts in this way dramatize the ways in which writing and reading transcend the divisions between languages and cultures in more ways than might be evident at first glance. His discussions both of mistranslation and of cultural and linguistic transfer also exhibit the difficulty of this linguistic interaction, and highlight at once the weight of the writer or reader's baggage and the creative, intercultural opportunities to which it might give rise. Kilito's work is by no means an easy read, his "world literary" texts are not those that Gramling saw fetishized by the global publishing market as a result of their exotic and easily assimilated incorporation of digestible foreign terms. Rather, he foregrounds the presence of one language within another, not to smooth over its difference but to emphasize both its particularity and its ability to engender new stories and new readings. The provocative statement "je parle toutes les langues, mais en arabe" is developed in the work of that name and beyond in order to reveal the portability of language and culture but not a smooth process of fusion. As Kilito suggests in relation to Said, our languages and the memories they carry are both a burden and a creative opportunity. Their inventive deployment through writing and reading most importantly constitute an apt performance of the manner of their interaction beyond the paradigms of monolingualism and multilingualism.

Works Cited

Apter, Emily. 2013. *Against World Literature: On the Politics of Untranslatability*. London: Verso.

Barthes, Roland. 1977. *Fragments d'un discours amoureux*. Paris: Seuil.

Deleuze, Gilles, and Félix Guattari. 1986. *Kafka: Towards a Minor Literature*. Translated by Dana Polan. Minneapolis: University of Minnesota Press.

elhariry, yasser. 2017. *Pacifist Invasions: Arabic, Translation and the Postfrancophone Lyric*. Liverpool: Liverpool University Press.

Flaubert, Gustave. 2001 [1869]. *L'Education sentimentale*. Paris: Flammarion.

Gramling, David. 2016. *The Invention of Monolingualism*. London: Bloomsbury.

Helgesson, Stefan, Annika Morte Alling, and Yvonne Lindqvist. 2018. *World Literatures: Exploring the Cosmopolitan-Vernacular Exchange*. Stockholm: Stockholm University Press.

Khatibi, Abdelkébir. 1983. *Maghreb pluriel*. Paris: Denoël.

Kilito, Abdelfattah. 2008. *Tu ne parleras pas ma langue*. Translated by François Gouin. Arles: Actes Sud.

——. 2010. *Dites-moi le songe*. Arles: Actes Sud.

——. 2013. *Je parle toutes les langues, mais en arabe*. Arles: Actes Sud.

Letellier, Bénédicte. 2014, "La Bibliothèque de Schéhérazade: enquête sur les lectures assassines," Fabula—LhT. www.fabula.org/lht/13/letellier.html. Accessed April 2, 2021.

Nothomb, Amélie. 1999. *Stupeur et tremblements*. Paris: Albin Michel.

Orsini, Francesca. 2015. "The Multilingual Local in World Literature," *Comparative Literature* 67 (4): 345–74.

Rice, Alison. 2006. *Time Signatures: Contextualizing Contemporary Francophone Autobiographical Writing from the Maghreb*. Lanham, MD: Lexington.

Said, Edward. 2000. *Reflections on Exile*. Cambridge, MA: Harvard University Press.

Warner, Marina. 2014. "Story-Bearers," Review of Abdelfattah Kilito, *Je parle toutes les langues, mais en arabe*, *London Review of Books* 36 (8) (April 17, 2014): 19–20.

Yildiz, Yasemin. 2012. *Beyond the Mother Tongue: The Postmonolingual Condition*. New York: Fordham University Press.

Young, Robert. 2016. "That which is casually called a language," *PMLA* 131(5): 1207–21.

CHAPTER FIVE

Intersignes du Maroc
Toward A Plural Cultural Aesthetic

Claudia Esposito

In a nation where government institutions and commercial venues systematically exhibit portraits of the current monarch, the relationship between image and power is hauntingly ubiquitous. What happens when embedded in that image/power dyad lies the trace of a traumatic past, one that is both visible in its metonymic representation and invisible in its lack of direct portrayal? This chapter investigates the practices of a cultural aesthetic in the Maghreb—in Morocco in particular—that relies on multiple creative forms of expression and that questions the artistic frameworks from which situated historico-political critiques arise. Through an examination of the sustained ties between Abdellatif Laâbi (1942) and Mahi Binebine (1959), two writers/painters who are individually well known for their social and political commitment, I suggest that it is in the interstices of form, or in the transpositions of mediums, that the two artists address several specific characteristics at the heart of Moroccan cultural production today. First of all, they model a form of historical repair through aesthetic innovation; secondly, their works carry out an unremitting reflection on questions of disappearance and (in)visibility; and finally, both elucidate what it means to be both inside and outside language. Both artists place the visual—and their politics—at the heart of their work and probe what Abdelkébir Khatibi calls the *intersigne*, a dynamic movement between semiotic systems that relies, I maintain, on a long-standing tradition in the Maghreb of continued connections between sculpture, writing, calligraphy, tapestry, painting, and more recently video art.[1]

---

1   See for instance, Abdelwahab Meddeb's *Talismano* (1979), Assia Djebar's

Engagement and Social Commitment

In *Le métier d'intellectuel*, Fadma Aït-Mous and Driss Ksikes[2] reflect on what it means to be an intellectual in contemporary post-2011 Morocco; the picture that emerges is one of an aggrieved country plagued by a gravely deficient education system, and at the mercy of a still repressive monarchy. In the midst of this "désastre culturel" (Aït-Mous and Ksikes, 2014, 25) and "maelstrom" (26), however, only a dozen or so voices have come to the fore with vision and vehemence. This is a trivial number, Aït-Mous and Ksikes maintain, and the fact that we keep coming back to Khatibi and Al-Jabri, for instance, in search of "nouvel élan," means there hasn't been much renewal since the first decades after independence. Aït-Mous and Ksikes decry the status quo all the more given the relative autonomy (from politics) of which intellectuals had availed themselves, they write, as the monarchy has never attempted to forge close ties with an intellectual body, unlike in post-independence Tunisia, for instance. The authors conclude that rather than having a "role" to play, the intellectual in Morocco should be called upon to practice their *métier* via a "palettes de pratiques à étaler" (2014, 31). Quite fittingly for the purpose of this chapter, the expression they use is suggestive of an artist spreading paint from a palette of colors, or of a writer laying out words on paper. Much like Bourdieu and his notion of an "intellectuel collectif," they situate the responsibility of the intellectual "entre savoir, conscience du public et souci de la collectivité" (2014, 24).

Laâbi and Binebine fit into the picture painted above in vastly different modes and at different critical junctures of Morocco's contemporaneity, but both have taken their artistic roles beyond the creative realm to generate political and social change. That is to say, while their writing, painting, and other creative works may carry the more complex and interesting thrust, their activism also allows us to parse out a number of significant critiques of a nation in flux. Laâbi's activism, as is well known, lies in part in the revolutionary work carried out with the journal *Souffles* (1966–1972). Along with its many

---

L'amour, la Fantasia (1985), Abdelkébir Khatibi's *L'amour bilingue* (1983), Tahar Ben Jelloun's *Le labyrinthe des sentiments* (1999).

2   Driss Ksikes is the former editor of *Nichane*, a magazine in Darija and MSA, which was founded in 2006 and banned in 2010. Although different in scope and subject from *Souffles*, its fate was similar.

other attributes, *Souffles* was a post-independence manifesto for a new aesthetic, a fierce experiment and a *cri de cœur* that launched some of the most dissenting voices and exciting artists. For his part, Binebine has founded, with filmmaker Nabil Ayouch, a number of cultural foundations, which aim to promote youth literacy in and through the arts.[3] Fondation Ali Zaoua/Les Étoiles de Sidi Moumen was the first to open outside of Casablanca in 2014, followed by Les Étoiles du détroit in Beni Makada outside Tangier in 2017, and then by centers in Fes and Agadir. The fifth, Les Étoiles de Jemaa el Fna, is slated to open in Marrakech in late 2021. Open to all young people in their respective areas, the centers of the Fondation Ali Zaoua are invested in offering access to—and freedom of—creative expression in an effort toward, according to their mission statement, "réhabilitation psychosociale."[4] It is this social, collective conscience of the intellectual that has, I believe, been at the root of a central concern for both Laâbi and Binebine. That is to say, a sustained engagement with the figuring of constraint and silencing. As a case in point, one of the latest instances comes from Laâbi's Facebook post from December 27, 2019, where he writes:

> Deux événements douloureux m'interpellent: le premier est devenu hélas presque banal au Maroc. Il s'agit de l'arrestation et de journalistes, d'humoristes et de blogueurs. Jeudi dernier, c'était au tour du journaliste Omar Radi, accusé d'outrage à magistrat. Son tort? Avoir écrit un texte, il y a de cela des mois, où il s'indignait contre les lourdes peines de prison infligées à des dizaines de participants au Hirak citoyen du Rif.

Laâbi's post on the silencing of journalist Omar Radi and Palestinian poet Ashraf Fayad echoed the words of Khadija Ryadi, former president of AMDH (Association Marocaine des Droits Humains), on the heels of the Hirak, "nous sommes tous en liberté provisoire" and "les années de plomb sont de retour."[5] If the feeling that the Years of Lead are looming once again, it is in great part due to the minatory threat of arrest and imprisonment issued forth by the state.

3   The second center was opened thanks, in part, to funds generated from an auction organized by a group of contemporary Moroccan visual artists, also in 2017.

4   See https://www.annalindhfoundation.org/members/fondation-ali-zaoua, accessed April 22, 2021.

5   See https://foreignpolicy.com/2019/01/16/moroccos-crackdown-wont-silence-dissent-maroc-hirak-amdh/, accessed April 2, 2021.

Laâbi and Binebine are no strangers to incarceration and the question of constraint unequivocally emerges from their dissimilar but nonetheless direct experiences. Laâbi spent eight years in prison during the 1970s on charges of crimes of opinion for his political views, and Binebine closely and personally witnessed the effects of his brother Aziz Binebine's incarceration in a two-by-three-foot underground cell for over 18 years in the infamous penitentiary Tazmamart. An officer in the military, Aziz Binebine was accused of being part of a plot to overthrow King Hassan II that culminated in a failed *coup d'état* in 1972. If speaking out against being silenced began, for Laâbi, as an anticolonial move directed in part at French imperialism, it quickly transformed into a critique of national politics in the immediate wake of independence. For Mahi Binebine, the critique of silencing also emerged from an anticolonial stance but manifested itself more trenchantly after his brother's incarceration and release from prison in 1990. At present, both continue to forge a wider critique of constraint that draws its more distant roots in the struggle for decolonization and Hassan II's repressive regime. If, in his poem "Chebaâ" (a contemplation of a piece by painter Mohammed Chebaâ) Laâbi "describes Moroccan intellectuals as former *prisoners* of a colonial system that *restricted* their view" (Pieprzak 2010, 174, emphasis added), Binebine solemnly reminds us of Hassan II's infamous statement "Il n'y a pas de danger aussi grave pour l'Etat que celui représenté par un prétendu intellectuel. Il aurait mieux valu que vous soyez des illettrés" (Lindsey 2017). I maintain that for Laâbi, as for Binebine, intellectual emancipation through a form of historical repair, a term I will explain shortly, has been a visionary way forward. Their approach has been visionary both in the sense of being based in the faculty of sight but also because both artists have ambitiously situated themselves in a transmedial practice.

Historical Repair/*Repère*

As Olivia Harrison and Teresa Villa-Ignacio state in their introduction to the critical anthology of *Souffles-Anfas* in English translation (2015),

> reading *Souffles-Anfas* in the wake of the global revolts that began in 2010 is simultaneously thrilling and chilling. Thrilling by virtue of the journal's uncompromising advocacy for democratic transformation across the region. Chilling in that its endeavors were so abruptly put to an end—or suspended, if we agree with Laâbi that the fight continues today. (Harrison and Villa-Ignacio 2015, 12)

Laâbi's 2013 essay *Un autre Maroc* clearly addresses a "new Morocco" and shows that the ongoing fight for greater social equality continues as a process of rehabilitation. Here, I draw on the work of visual artist Kader Attia, who conceives of historical repair as acts of cultural resistance that are both symbolic and physical. Repair "as a methodology offers the potential for colonized or oppressed peoples to reinstate their freedom" (Exhibition Notes 2018). In other words, it is a call for liberation from—and acknowledgment of—constraint. For Attia, who was born in France to Algerian parents and spent several years in Algeria and in Congo-Brazzaville, Western rationalism has favored an aesthetics of control and clean order, and in moving increasingly toward a capitalist mode of thought has privileged the "new" over the repaired. How this pertains to daily life in much of Europe or the United States needs no explanation; how it manifests in the rest of the world and in the arts, however, is not as straightforward. Attia takes as his most explicit model the reconstruction of Japanese ceramics, known as *kintsugi*, a method that expressly emphasizes the fragmentation of the object and that in no way attempts to mend the fracture, or to render it invisible. In a quite different vein, although along the same lines of critical thought, Attia juxtaposes photographs of facially injured First World War soldiers—the *gueules cassées*—with African masks that were broken and repaired, as a way of bridging traditional forms found in mask carving and Western reconstructive surgery. Repair, he maintains, is subtended by the "illusion that in controlling the injury by removing it, you have superiority over time and history" (Scher 2017, 1). Thus, by reconstructing the faces of the wounded, time would be metaphorically turned back and the historical traces of war effaced. Laâbi and Binebine's works grow out of a symbolic injury that can be traced, in part, back to the lesions left by colonialism, discernable in the educational, political, institutional legacies of French imperialism. But both make a point of rendering the injury visible, placing it squarely in a discursive space of constraint and imprisonment. For Laâbi and Binebine, like for Attia, the injury must be seen. To remove it would be tantamount to negating its origin and the memory of it. Repair, in this sense, is also *repérer*, it is what allows us to see not only the (historical) injury but our own blindness as well.

In *Visual Occupations*, Gil Hochberg analyzes the visual politics of the Israeli–Palestinian conflict, deciphering who has the right to see and be seen in this deeply asymmetrical crisis. While the conditions are not wholly comparable, I believe that similar politics of seeing are brought to the fore in a Moroccan cultural aesthetic fraught with critiques of constraint and conflict with the all-seeing state. Reshaping a visual field that "dominates and sustains" (Hochberg 2015, 3) such a conflict, writes Hochberg,

> involves not just tactical, physical interventions into the landscape, but also the manipulation of visual positions, new settings for spectatorship, new modes of appearance, and at times new modes of disappearance, concealment, or refusal to appear. It also involves the ability to see one's own blindness and render visible one's failure to see. (Hochberg 2015, 3)

I tie the critique of constraint to the image of incarceration to demonstrate how Laâbi and Binebine mobilize empowerment, which is, Hochberg suggests, "dependent on opacity, the ability to disappear, blindness, failed vision, and invisibility at least as much as ... on visibility, being visible, or having access to the gaze" (2015, 7). Put differently, cultural interventions, such as poetry and painting, for instance, have the strategic power to escape the reifying and already understood representations of the constrained or the imprisoned.

Turning the Page

The dark and inhumane conditions of Moroccan prisons under Hassan II's reign are well documented, and it is not my intention to rehearse that history here.[6] In a well-known speech given in July 1994, Hassan II memorably announced "We have decided to definitively turn the page on what is called 'political prisoners'" (quoted in Slyomovics 2005, 75). It wasn't until 2004, however, that the governmental organization l'Instance Equité et Réconciliation (IER) was set up to deal with Morocco's "subtle gradations of disappearance" (Slyomovics 2005, 47).[7] As Susan Slyomovics writes, "to designate someone as 'disappeared,' if only on the printed page, new grammatical forms, notations, and distinct writing styles have evolved in many languages. The body of the 'disappeared person,' for example, lies between quotation marks"

---

6   In *L'ombre du bagne,* Semlali recalls Kristeva's notion of the abject to describe Moroccan prisons: "Lieu d'un surgissement massif et abrupt d'une étrangeté," le bagne est "là où le sens s'effondre" (2017, 9).

7   For an analysis of earlier commissions and investigations, see Slyomovics's *The Performance of Human Rights in Morocco* (2005).

(2005, 43). Those who were imprisoned literally vanished from their surroundings and figuratively disappeared from any form of representation. What is compelling here, is that first, as I mentioned earlier, Laâbi and Binebine wage critiques of silencing and constraint through the prism of incarceration but more significantly, their works tie the question of constraint to a reconceptualization of (both theirs and our) visibility. At the most literal level, Moroccan prisons were frequently secluded places, often underground, typically out of sight. Prisoners often vanished overnight and were forcibly disappeared. Prisons of the Years of Lead such as Derb Moulay Cherif, Dar el Moqri, and Kalaat M'Gouna, were shrouded in silence, invisibility, and denial, sometimes in actual underground chambers, disconnected from surrounding space and time. In 2006, Tazmamart, the prison in the middle of the southeastern Moroccan desert, was razed to the ground, as if eradicating the physical building would efface 18 years of what happened within its walls. For the most part, Moroccan prisons were virtually inaccessible, invisible, and unseeable. Paradoxically, it was in the penitentiary, a sort of *repaire*, that many prisoners found a sense of repair in their encounters with literary texts.

In *Pourquoi cours-tu après la goutte d'eau*, a small collection of prosoèmes (a form between prose and poetry) published in 2006, Abdellatif Laâbi reworks a series of pieces published in the mid-1980s entitled *L'écorché vif*.[8] In it he writes imagined letters to Fyodor Dostoïevski, Nazim Hikmet, Vladimir Maïakovski.[9] If the original title points to being skinned alive, to wounds that have not healed, the 2006 re-edition takes its title from one of the poems, which reads "Pourquoi cours-tu après la goutte d'eau, alors que tu te diriges vers la mer?" (Laâbi 2006, 54), a citation from Farid Al-Din Attar's *The Conference of the Birds*, a poem that is well known for its critique of ruling parties. The second edition includes fewer prosoèmes, and four sketches by Mahi Binebine. The poet states in the opening poem, "Mais je reviens. Du moins cette fois-ci encore. Parce que je le veux. Parce que j'ai besoin de mille descentes comparables pour *voir ce que je n'ai pas vu et ne verrai*

8   As journalist Mustapha Bourakkadi puts it alluding to yet another transposition, the author reveals "une idée originale de l'écriture littéraire tel un musicien de jazz qui s'évertue à explorer les possibilités de son instrument au-delà de la mélodie" (2006, 1).
9   As the poetic "I"/eye writes in *Pourquoi cours-tu*, he "met" Dostoïevski in Laâlou, a Rabat prison of the Years of Lead.

peut-être jamais" (Laâbi 2006, 9, emphasis added). Laâbi underscores the critical importance of seeing in order to know. The 2006 edition interrupts and reworks dominant visual fields in its blending of genres, causing the reader to stop reading and join the poet in looking at, and in seeing, the images in front of her. The reader is called upon first to see, as the cover of the edition features one of the sketches, and then to read.

The person in the sketch appears constrained, his hands presumably tied behind his back, yet disquietingly mobile (Figure 5.1). There is, in these three images, a deliberate refusal to see and be seen; in each case the subject looks down, refuses to engage, and is fleeting, moving out of the frame, carried either by someone or by a device (in Figure 5.1, a wheel). The injury is in plain sight; amputated arms, missing facial features and bent backs (this was a common condition of Tazmamart survivors as the ceilings of the cells were often not high enough for them to stand up straight). The faces are covered in dark lines, reminiscent of the blindfolding and the darkness to which the prisoners were regularly consigned. In many ways, Binebine's is a distinct endeavor to represent the Tazmamart prisoner; it is an attempt to visualize him, to see and show. In another way, however, he refuses representation of the incarcerated by way of inscribing a refusal to be seen and to be known, as Hochberg would put it. The tension between visibility and invisibility is mobilized here, hanging almost by a broken thread (Figure 5.3), a dotted line, as we visualize the prisoner and at the same time come face to face with the denial of "a so-called proper or restorative representation" (Hochberg 2015, 59). As Levinas (1979) contends, it is the face that constitutes a call to moral responsibility and that brings us into an ethical encounter with the other. Judith Butler goes further, deeming the face the site that alerts us to suffering and to the precariousness of the other: "the face, if we are to put words to its meaning, will be *that for which no words really work*; the face seems to be a kind of sound, the sound of language evacuating its sense" (Butler 2004, 134, emphasis added). If, for Butler, the face is the site of the expression of suffering, one that expresses something that words cannot possibly represent, the images above urge us to grapple further with the fact that it is not actually in the recognizable face itself that empathy and a bridge to the other originate. She reminds us that for Levinas, "the human is not *represented by* the face … For represen-tation to convey the human, then, representation must not only fail, but it must *show* its failure" (Butler 2004, 144, emphasis added). Butler concludes that this paradox must be retained in any representation

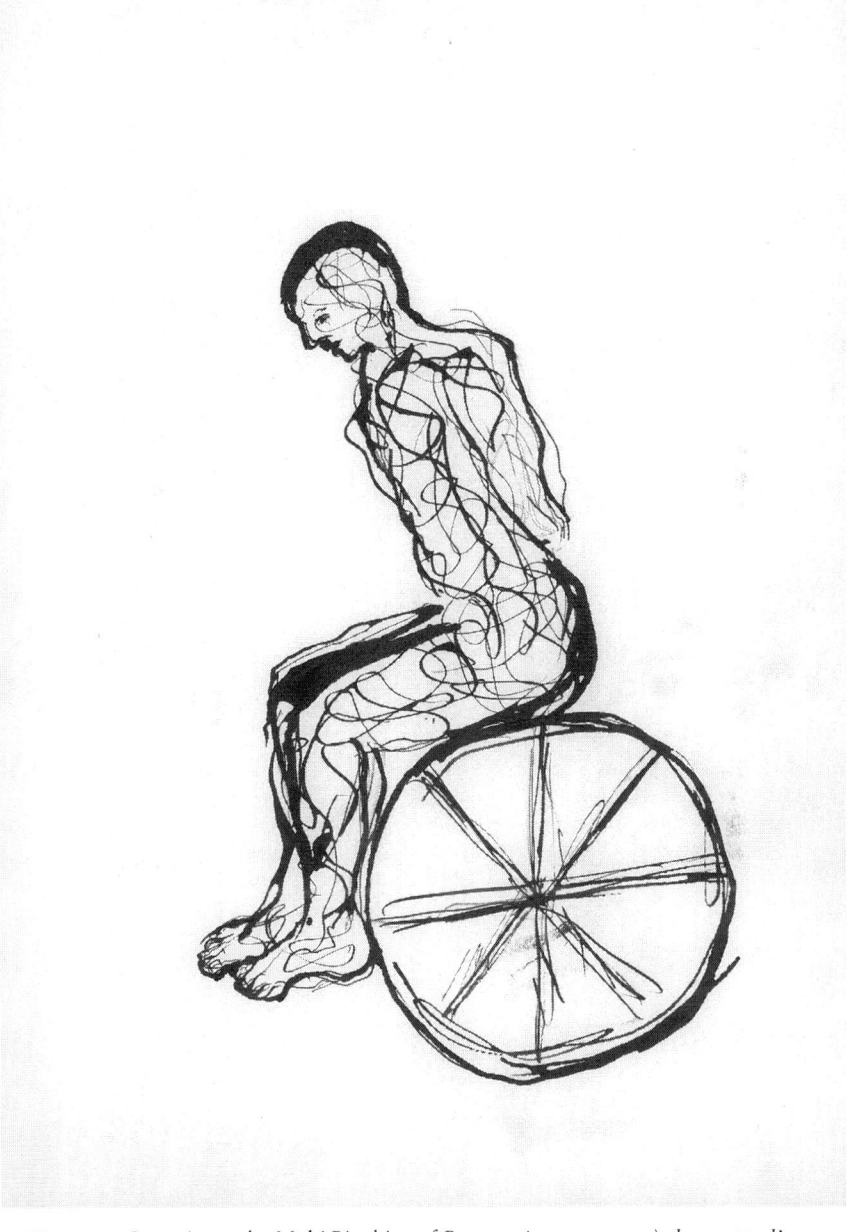

Figure 5.1 Cover image by Mahi Binebine of *Pourquoi cours-tu après la goutte d'eau*.

Figure 5.2 Sketch by Mahi Binebine in *Pourquoi cours-tu après la goutte d'eau*, p. 26.

Figure 5.3 Sketch by Mahi Binebine in *Pourquoi cours-tu après la goutte d'eau*, p. 20.

that aspires to convey what is human. It is here that the obscurantist Moroccan state apparatus gravely failed its citizens as it shrouded the Years of Lead in darkness, providing prisoners with "no image, no name, no narrative, so that there never was a life and there never was a death" (Butler 2004, 146). Slyomovics details the painstaking process that has been undertaken since 1999 of bringing justice to those who were forcibly disappeared during the Years of Lead, and explains how "as with other projects in which a state appears to declare war against its own citizens, the attempt to analyze such an historical past tests the limits of our ability to portray such experiences" (Slyomovics 2005, 2). These limits continue to take on new forms and functions in a current cultural aesthetic that has nonetheless seen a significant shift after Hassan II's death in 1999.[10]

As readers/viewers, we both see constraint in these images and fail to perceive it. We are faced with the possibility that the pain and the suffering of constraint is ever-present and not only a feature of the past. Further, we interrogate our own ethical failure. Following Hochberg reading Cathy Caruth, we are held to reckon with our "own (ongoing) failure to see (on time)" (Hochberg 2015, 146). Caruth maintains that this sort of realization is "itself the site of a trauma, the trauma of the necessity and impossibility of responding to another's death" (Caruth 1996, 100). Before even reaching the question of death, it is in the impossibility of response, signaled by Caruth, that trauma lies. Like Freud, she maintains that trauma is always experienced belatedly, after the event, and in the form of compulsive repetition. Drawing on this, Hochberg emphasizes:

> it can be argued that trauma is *innately scopic* and that it is accessible only insofar as it appears in the form of images of an otherwise missed (unseen) event. In other words, trauma may only be experienced in delay through one's compulsion to see what one failed to see, and this experience inevitably involves coming to terms with one's previous failure to see *on time*. (Hochberg 2015, 141, emphasis added)

For Laâbi, this so-called failure materializes in the re-edition of his poems with sketches by Binebine "pour voir ce que je n'ai pas vu" (Laâbi 2006, 9) and for Binebine, it manifests as the compulsive repetition of constrained individuals in his sketches, paintings, and sculptures.

---

10   Laâbi's own novel about his imprisonment, *Les chemins de l'ordalie*, published in Paris in 1982, was published in Morocco only in 2000.

Figure 5.4 "Untitled" by Mahi Binebine.

Even a cursory visit of the works on his website reveals the ubiquity of confinement, constraint, and fragmentation.[11]

Dynamiting the Prison-house of Language

If above I suggest that Laâbi's re-edition of *L'écorché vif*, which is inclusive of the Binebine sketches, provides both an enhanced view and the recognition of the state's, the public's, and our failure to see (on time), what else does it tell us? First, I believe that it signals a reckoning not only with the limits of language, but with the limits of writing (possibly for a specifically Moroccan public given the prohibitive cost of books and depressed literacy rates), a sort of *prise de conscience*. As Laâbi notes even in the early days of his incarceration in the aptly titled poem "Sous le bâillon, le poème," writing is always movable but insufficient: "Écrire. Dois-je l'avouer. Je n'ai qu'une relative confiance en les mots, quand bien même je les tourne et les retourne dans tous les sens ..." (Laâbi 1983, 101). *Pourquoi cours-tu* opens with the poet's reflection on the limits of the written word. In confronting his "geôliers de l'espoir" (Laâbi 2006, 8), again adopting a prison metaphor, Laâbi states "je deviendrai orateur," "je me joindrai aux analphabètes de Jamaâ Lafna" (Laâbi 2006, 9). Making a gesture toward the future rather than toward the past, Laâbi nevertheless looks back: "Et me voilà, tête nue, pieds nus, parlant alors que j'aurais dû épouser votre silence" (Laâbi 2006, 33). In using the conditional past "j'aurais dû," is the poet not underscoring what should have been? Is he not suggesting that it should have been otherwise? But should the poet remain silent? In the reparative *prosoème* to Hikmet, Laâbi seems to answer with a resounding no, and yet he returns to the constraints of writing:

> Mon cher Nazim, Excuse-moi d'avoir tellement tardé à te répondre.

---

11   In an article entitled "Zones of perceptual enclosure: The Aesthetics of Immobility in Casablanca's Literary Bidonvilles" (2016), Katarzyna Pieprzak convincingly analyzes the question of immobility in Binebine's novel *Les étoiles de Sidi Moumen*. Interestingly, she concludes that "human being and human meaning remain captive in a representational system that does not allow for self-creation or self-revision" (41). To be sure, Binebine's novel does present a somewhat diminishing picture of the inhabitants of Sidi Moumen. Placing this work in dialogue with his paintings, sketches, and sculptures, however, brings us to a dynamic and reparative reading of what Pieprzak reads as immobility.

Diverses sollicitations (tu les connais bien, ces moments où on se trouve débordé en prison) … Et puis surtout une sorte d'impossibilité à t'écrire comme j'ai l'habitude de le faire avec d'autres amis. S'agissant de toi, l'idée même du censeur entre nous me paralyse. Et ce "métalangage" que j'ai forgé au cours des années pour communiquer un certain essentiel en évitant le piège des mots-vedettes s'est avéré inopérant chaque fois que j'ai voulu t'écrire. (Laâbi 2006, 45)

Laâbi "se pretend[re] libre de toutes les prisons" (Laâbi 1986, 64) nowhere more freely than in *Petit musée portatif* (2002), another hybrid book composed of 31 poems and 32 images (18 gouache illustrations by Abdallah Sadouk, photos by Laydi Maroufi and reproductions of various paintings by Mohamed Kacimi, among other artists). Pieprzak calls the book a "museum in exile" and a "physical realization of the discursive museum of the 1960s produced by *Souffles*" (2010, 172). Here, Laâbi probes the link between writing and painting, and revives Khatibi's *intersigne*, not necessarily as contact between different semiotic signs but as their moving and dynamic imbrication. The spark set off by the dialogue between writing and painting owes its force to *Souffles*. The first issue was explosive: "Ce mince opuscule contient de la dynamite" declared the newspaper *Politique Hebdo* in 1966 (quoted on Laâbi's website). Yet another commentator for *Notre libraire* (1986) affirmed "les poètes de *Souffles* sont doublement hérétiques: ils utilisent la langue française, et ils la sculptent à la dynamite." The *Souffles* blast was forceful, not least because it grappled with questions of medium and form all while "sculpting" and exploding the French language. The linguistic dynamiting had as much to do with the choice between French and Arabic—a "guérilla linguistique" as Mohamed Khair-Eddine called it—as it did with the very possibilities and constraints of writing.

In *L'Écriture au tournant*, a short essay published by Editions Al Manar, and also featuring Binebine's work, Laâbi raises the possibility of writing as utopia, as a "quête perpétuelle du sens" in the "tableau apocalyptique" (Laâbi 2000, 22) that is the world the writer is forced to inhabit today. Clearly and deliberately dating a shift in consciousness and freedom to the aftermath of the Gulf War, Laâbi implicitly evokes a time when the role of the image took on a radically new valence. In the incipit he pays homage to Tahar Djaout, a writer who was gunned down for his words, and who in *Le dernier été de la raison* writes: "On ne se défait pas facilement de l'utopie: c'est un acide qui creuse dans l'opacité du dogme, des trous où se logent les controverses, où prolifèrent les questions" (1999, 124). If Laâbi raises more questions than answers in his book, he is categorical in his belief that "le champ de la pensée s'est énormément rétréci" (Laâbi 2000, 18) and that outside of the West, in the "pays du Sud," the writer/intellectual is a minority, "privé de ses droits essentiels" (Laâbi 2000, 19). In a poetic ending addressed to himself, and to all writers, Laâbi concludes, "Si tu écris, c'est par respect pour le pacte d'honneur que tu as signé avec toi-même dès ton éveil à la conscience. Le plus grand échec serait que tu puisses un jour perdre la face, ta face humaine" (Laâbi 2000, 24). As if writing were no longer sufficient to draw the reader into an encounter with the humanity of the other, the facing page to these closing lines asks the reader to contemplate a painting by Binebine. An unrecognizable face is cut through by a disfiguring line, in the very place where words are emitted; a yellow line severs the mouth in two as if to acknowledge a fault line in the power of the word. The laceration is, however, clearly and painfully visible; the face is still entirely there.

If repair is to occur, it finds its most effective expression at the intersection of writing and the image, in the interstices and imbrication of mediums. As Laâbi writes about the perils of being an intellectual in today's Morocco, "On dirait que ce qu'il (l'intellectuel) écrit se grave immédiatement dans le marbre" (Laâbi 2013, 75). Warning of writing's potential to be stuck, again in the hard sculpting of marble, he advances a dynamiting of forms. If the French verb *plastiquer* is suggestive—and reminiscent—of the visual arts, *les arts plastiques*, it simultaneously carries with it the expression of blowing up or dynamiting. The fragments of dynamited language must be molded and shaped, recomposed for us/them not only to read, but also to see.[12] As journalist Abdeslam Maghraoui writes, in conversation with former Tazmamart prisoner Ahmed Marzouki, "today, Moroccan democrats worry that a new but no less vicious version of the Years of Lead is creeping into Moroccan social and political life" (2015).[13] As Hochberg suggests, "an effective political act necessitates an interruption and reworking of dominant visual fields, and … generating new ways of seeing is the precondition

---

12   "La langue d'un poète est d'abord sa propre langue, celle qu'il crée et élabore au sein du chaos linguistique, la manière aussi dont il recompose les placages de mondes et de dynamismes qui coexistent en lui" (Laâbi 1966).

13   See http://www.jadaliyya.com/Details/32415/The-Moroccan-Non-Exception-A-Conversation-with-Ahmed-Marzouki,-Former-Tazmamart-Detainee, accessed December 27, 2019.

Figure 5.5 "Untitled" by Mahi Binebine,
from Abdellatif Laâbi, *L'écriture au tournant*, p. 25.

for overcoming oppressive geo-sociopolitical orders" (Maghraoui 2015, 3). While Laâbi and Binebine voice a call to see, it is a call that refuses the seeing we experience through the majority of traditional media outlets or mainstream depictions, that is to say, a form of seeing that relies on the reification of trauma and on the entrenchment of an already understood representation, in this case of the prisoner, but the same might be said of the migrant and the refugee, for instance.[14] Theirs is a call that invokes the very opposite of what Butler defines as "the media's evacuation of the human through the image" (Butler 2004, 146).

The role of the writer, the artist, the intellectual, in social and political life continues to be central to Moroccan cultural production today. Laâbi and Binebine invoke a deliberate insistence on mobilizing and on seeing, on not sanitizing the wounds of history, and on visibility. To some degree this seems like an organic progression in an era where images appear to carry more weight and garner more attention than words, in a context where the visual landscape has been—and can still be—oppressive, and where the most recurrent images continue to be portraits of the king and mainstream television reporting.[15] The challenge, if we are to heed cultural theorist Wendy Kozol's work on the ambivalence of witnessing (2014), is to become ethical spectators, an indubitably paradoxical idea that takes stock of the contemporary society of the spectacle and its dangers. Kozol and Hochberg refer specifically to mainstream media representations in their critiques of the reification of suffering and look toward cultural productions (film, in particular) that escape such approaches. Laâbi and Binebine continue to confront and challenge what we should not and cannot ignore; that is, how to be ethical readers of images, what it means to experience bystander trauma, and how to continue to cultivate empathetic seeing. Yet, to what extent does their work call to account for what happened during the Years of Lead, and for the autocratic measures that continue to transpire, as Laâbi reminds us in his Facebook post cited at the beginning of this chapter, without letting the viewer achieve what would ultimately be egotistical ethical satisfaction? To engage with *all* others, says Butler following Derrida, "can only result in a situation of

---

14   In Hochberg's work, the Palestinian.

15   The internet presents another arena altogether for images to play a defining role in the mobilization "from below" of collective engagement with otherness. In the Moroccan context, one might consider such mobilization as a productive form of *sousveillance,* a tactical response to the ubiquitous gaze of the Royal Palace.

radical irresponsibility" (Butler 2004, 118). We must choose our ethical engagements, and ethical responsibility must be situated. Part of that responsibility is to reframe our ways of seeing, and to this end Laâbi and Binebine work cogently in the interstices of forms, transposing points of view, to retrace and repair the contours of a still-fractured Moroccan cultural and historical landscape.

Works Cited

Aït-Mous, Fadma, and Driss Ksikes. 2014. *Le métier d'intellectuel*. Casablanca: Presses de l'Université Citoyenne.

Attia, Kader. 2018. "The Field of Emotion." http://kaderattia.de/the-field-of-emotion/. Accessed December 27, 2019.

Bourakkadi, Mustapha. 2006. "Abdellatif Laâbi construit un pont entre prose et poésie." Rabat: Le Matin. Accessed December 29, 2019.

Butler, Judith. 2004. *Precarious Life: The Powers of Mourning and Violence*. London and New York: Verso.

Caruth, Cathy. 1996. *Unclaimed Experience: Trauma, Narrative, and History*. Baltimore: Johns Hopkins University Press.

Djaout, Tahar. 1999. *Le dernier été de la raison*. Paris: Éditions du Seuil.

"Exhibition Notes—The Power Plant." 2018. https://www.goethe.de/ins/ca/en/m/sta/tor/ver.cfm?fuseaction=events.detail&event_id=20998923. Accessed November 13, 2020.

Harrison, Olivia, and Teresa Villa-Ignacio. 2015. *Souffles-Anfas: A Critical Anthology from the Moroccan Journal of Culture and Politics*. Stanford: Stanford University Press.

Hochberg, Gil. 2015. *Visual Occupations: Violence and Visibility in a Conflict Zone*. Durham: Duke University Press.

Khari Eddine, Mohammed. 1970. *Moi l'aigre*. Paris: Editions du Seuil.

Kozol, Wendy. 2014. *Distant Wars Visible: The Ambivalence of Witnessing*. Minneapolis: University of Minnesota Press.

Laâbi, Abdellatif. 1966. *Souffles*. Numéro 1 "Prologue." http://laabi.net/index.php/evenement/. Accessed April 2, 2021.

——. 1983. *Chronique de la citadelle d'exil: Lettres de prison 1972–80*. Paris: Denoël.

——. 1986. *L'écorché vif*. Paris: L'Harmattan.

——. 2000. *L'écriture au tournant*. Casablanca: Editions Al Manar.

——. 2002. *Petit musée portatif*. Casablanca: Editions Al Manar.

——. 2006. *Pourquoi cours-tu après la goutte d'eau?* Casablanca: Editions Al Manar.

——. 2013. *Un autre Maroc*. Paris: Editions de la Différence.

Levinas, Emmanuel. 1979. *Totality and Infinity*. Heidelberg: Springer.

Lindsey, Ursula. 2017. "Culture is the Solution." The Century Foundation. https://tcf.org/content/report/culture-is-the-solution/?agreed=1#easy-footnote-bottom-30. Accessed March 29, 2021.

Maghraoui, Abdeslam. 2015. "The Moroccan Non-Exception: A Conversation with Ahmed Marzouki, Former Tazmamart Detainee." https://www.jadaliyya.com/Details/32415/The-Moroccan-Non-Exception-A-Conversation-with-Ahmed-Marzouki,-Former-Tazmamart-Detainee. Accessed April 2, 2021.

Pieprzak, Katarzyna. 2010. *Imagined Museums*. Minneapolis: University of Minnesota Press.

——. 2016. "Zones of Perceptual Enclosure: The Aesthetics of Immobility in Casablanca's Literary Bidonvilles." *Research in African Literatures* 47 (3): 32–49.

Scher, Robin. 2017. "In the Service of Repair: Kader Attia on Systems of Belief and 'Reason's Oxymorons.'" http://www.artnews.com/2017/02/24/in-the-service-of-repair-kader-attia-on-systems-of-belief-and-reasons-oxymorons/. Accessed November 12, 2020.

Semlali, Mohamed. 2017. *L'ombre du bagne: La littérature carcérale du Maroc et ailleurs*. Fès: Université de Fès.

Slyomovics, Susan. 2005. *The Performance of Human Rights in Morocco*. Philadelphia: University of Pennsylvania Press.

PART III

Performance Arts

CHAPTER SIX

Minor Transpositions
Mohamed Rouabhi Stages the Colonial Cliché

Olivia C. Harrison

Minor Transpositions

Like its cousins, translation and metaphor, transposition evokes movement from one place to another. A body in movement can, according to the Trésor de la langue française, figuratively be said to be transposed. Migration, exile, flight, are in this sense figures of transposition. At the same time, the mass displacements that peaked in the 2010s have lent new urgency to what, in the aftermath of decolonization, Frantz Fanon called "the question of minorities," but on a transnational scale (1968, 80). Today's European minorities are the bodies transposed from south to north under the pressures of industrial capitalism, poverty, and war.

Against the expression *migrant crisis*, which produces displaced persons as external to the body politic—the nation-state, the EU—this chapter situates contemporary mass displacements within a much longer history of colonial and postcolonial population transfer across and between imperial formations. The migrant question demands a transnational, transcolonial approach to forced displacement and enforced immobility, one that begins, as Achille Mbembe (2016, 85–86) and Patrick Chamoiseau (2017, 23, 27) remind us, with transposition on a mass scale: the removal of indigenous peoples and the deportation of Africans after 1492.[1] But if

---

1   I borrow the term "transcolonial" from Françoise Lionnet and Shu-mei Shih, who describe transcolonialism as "the shared, though differentiated, experience of colonialism and neocolonialism (by the same colonizer or by different colonizers)" (2005, 11).

there is ample historical evidence for the transposition—in the sense of substitution but also intermingling—of indigenous and African peoples in the Americas (Forbes 1993), I want to suggest that the figure of transposition also makes legible forms of migrant relationality that do not fit neatly into empirically driven frameworks for the study of mass displacement. What might it mean to transpose a singular experience of migration across heterogeneous national contexts or imperial formations? What might such transpositions reveal about the migrant question, writ large to include the *longue durée* history of European imperialism?

In order to begin answering these questions, I take the theatrical *œuvre* of Franco-Algerian playwright Mohamed Rouabhi as a case study in what I call *minor transpositions*, focusing on three performances that stage Palestine, Algeria, Native America, and France in a multidirectional critique of colonialism and racism: *Les nouveaux bâtisseurs*, *El menfi/L'exilé*, and *Darwich, deux textes*.[2] As I will argue, the characters Rouabhi stages in these plays—Algerians, Palestinians, and Native Americans—are not arbitrary figures of (post)colonial exile. Through a complex dramaturgy that mobilizes a range of media (photography, film, dance, music, spoken word) and languages (French, Arabic, sign language), Rouabhi transposes the experience of exile across heterogenous but overlapping imperial formations: France-Algeria, Israel-Palestine, and the US. Drawing on Ariella Azoulay's writings on photography in the colonial contact zone and W. J. T. Mitchell's notion of race as medium, I further analyze the ways in which Rouabhi transposes the medium of photography on the stage in order to draw attention to, and critique, the production of migrants/refugees as racialized strangers/outsiders.

2   The phrase "minor transpositions" intentionally echoes Lionnet's and Shih's productive notion of "minor transnationalism," which aims at "looking at transnationalism from [a] 'minor' perspective." As they note, "minor cultures as we know them are the products of transmigrations and multiple encounters, which implies that they are always already mixed, hybrid, and relational ... The minority and the immigrant are constitutive of the national in its status as the object of interior exclusion, integral to what the national means and how citizenship is defined" (2005, 5; 10–12).

Children of the Colonies

Although Rouabhi's work is clearly inscribed in a decades-long tradition of militant theater by and for postcolonial migrants, it is not easily classifiable as *Beur* or *banlieue* literature.[3] On the contrary, his plays put pressure on these nomenclatures, resisting the critical impetus to separate *Beur* and *banlieue* writings—implicitly cast as migrant literature—from writings by non-racialized French nationals. Because his method is inherently transnational and comparative—transposing the question of race in the US, for example, onto a French imperial context (*All Power to the People!*), or the Palestinian question across Native America and postcolonial France (*El menfi/L'exilé*)—his work is not immediately legible as French, or even Algerian. Why write about Palestine, and not his parents' native country? critics wanted to know when they saw *Les nouveaux bâtisseurs*, his first play on Palestine (Rouabhi 1997a).

Perhaps in reaction to the expectation that he should write about Algeria, Rouabhi devotes the bulk of his preface to the published version of *Les nouveaux bâtisseurs* to the question "why Palestine?" Titled "Les enfants des colonies," the preface offers a stark assessment of Rouabhi's place in a country that has forgotten the conditions that turned him, *nolens volens*, into a French citizen. Born in France to parents who had until 1962 been colonial subject-citizens of France, Rouabhi is not *issu de l'immigration* but *issu de la colonisation*: "Mon père me disait: 'Avant d'être algérien, j'étais français.' Quant à moi, avant d'être français j'étais algérien." Citing the Palestinian poet Mahmoud Darwish, Rouabhi articulates the paradoxical position of French citizens of colonized descent through a minor transposition of (post)colonial exile:

> "Inscris sur tes papiers, je suis arabe," dit un vers célèbre de Mahmoud Darwich. Alors j'écris, en français, sur mes papiers, que je suis arabe … c'est ce qui constitua pour moi un point de départ: une démarche plus ou moins consciente, pour un Arabe vivant en France, d'écrire une pièce se déroulant en Palestine. (Rouabhi 1997b, 9–10; Darwish 1964, 5)

---

3 Born to Algerian migrants in Paris in 1965, Rouabhi is the author of more than 30 plays, most of them unpublished, on topics ranging from the HIV/AIDS crisis to domestic abuse, race in America, French colonial history, and the question of Palestine. The website of Rouabhi's company, Les Acharnés, contains a wealth of information on his plays, including visual documentation, press reviews, workshop notes, and detailed production information: http://www.lesacharnes.com/, accessed October 8, 2020.

In Rouabhi's telling, the experience of racialization in postcolonial France—the perpetual designation of the children of the colonies as immigrants, and of French citizens of Maghrebi parentage as Arabs—is part of the *longue durée* history of European colonialism, including the settler-colonies of French Algeria and Israel.

Dedicated to "mes frères de colère mes sœurs d'amour mes semblables enfants de la colonisation nés ici … pour les enfants de la Palestine," *Les nouveaux bâtisseurs* excavates traces of Palestine for the children of France's colonies. "Les traces sont de toute nature et s'affichent sur tous les supports," explains Rouabhi, "des photographies, des livres échappant à l'autodafé, des dessins d'enfants, des fac-similés, des plans, des cartes, un film qui se tourne, des poèmes, des témoignages" (Rouabhi 1997b, 10–11). The theater represents, through a simulacrum of traces, what has been removed from the domain of visibility, a way of reconstituting the traces of what has been destroyed, a way of presenting on the stage what has been absented from the ground. Derived from the Greek *theasthai*, to contemplate or to behold, theater offers a new mode of seeing that which has been removed from the field of visibility: Palestine.[4] In metatheatrical terms, *Les nouveaux bâtisseurs* also evidences something that is not legible in mainstream accounts of the Israeli–Palestinian conflict in France: a strong political and affective investment in Palestine in the French *banlieue*. The following year, Rouabhi would begin working on *El menfi*, a play that transposes the Palestinian question into an American context through the subversive remediation of colonial photography.

Workshops in Ramallah

In 1999, Nadine Varoutsikos, the director of La Maison du Théâtre et de la Danse (MTD) in Epinay-sur-Seine, invited Rouabhi to write a play in collaboration with Epinay's sister city, Ramallah.[5] In May and June 1999, Rouabhi held writing workshops in Epinay, Ramallah,

4   My understanding of the theater is close to that developed by Alain Badiou and Denis Guénoun, who both insist on theater as a medium that makes visible the process of representation itself. "The theater doesn't give explanations, it shows!" (Badiou 2015, 68). "Le théâtre (les gradins) est le lieu d'où l'on voit … lieu où se pose la question du rapport du visible à l'invisible, du sensible au non-sensible" (Guénoun 1998, 25, 37).

5   Epinay-sur-Seine is in the Seine-Saint-Denis department northeast of Paris, best known as the epicenter of the 2005 urban rebellions that were triggered by the

and East Jerusalem, working with schoolchildren, university students, incarcerated youth, and refugees. The figure of the Native American appears in the course of one of the most interesting writing exercises that was assigned to each group. Students were asked to choose a photograph from a selection of six to 11 photos, describe the subject(s) it represents, and imagine their autobiography. Badawi Qawasmi, a 20-year-old Birzeit University student who would travel to Epinay-sur-Seine for the French premiere of *El menfi*, chose to write about a close-up photographic portrait of an elderly man, his face angled *de trois quarts*, head held high, gaze cast downward, lips sealed in an upside-down smile.

This photograph resembles the iconic clichés taken by photographers on the colonial frontier, in the wake of the catastrophic conquest of North America. Though Rouabhi did not provide any captions or contextual information for the images, Qawasmi instantly recognized the photographic subject as a conquered Native American.[6] Written in slightly ungrammatical but fluid English, Qawasmi's photo-essay reveals the close affinity he must have felt when he saw the face captured in the colonial cliché. For the photograph tells a story remarkably close to that of the occupied Palestinian:

> My story is the story of most Indien-American. We were living in peace and prosperity, our tribes we spread through the plains, hills and mountains of what we believed was our land. We had no borders, no prisons, no killing, and the only thing we thought about was hunting and raising horses. Our civilization grew slowly and steadily untill and at a sudden, we were confiscated from our freedom. These new comers killed our children, stole all our possessions and most importantly our freedom. Instead of setting down as a leader of my tribe I am setting in the occupier's prison not knowing what is waiting for me out of this door [*sic*]. (Rouabhi 1999, 93)[7]

death of Zyed Benna and Bouna Traoré during a police chase in the neighboring commune of Clichy-sous-Bois.

6 Rouabhi lost the photographs he used during the Palestine workshops, but provided me with a facsimile of Qawasmi's photo-essay, written below a reproduction of the photograph. Personal communication with the author, June 27, 2018. One of Edward Curtis's lesser-known photographs, this cliché bears the title "Lone Tree—Apsaroke"—presumably the name and nation of the photographed subject—and is included in Volume IV of Curtis's photographic encyclopedia *The North American Indian*, published in 1909 (Curtis, 1997: 203).

7 I have transcribed this passage from the facsimile Rouabhi sent me of Qawasmi's handwritten composition.

Figure 6.1 Edward S. Curtis, Lone Tree – Apsaroke, 1908.
Photogravure plate. National Museum of the American Indian,
Smithsonian Institution (080_F08_plate_143).

Qawasmi's transcolonial "autobiography" as a Native American activates some of the same romanticized stereotypes we find in the writings of Palestinian as well as Algerian and Beur writers and activists: an idealized view of pre-colonial life, torn asunder by the violent intrusion of the colonizer.[8] But it also requires us to reflect upon the mediation of indigenous America in Palestine, and the modalities of its transposition in a Franco-Palestinian play.

What interests me here is the medium of identification: photography. Unlike the stereotype—which derives etymologically from an early technology of mechanical image reproduction—photography is a relational medium, involving photographer, photographed, and, as Ariella Azoulay argues in her remarkable analysis of "photographing on the verge of catastrophe," the spectator.[9] If the reproduced image still belongs to the artist, the photograph eludes authorship, not because of its reproducibility, but because of its relationality. The photograph

> [is] always, of necessity, the product of an encounter—even if a violent one—between a photographer, a photographed subject, and a camera, an encounter whose involuntary traces in the photograph transform the latter into a document that is not the creation of an individual and can never belong to any one person or narrative exclusively. (Azoulay 2008, 13)

Qawasmi's appropriation of a colonial-era photograph of an indigenous American participates in what Azoulay calls "the citizenry of photography": a civil contract linking not only the imagined photographed subject (a Native American after conquest) and photographer (a white occupier), but also the spectator (the Palestinian) in an unequal but potentially transformative relationship. Crucially, the photograph is not only a record of what "was there," and is no longer. It

---

8 "Je marche comme une indienne," the narrator of Farida Belghoul's novel defiantly proclaims, "A poil comme les sauvages!" (Belghoul 1986, 71–72). Looking at an old photograph of her maternal grandmother, Zahia Rahmani imagines her to be "la petite-fille d'un grand chef indien. Un Cherokee éloigné de ses terres américaines" who sees in the Algerians "une certaine familiarité avec ses frères" (Rahmani 2006, 51–52). On transcolonial identification with Native Americans in *Beur* literature, see Harrison 2018.

9 "Photographing the Verge of Catastrophe" is the title of one of the chapters of Azoulay's book *The Civil Contract of Photography* (2008), which analyzes photographs from the Occupied Territories, antebellum America, the second Gulf War, and other sites of disaster.

also addresses the spectator. The photographed subject speaks through the Palestinian student observing the image to address a grievance, in non-idiomatic English, to a community of empathetic spectators.[10]

On the last page of his photographic essay about Jean Mohr's photographs of Palestinians, Edward Said invites the viewer to see that the photographed subjects are in fact also "looking at [their] observers" (Said 1986, 166). Here, the observer casts a transcolonial gaze on the photographed, identifying with the subject of another colonial power. But Azoulay's performative account of civil spectatorship—the kind of careful watching that makes possible an imagined citizenry of photography—is also subject to minor transposition in Qawasmi's autobiography: the remediation of spectatorship into a written grievance transposes native dispossession into the terms of Palestinian occupation. For this ventriloquized account of colonization "palestinianizes" the indigenous subject's experience by introducing a term, "the occupier," that is not usually found in the context of native dispossession and genocide. In this sense, it also beckons Qawasmi's gaze into the image, as if the spectator were not simply witnessing, but also participating in the citizenry of photography. Qawasmi's performance as a Native American will find its way into *El menfi* in the mouth of a character whose name, Kawani, echoes that of its author, and whose photograph—which now includes a Palestinian spectator *within* its frame—will structure the play from beginning to end.

Enter the Colonial Cliché

El menfi begins with a photographic encounter between a Palestinian and a Native American. A concatenated tableau of exilic encounters across the United States, France, Lebanon, and Palestine, the play is

---

10   Azoulay's notion of the civil contract of photography is explicitly articulated as a challenge to Roland Barthes's theorization of photography as an irremediably irretrievable trace of what has vanished. Against Barthes's nostalgic view of photography, and beyond the humanitarian uses of photography as archive or witness, Azoulay proposes a performative understanding of the medium that implicates the spectator in a political and ethical relationship with the object of photography. "The civil contract of photography enables citizens and noncitizens alike to produce grievances and claims that otherwise can't be seen and to impose them by means of, through, and on the citizenry of photography" (2008, 192). On Barthes, see Azoulay (2008, 93–94) and Roland Barthes (2000, 76).

framed by the life story of a Palestinian writer named John Walid Jaber, who tells the "singular story" of his encounter-in-photography with a man named Kawani:

> Je m'appelle John Walid Jaber. Quand j'étais petit il m'est arrivé une histoire singulière qui marqua pour la première fois mon enfance: j'ai été enlevé par un Indien Pawani. Cela s'est passé à New York, à l'aéroport John Fitzgerald Kennedy.
>
> Il y avait un photographe qui venait voir les gens et qui leur demandait s'ils voulaient poser à côté d'un vrai Indien Pawani, s'ils voulaient ramener chez eux une photo souvenir de l'Amérique mythique. J'ai demandé à ma mère un dollar et je me suis assis à côté du vrai Indien Pawani. L'homme qui l'accompagnait a pris la photo et après l'Indien Pawani m'a demandé si je voulais écouter une histoire Pawani, une histoire comme il n'en existait plus et je lui ai dit: oui.
>
> Alors il m'a demandé de le suivre et nous sommes sortis de l'aéroport avec l'Indien Pawani et nous sommes montés dans une Buick noire modèle 69 avec des jantes dorées à rayons et nous avons pris la direction de Southtown Avenue et après nous avons pris l'autoroute 927 et je ne me rappelle plus combien d'heures ni combien de jours nous avons roulé mais il faisait nuit lorsque Kawani me dit que nous étions enfin arrivés dans ce qui avait été jadis, le pays des Indiens Pawani.

Kawani and John stop at a gas station for coffee and donuts. The boy sees a newspaper lying on the counter and exclaims: "Oh regarde, c'est toi sur la photo." The "souvenir photo" has been printed in the paper and now bears the double function of a missing child advertisement and wanted mug shot. "Pourquoi tu me dis que c'est mon visage pourquoi tu me dis que çà, sur ce papier, c'est moi?" asks Kawani. Against the partial, static, lifeless photographic image, Kawani evokes the living faces he has known, faces that bear the imprint of the land that was theirs: "J'ai vu des hommes aux visages de toutes les couleurs, aux visages de toutes les formes, des visages froissés par le temps, rayés par le temps, des hommes qui avaient le cuir du visage comme la terre plissée de notre terre, la terre des indiens Pawani." But this land, and these faces, no longer exist. Sitting at a gas station built on Pawani land, Kawani is interrupted by its new occupants:

> DOUG, *l'employé de station-service*
> > Bon dis donc le vieux t'aurais pas bientôt fini d'enquiquiner le monde avec tes salades par hasard? Laisse ce gosse tranquille tu veux.
> JOHN, *enfant* Raconte-moi l'histoire que tu m'a promis.

KAWANI	Elle a déjà commencé ton histoire. Viens John, allons-nous-en. Combien je vous dois jeune homme?
DOUG	Hé là Peau-Rouge, y me semble que je viens d'te dire quelque chose … . Attends un peu mais j't'ai déjà vu quelque part …
KAWANI	Hum hum.

DOUG, *sortant un fusil de dessous le comptoir.*

	Bon Dieu mais c'est qu'il est en train d'se payer d'ma tronche hé Mike viens voir un peu par ici.
KAWANI	Repose cette arme.
DOUG	Tu donnes des ordres maintenant? … Je vais te faire la peau mec!
MIKE	Vas-y Doug, fais-lui la peau à c't'indien! (Rouabhi 2000, 6–10)[11]

The intrusion of the racist gaze in this scene—"j't'ai déjà vu quelque part"—has a double valence: if Doug recognizes Kawani, it is not only because he has seen the photograph of the wanted child kidnapper in the newspaper, but also because he recognizes in that picture, and in Kawani himself, the cliché of the Native American popularized through the staged ethnographic photographs taken at the turn of the nineteenth century—the very sort of "souvenir photo of mythical America" that the airport photographer sells for a dollar to unsuspecting foreign tourists and, unwittingly, Palestinian refugees. But now John is in this picture too: a second racialized, occupied subject has entered the colonial cliché. The story of colonial racism told here is, as John's request implies, also his story, the story of Palestine: "Tell me the story you promised," he implores. "The story has already begun," replies Kawani, sending him back to the car. When John awakens, Kawani is gone, the two racist men are dead, and his body is tattooed—indelibly "marked"—with intricate Pawani motifs.

It is important to note that the Pawani tribe is a fictional Native American nation. When I pressed Rouabhi to explain why he decided to "invent" a tribe rather than use one of the numerous extant names still in use—indigenous Americans have not disappeared, contrary to settler colonial fantasies of total conquest—Rouabhi responded that, for

---

11   The first and last elision are mine. I am grateful to Mohamed Rouabhi for sharing the typescript of the French version of the play along with annex materials from his Palestinian workshops. All translations are mine unless otherwise indicated.

him, Kawani is a survivor of genocide, a being who should not be there but remains.[12] The name Kawani sounds like it could be derived from the Arabic trilateral root *ka-wa-na*, which gives us both the verb *kan*, "to be, to exist" and *kan wa ma kan*, literally "there was and there was not" or, more idiomatically, "once upon a time." Like the photographs of Native Americans taken on the cusp of dispossession, or the tattoo that will magically appear on John's body at the end of this scene, his presence indexes both what was and is no longer, and an impossible encounter between two heterogeneous subjects of photography: the Native American and the Palestinian.

The ghostlike figure of Kawani returns to haunt Jaber in the final tableau of the play. Standing alone on stage, Jaber sees Kawani seated on a chair. "L'histoire reprend toujours là où elle s'est arrêtée," explains Kawani as he beckons to him: "viens mon petit John, viens ..." John, now a child, comes to sit on his lap, as we hear the adult Jaber reading the beginning of the memoir:

> Je m'appelle John Walid Jaber. Quand j'étais petit il m'est arrivé une histoire singulière qui marqua mon enfance: j'ai été enlevé par un Indien Pawani ... Il y avait un photographe qui venait voir les gens et qui leur demandait s'ils voulaient poser à côté d'un vrai Indien Pawani, s'ils voulaient ramener chez eux une photo souvenir ... (Rouabhi 2000, 51–52)

The flash of a photo camera illuminates the pair one last time, and the lights go out.

The encounter between the colonized photographic subject and the Palestinian spectator, turned, in *El menfi*, co-subject of the colonial cliché, is, I have argued, what makes possible a relational, multidirectional critique of colonialism and racism across imperial histories and geographies. If, as Cécile Bishop argues, photography is a medium that produces race (in this case, the cliché of the "Red Skin") it is also a medium that is subject to subversive remediation (Bishop 2018).[13] For W. J. T. Mitchell, race itself is a medium:

> race is not merely a content to be mediated, an object to be represented visually or verbally, or a thing to be depicted in a likeness or image ...

12 Mohamed Rouabhi, in conversation with the author, November 21, 2016.

13 Bishop compellingly argues that photography is evidence not of the visibility of race—the photograph of the Native American as empirical proof of his persistent presence—but of "the 'visuality' of race: the cultural practices and ideological structures that underpin [race's] visibility" (Bishop 2018, 197).

race itself is a medium and an iconic form—not simply something to be
seen, but itself a framework for seeing through or (as Wittgenstein would
put it) seeing as.

As such, "the medium of race is always open to *remediation*, to a
secondary representation, a double take, a critical reflection" (Mitchell
2012, 13; 89; original emphasis). What we might call the minor transposition of photography in the play—remediation as transposition—is
all the more remarkable given the role that photography has played in
developing the cliché of race, be it that of the "Red Skin" or the "Arab."
As scholars have documented, photography was, from its beginnings, a
race-making medium at the imperial frontier, albeit one that is subject
to recuperative remediation (Alloula 1986; Behdad 2016; Hannoush
2016; Moser 2017). An instrument of racial science, the colonial cliché
becomes a medium of minor transposition in *El Menfi*, much like
the racial nomenclature *Arab* in Rouabhi's reading of Darwish: "so I
write, in French, on my papers, that I am Arab." In the final section of
this chapter, I turn to Rouabhi's performance of Native Americanness
through the poetry of Mahmoud Darwish.

Exit the Colonial Cliché

In 1996, while he was completing *Les nouveaux bâtisseurs*, Rouabhi
staged Darwish's "Discours de l'indien rouge," a long prose poem he
discovered in 1993 in the pages of the *Revue d'Études Palestiniennes*,
in what he describes as a theatrical *coup de foudre*: "je me souviens
qu'entre l'instant où je venais de finir la lecture de ce récit … et l'instant
où je savais que je le dirai un jour à haute voix devant un public, il
s'est écoulé quelque chose comme une nanoseconde" (Rouabhi 2009,
4). Rouabhi would return to "Discours de l'indien rouge" on a number
of occasions: in 2003, with co-director Carlo Brandt, and again after
Darwish's death, in 2009 and 2010, for a solo performance titled
Darwich, deux textes, a double bill featuring "Discours de l'indien
rouge" alongside Darwish's memoir of the 1982 Israeli bombing of
Beirut, *Une mémoire pour l'oubli*.

Inspired by Chief Seattle's 1855 address to Governor Stevens, Darwish
originally included "The 'Red Indian's' Penultimate Speech to the White
Man" in his 1992 collection *Ahad ashar kawkaban*, which marked the
quincentennial of the conquest of the Americas and the Reconquista of

Muslim Spain.[14] Darwish's poem mobilizes a relational, comparative understanding of coloniality: a Palestinian poet addresses the white man in the name of the Native Americans, and in so doing, reinscribes Palestine within the *longue durée* history of European colonialism.[15] Like Qawasmi's Native American autobiography, "Discours de l'indien rouge" also surreptitiously transposes the language of Palestinian resistance. The Red Indian's first address to the white man recalls Darwish's musings about the tragic irony that has irremediably tied Palestinians to Israelis: "N'est-il pas venu le temps que nous nous retrouvions, l'Etranger? Deux étrangers en un même temps, en un même pays, comme se retrouvent les étrangers sur un abîme?" (Darwish 1993, 4). In a 1996 interview with the Israeli poet Helit Yeshurun, who has just asked him about the meaning of exile, Darwish characterizes his own relationship to the colonizer in strikingly similar terms: "Moi et l'occupant, nous souffrons tous les deux de l'exil. Il est exilé en moi et je suis la victime de son exil" (Darwish 1996, 56).

"L'exilé," of course, is the French translation of *El menfi*. If Badawi Qawasmi played an important role in the genesis of the play's Native American character, Rouabhi clearly had in mind Darwish's "Discours de l'indien rouge" when he drafted Kawani's poetic evocation of "the land of the Pawani Indians" (Rouabhi 2000, 7). His desire to dramatize the traces of Palestine beneath the all-too-visible image of Israel in *Les nouveaux bâtisseurs* also echoes the phantasmatic traces of Native America in Darwish's poem, the could-have-been of the pluperfect conditional: "Là nous aurions encore bâti, n'étaient les fusils anglais, le vin de France, et les fièvres … Ici les Etrangers nous vainquirent, et il ne nous reste rien dans le temps nouveau" (Darwish 1993, 8–9).

Beyond the intertextual echoes of Darwish in Rouabhi's plays, Rouabhi's production of "Discours de l'indien rouge" is crucial to the

14 I use Fady Joudah's word-for-word translation of the title of Darwish's epic poem, "khutbat 'al-hind al-ahmar' – ma qabl al-akhir – amam al-rajul al-abyad" (Darwish 2009, 69–77). In an interview with Rouabhi, Elias Sanbar explains that he was the one to suggest that Darwish write "a sort of response" to Chief Seattle's address to Governor Stevens (Rouabhi 2009, 10).

15 Darwish's poem also performatively transposes the "cultural erasure" encoded in the transmission of Chief Seattle's speech. As Rebecca Dyer and François Mulot point out, this address was already multiply mediated, from Duwamish to Chinook to English, and from a simultaneously translated speech to Henry A. Smith's transcribed notes, which served as the basis for the text he published three decades later in the *Seattle Sunday Star* on October 29, 1887 (Dyer and Mulot 2014, 80).

notion of minor transposition that I have elaborated in this chapter. In theatrical terms, "an Arab living in France" plays the role of a Palestinian poet playing the role of a Native American, addressing "the white man" from a triply (post)colonial subject position. Formally speaking, the transposition of Darwish's poem on a French stage enables the performance of indigeneity via Palestine and Native America: a French Algerian man, whose only costume is the glimmering silver and bright blue turquoise bolo tie appended to the collar of his linen suit, declaims Darwish's Native American address to the white man in eloquent French, simultaneously translating his peroration in sign language, an indigenous American form of gestural semantics (Figure 6.2). Rouabhi's embodiment of Darwish as a Native American also remediates colonial photography in a way that elucidates the minor transpositions of *El menfi*'s photographic encounter in the intimacy of an impromptu theater space that makes visible, and audible, the indigenous subject for a public too close not to see and hear.

Haloed by a spot that illuminates his face and torso, this character looks hauntingly like Kawani, sitting on the verge of the souvenir photograph of mythical America. Remember Kawani's rebellion against the reduction of his identity to a still image:

KAWANI   Pourquoi tu me dis que çà, sur ce papier, c'est moi?
JOHN, *enfant* Parce que c'est vrai. C'est toi qu'est là et là c'est moi.
KAWANI   Moi je crois que je ne suis pas sur ce papier. Moi, je te
              parle et mon corps tout entier est habité par la vie …
              Regarde mes mains. Mes mains sont vivantes non? Cet
              homme sur le papier ne possède pas de mains pareilles aux
              miennes. Il n'a ni bras ni jambes et il lui manque la moitié
              du visage … Ses cheveux sont immobiles, les miens sont
              animés non? … Je parle, je m'exprime, je peux m'adresser
              à cet homme sur ce papier si celui-ci est aussi vivant que tu
              le dis. Mais cet homme sur ce papier ne me répond pas. Il
              est muet. (Rouabhi 2000, 7–8)

Unlike the photographed subject, Kawani can speak; he can address the spectator, John, even after the Palestinian has entered the frame. Sitting almost perfectly still, barring his hands, which trace words and images in the sky, Rouabhi embodies the Native American captured in colonial photography, animated in turn by the Palestinian poet, the Birzeit student, and the French Algerian actor and director who speaks in his place—at first sitting squarely before the audience, then sitting *de trois quarts*—like Qawasmi's Native American—and finally upright, as

Figure 6.2 *Darwich, deux textes*, Chapelle du Verbe Incarné, Avignon,
July 2010. Courtesy of Mohamed Rouabhi. Source: Vimeo.

if exiting the colonial cliché (Figure 6.3). Standing beside the empty chair
in which he posed moments earlier, Rouabhi declaims the final verses of
Darwish's poem: "Laissez donc, ô invités du lieu, quelques sièges libres
pour les hôtes, qu'il vous donnent lecture des conditions de la paix avec
les défunts" (Darwish 1993, 10).

Figure 6.3 Final tableau of *Darwich, deux textes*.
Courtesy of Mohamed Rouabhi. Source: Vimeo.

In the promotional materials for *Darwich, deux textes*, Rouabhi explains his decision to embody Darwish's "Red Indian" in the guise of a Native American posing for a studio photograph. For Rouabhi, photography simultaneously marks the obliteration of a world, and paradoxically enables its preservation, albeit as cliché:

> Avec le massacre de Wounded Knee, une des dernières grandes batailles du 19ème siècle et la mort du chef sioux Big Foot à la fin de l'année 1890, c'est un peu la fin d'un monde, le crépuscule de l'Amérique précolombienne … . L'ironie voudra que la photographie, qui vient juste de voir le jour, capturera à jamais sur les plaques argentées de ses entrailles, les visages et les corps de ceux qui ne sont déjà plus que des fantômes, halos de lumière qui impressionnent le papier, esprits ailés visitant nos rêves. (Rouabhi 2009, 15)

Roaubhi's performance as a Native American subject of photography in "Discours de l'indien rouge" elucidates the stakes of the photographic encounter in *El menfi*: the Palestinian boy has entered the colonial cliché, the French Algerian dramaturge will exit it. From *Les nouveaux bâtisseurs* to *El menfi* to *Darwich, deux textes*, the photographic traces of those who have been removed from the field of visibility provide paradoxical proof of transcolonial identification in the present between Native Americans, Palestinians, and post-colonized Algerians in France.

Rouabhi's plays transpose the experience of exile across France, Algeria, Palestine, and Native America through the medium of photography, vehicle and witness to the overlapping colonial histories that have produced the figure of the migrant/refugee as racialized stranger/outsider. In so doing, they illustrate what I have been calling *minor transpositions*—the representation of one colonial situation (Palestine, Native America) on another (post)colonial stage (France)— elucidating a transcolonial genealogy that remains invisible on a national scale. For migrants and refugees are not unexpected guests in Rouabhi's plays. They are the traces of displacement—transposition—on a mass, global scale, connecting the many coordinates of our unacknowledged imperial map.

Works Cited

Alloula, Malek. 1986 [1981]. *The Colonial Harem*. Translated by Myrna Godzich and Wlad Godzich. Minneapolis: University of Minnesota Press.

Azoulay, Ariella. 2008. *The Civil Contract of Photography*. Translated by Rela Mazali and Ruvik Danieli. New York: Zone Books.

Badiou, Alain. 2015. *In Praise of Theatre*. Translated by Andrew Bielski. Cambridge, UK: Polity Press.

Barthes, Roland. 2000. *Camera Lucida: Reflections on Photography*. Translated by Richard Howard. New York: Vintage Press.

Behdad, Ali. 2016. *Camera Orientalis: Reflection on Photography of the Middle East*. Chicago: University of Chicago Press.

Belghoul, Farida. 1986. *Georgette!* Paris: Barrault.

Bishop, Cécile. 2018. "Photography, Race and Invisibility." *Photographies* 11 (2–3): 192–213.

Chamoiseau, Patrick. 2017. *Frères migrants*. Paris: Seuil.

Curtis, Edward. *The North American Indian: The Complete Portfolios*. Cologne: Täschen, 1997.

Darwish, Mahmoud. 1964. "Bitaqat hawiya." In *Awraq al-zaytun*, 5–10. Haifa: Matba'at Al-Itihad Al-Ta'awuniya.

——. 1992. *Ahad 'ashar kawkaban*. Beirut: Dar Al-Jadad.

——. 1993. "Discours de l'indien rouge." Translated by Elias Sanbar. *Revue d'Etudes Palestiniennes* 46 (Winter): 3–10.

———. 1996. "Je ne reviens pas, je viens." Interview with Mahmoud Darwish. By Helit Yeshurun. Translated by Simone Bitton. *Revue d'Etudes Palestiniennes* 9 nouvelle série (Fall): 53–80.

———. 2009. *If I Were Another*. Translated by Fady Joudah. New York: Farrar, Straus and Giroux.

Dyer, Rebecca, and François Mulot. 2014. "Mahmoud Darwish in Film: Politics, Representation, and Translation in Jean-Luc Godard's *Ici et ailleurs* and *Notre musique*." *Cultural Politics* 10 (1): 70–91.

Fanon, Frantz. 1968 [1961]. *The Wretched of the Earth*. Translated by Constance Farrington. New York: Grove Press.

Forbes, Jack D. 1993. *Africans and Native Americans: The Language of Race and the Evolution of Red-Black Peoples*. Urbana and Chicago: University of Illinois Press.

Guénoun, Denis. 1998. *L'exhibition des mots et autres idées du théâtre et de la philosophie*. Paris: Circé.

Hannoush, Michèle. 2016. "Practices of Photography: Circulation and Mobility in the Nineteenth-Century Mediterranean." *History of Photography* 40 (1): 3–27.

Harrison, Olivia C. 2018. "Whither Anti-Racism? Farida Belghoul, les Indigènes de la République, and the Contest for Indigeneity in Postcolonial France." *Diacritics* 46 (3): 54–77.

Lionnet, Françoise, and Shu-mei Shih. 2005. "Thinking Through the Minor, Transnationally." Introduction to *Minor Transnationalism*, eds. Lionnet and Shih, 1–23. Durham, NC: Duke University Press.

Mbembe, Achille. 2016. *Politiques de l'inimitié*. Paris: La Découverte.

Mitchell, W. J. T. 2012. *Seeing Through Race*. Cambridge, MA: Harvard University Press.

Moser, Gabrielle. 2017. "Developing Historical Negatives: The Colonial Photographic Archive as Optical Unconscious." In *Photography and the Optical Unconscious*, eds. Shawn Michelle Smith and Sharon Sliwinski, 229–63. Durham, NC: Duke University Press.

Rahmani, Zahia. 2006. *France, récit d'une enfance*. Paris: Sabine Wespieser.

Rouabhi, Mohamed. 1997a. "Le dramaturge Mohamed Rouabhi dévoile les écorchures des errants d'aujourd'hui." Interview by Alexandre Demidoff. *Tribune de Genève*, October 25, 1997.

———. 1997b. *Les nouveaux bâtisseurs*. In *Les nouveaux bâtisseurs suivi de Ma petite vie de rien du tout*, 13–62. Paris: Actes Sud.

———. 1999. "Ateliers d'écriture." Typescript. Ramallah and Jerusalem.

———. 2000. *El menfi / L'exilé*. Typescript. Ramallah.

———. 2009. *Darwich, deux textes*. Dossier de vente. Paris.

Said, Edward. 1986. *After the Last Sky: Palestinian Lives*. Photographs by Jean Mohr. New York: Pantheon Books.

CHAPTER SEVEN

In Search of the Ghost Country

The Artistic and Literary Transpositions of Exile

Olivier Morel

Je sens-sais comment l'Algérie t'a abandonné (voilà un exemple de *felix culpa*, d'heureux malheur) (ce que Joyce éprouve à propos de l'Irlande, 'la vieille truie qui dévore ses petits:' il quitte celle qui le quitte, le nie, et il fait de l'exil son pays fantôme). Je n'ai même jamais été, pu être, abandonnable pas l'Algérie: j'étais en exclusion-interne à ce pays, magnifique, chargé de chaînes, et qui cultive les baîllons.

(Hélène Cixous, *Insurrection de la Poussière*)

Un écrivain est tout nourri d'horreur.

(Hélène Cixous, "Obstétriques cruelles")

—Et si on n'y arrive pas? C'est la question du réfugié en son voyage.

(Cixous and Théâtre du Soleil, *Le Dernier Caravansérail* [DVD booklet])

Tu abandonneras toutes les choses que tu aimes le plus: c'est le premier dard que te lance l'arc de l'exil.
Tu goûteras combien amer est le pain d'autrui et combien dur est le chemin
Qui te mène à monter et descendre les escaliers d'autrui.

(Dante Alighieri, *La Divine Comédie*)

Figure 7.1 *Le Dernier Caravansérail*, Théâtre du Soleil, 2006
(screen capture of the film).

Prolog : Nomen Nescio
Au pied du mur, the artist awakens to the wall

Hit the wall. What does it mean to hit the wall?

In 1995, nearly 30 years ago, the biggest humanitarian crisis since the outbreak of the Second World War started when the Schengen agreement became effective. In 1998, a cartoon published in a magazine issue of the Italian newspaper *Il Manifesto* showed a map of the European continent whose "external borders" were materialized by a wall surmounted with barbed wire, as if Europe had become a vast prison-camp. In this cartoon, Europe was represented as *the inside* of the prison surrounded by this tall wall. The title of this issue of *Il Manifesto* was "Il Muraglia," *La muraille* in French, meaning the big wall, the wall of a fortified place, of a fortress. This is the story of the wall: it forces us, everyone, to take a stand. No one can remain indifferent, and those who refuse to choose are complacent. At the time, the term that was coined in France to name this wall was "l'Europe forteresse," fortress Europe, often used by non-profit organizations, especially the GISTI (Groupe d'Information et de Soutien des Immigrés) to materialize the new legal order created by the European Union. This notion of "fortress" had already been used to qualify walls, especially the Atlantic Wall, built by the Nazis in order to fortify occupied Europe during the Second World War. This word and the humanitarian crisis remind us of the fact that Europe re-entered a war-like situation due to its attitude to international migration. At the time when the Schengen agreement began to be enforced, the word "war" was also used on the European continent in the context of the violent disintegration of Yugoslavia, a war that generated waves of refugees.

Fast forward to April 6, 2018, when the International Organization for Migration (the UN migration agency) reported that during the first 95 days of the year 2018, 517 were dead (International Organization for Migration 2018). Six hundred and thirty-six people were either dead or missing (ibid.). The total death toll was 3,116 in 2017 and 5,143 in 2016 (ibid.) (that's 8,259, with a total 8,895 from January 1, 2016 until May 23, 2018). In 2017, a team of journalists from the Berlin newspaper *Der Tagesspiegel* established a list with the idea of going beyond the numbers—giving names, showing faces, tracing trajectories and human incarnations of the human disaster. Here is what *Le Monde* writes about the *Tagesspiegel*'s initiative, also named "travail colossal" (colossal piece of work) in the article:

> Il y a Samuel du Congo, Nouhou Doumbia du Mali, ou encore Faisal Imran, du Pakistan. Mais l'immense majorité de ces 33 293 personnes s'appelle "N.N.", pour 'nomen nescio' (nom inconnu). C'est pourtant leur existence que le quotidien allemand, *Der Tagesspiegel*, a voulu remettre en lumière, en publiant sur son site Internet l'identité des migrants morts en tentant de rejoindre l'Europe, entre 1993 et mai 2017. Dans cette immense liste qui couvre quarante-huit pages, les journalistes allemands ont tenté de rassembler les données disponibles: nationalité, âge, date et causes de la mort. On y trouve là les nombreux noyés de la Méditerranée, ceux morts dans les centres de rétention, ou encore ce Somalien de 17 ans, mort dans la ville allemande de Schmoellnhe, poussé par des militants d'extrême-droite depuis un immeuble le 21 octobre 2016. (*Le Monde* 2017).

The list:

> June 20, 2003: 209 dead. September 12, 2006: 250. June 7, 2008: 149. March 29, 2009: 235. April 1, 2009: 300. March 25, 2011: 295. March 27, 2011: 308. April 6, 2011: 220. June 1, 2011: 273. October 3, 2013: 373. October 11, 2013: 268 (including 100 children). May 12, 2014: 194. June 1, 2014: 400. August 22, 2014: 251. August 28, 2014: 153. August 31, 2014: 105. September 10, 2014: 487. September 14: 214. February 8, 2015: 329. April 13, 2015: 401 (including one pregnant woman). April 19, 2015: 846 (including 50 children and 250 women). August 6, 2015: 201. August 28, 2015: 200. April 9, 2016: 500. April 16, 2016: 520 (including 100 children).

April 18, 2016: 400. May 25, 2016: 107. May 26, 2016: 550. May 27, 2016: 522. September 21, 2016: 645. March 23, 2017: 257 (including five children). (Cennetoğlu 2017)

According to this report, in three single days (April 19, 2015; May 26, 2016, and September 21, 2016), 2,041 individuals, including 50 children and 250 women (as far as we know), were killed.

They hit the wall. The *Muraglia*, depicted by *Il Manifesto* over 20 years ago, has become more and more deadly in a cycle that seems to never end, which is indicative of the fact that it is a political goal to "let them die," meaning to kill them. At this level of indifference and neglect, nothing is accidental. Formerly and famously depicted as a liquid continent by the poet Gabriel Audisio in the mid-1930s, the Mediterranean Sea has turned into a liquid wall.[1] A big, extraordinary wall is deemed insurmountable. What does it mean to hit the wall? To hit the wall like "that?" To hit *that* kind of a wall? What exactly is a wall? Are all "walls" comparable? Is this specific wall similar to another wall? A wall in Berlin from 1961 until 1989, or the wall that an American president wanted to build along the US–Mexican border?

It seems intrinsic to the very notion of "wall" to always generate a highly disputed taxonomy, a proliferation of names encrypting a heated polarization that might bear witness to the essence of the "wall." "Wall of tears," *Murs des Lamentations* in French, *Al-Buraq Wall*, *Western Wall*, *Wailing Wall* in Jerusalem, "antifaschistischer Schutzwall" *Antifascist Wall of Protection* in East Berlin, *Schandmauer*, *Wall of Shame* in West Berlin in the 1960s … *Mur de la Honte* as it was named by activists in France, in order to qualify the structure designed by the British and the French in 2014 in the hope of blocking the refugees from reaching the haven of Calais … All those terms, all those "walls" are as disputed as if a harsh deconstruction of the wall was always at stake whenever a wall is built. The "wall" materializes the abstract

---

1   Here is how the writer and poet Gabriel Audisio defined the Mediterranean Sea in 1935: "Méditerranée, sixième partie du monde. Il ne fait pas de doute pour moi que la Méditerranée soit un continent, non pas un lac intérieur, mais une espèce de continent liquide aux contours solidifiés. Déjà Duhamel dit qu'elle n'est pas une mer, mais un pays. Je vais plus loin, je dis: une patrie. Et je spécifie que, pour les peuples de cette mer, il n'y a qu'une vraie patrie, cette mer elle-même, la Méditerranée." Gabriel Audisio, *Jeunesse de la Méditerranée* (Paris: Gallimard, 1935), 15. I am indebted to my professor and mentor Bruno Etienne, who used to quote this famous sentence often.

separation of language(s) as a refusal to translate, to speak the language of the other that the wall constitutes while defining and performing it as irreducible, as foreign. As a legal fiction, the wall always performs the separation it creates. I propose to call this structure the "obsidional complex." After all, diplomacy and warfare are always about walls, trenches, lines, borders, fortifications, lines of defense, fences, barbed wire. The wall unites in a common polemical fate the separated, the antagonized communities it creates. Within the two essential aporia— the utopia that everything is translatable—or the dystopia that nothing is translatable, the wall traces a line of demarcation that always falls on the dystopian side. From this aporia a non-deconstructible notion arises: one day the wall will fall. It is as certain as the fact that justice is not deconstructible. In other words, the fall of the wall is ingrained in the very concept of the wall.

The Obsidional Complex

The Mediterranean wall—*Muraglia*—is, strangely enough, not a wall of stone. It is a beautiful blue sea. A beautiful sea turned into, if I refer to the 48 pages of the *Tagesspiegel* investigation, a mass grave of mainly unknown, unidentified "NN" victims. They hit this liquid, vast, and deep wall as an *aporia* that is not only theirs, but more specifically the largely unaddressed *aporia* called "Europe" today. As if Europe, and more importantly, the construction of a multilingual Europe, had fallen on the wrong side of the aforementioned aporia. This multilingual Europe, with a parliament that speaks 24 languages,[2] had envisioned an entirely translatable political space, in fact, a political entity revolving around a general principle of transposition. The dystopian "aporia" that attempts to reduce, erase, diminish, and ultimately destroy any

2   As of 2020, the European Parliament has 24 official languages: Bulgarian, Czech, Croatian, Danish, Dutch, English, Estonian, Finnish, French, German, Greek, Hungarian, Italian, Irish, Latvian, Lithuanian, Maltese, Polish, Portuguese, Romanian, Slovak, Slovene, Spanish, and Swedish. News European Parliament, the official website of the European Parliament, indicates: "With 24 official languages, there are 552 possible language combinations. ... The Parliament employs about 270 staff interpreters and can also regularly draw on more than 1,500 external accredited interpreters. Between 700 and 900 interpreters are on hand for plenary session weeks. The Parliament employs about 600 translators" (European Parliament, 2019).

translation, any transposition, is another name for the "wall" that takes the place of the utopian "transpositional," active construction of Europe. It could very much be that after two devastating world wars and a genocide, speaking more than one language has long been the ultimate embodiment, *the* essence of the European project.

What carries the name of "Europe" in a whole tradition revisited by Derrida in *L'Autre cap* in 1991 is a story with which Derrida confronts the process of thought that kills refugees in Europe today, as part of Europe's criminal history. Derrida warns us about the fact that while attempting to establish an exclusive, self-centered "identity," Europe is in fact betraying its "identity." This identity is, can be, or even *has to be* an *aporia*, but Derrida is calling for the kind of Europe that can endure the *aporia* and not try to solve it or conjure it away. In other words, getting rid of the *aporia* is the vicious solution that lies underneath the attempt to build a self-assured, self-referential identity for Europe. The wall would be what erupts from a refusal to deal with the aporetic nature of *the idea of Europe*—I would add, the idea of a translatable, transpositional Europe. Being European would mean cultivating and enduring the aporia instead of materializing it. Derrida argues that Europe's identity should comprise an art of *cultivating the possibility of the impossible*, the possibility, the endurance, the beauty of the *aporia*. *Aporia*, in this sense, would be the other name for "culture," but if *aporia* implies that Europe conceives its identity as a "monogenealogical" process of self-identification, Europe will destroy itself. It is destroying itself when it turns its translatable nature into a monogenealogical identification, and when it turns its transpositional essence into a fortress. Enduring and cultivating the aporia is the condition *sine qua non* for the existence of an open Europe. This dark side of the *aporia*, understood as an attempt to reduce it through a monogenealogical ideology, is what generates the *Muraglia* when Derrida points out that:

> Le propre d'une culture, c'est de n'être pas identique à elle-même. Non pas de n'avoir pas d'identité, mais de ne pouvoir s'identifier, dire "moi" ou "nous," de ne pouvoir prendre la forme du sujet que dans la non-identité à soi ou, si vous préférez, la différence *avec soi*. … Il n'y a pas de rapport à soi, d'identification à soi sans culture, mais culture de soi *comme* culture *de* l'autre, culture du double génitif et de la *différence à soi*. La grammaire du double génitif signale aussi qu'une culture n'a jamais une seule origine. La monogénéalogie serait toujours une mystification dans l'histoire de la culture. (Derrida 1991, 16–17).

This segment of *L'Autre cap* could well define what our volume names "transposition." "More than one origin" is what transposition signals. A "transposition" is indeed the art of crossing while *keeping everything the same and different* in the same movement. This is art, this defines art, when a slight change in sign can reverse the whole meaning in a never-ending process of defamiliarization that deconstructs the wall in order to render it into creativity. It is translation, transmission, transcription, changing the signs, the codes, the encryption, varying the keys and let this play indefinitely ... Europe is in essence a constant deconstruction of the wall(s). It is, at the site of the *aporia*, in the capacity to endure it, the art of cultivating the possibility of the impossible, the idea that a non-monogenealogical Europe would be possible—that is, in other words, a Europe capable of confronting and deconstructing itself. There would be no European hope, no European utopia, no European hospitality, no Europe, without this double deconstruction of identity and of culture and the responsibility it implies: "Ouverture et non-exclusion, dont l'Europe aurait en quelque sorte la responsabilité même? Dont l'Europe *serait*, de façon constitutive, cette responsabilité même?" writes Derrida (22). The "responsibility itself" of Europe would lie in its capacity to *not be itself* (which means notably not speak "one" language) and more specifically to acknowledge that *if* there is a European culture, it is, it has to be, *a culture of the other*, of "ouverture," openness, non-exclusion. Europe is the other's culture. Derrida's Europe is a conjuration of monolingualism. That's the [anti-] privilege that Derrida is claiming for what he defines as "Europe" as a *deconstruction of the privilege*. The European plurality of languages is the daily utopia of its openness. This non-exclusiveness is what *constitutes* Europe, it is *the constitution of Europe*. One should really wonder about why such an open-minded "constitution" of Europe— as it has to be, in order to reunite so many different languages and cultures—can at the same time be so bolted, so adept in the engineering business and industrial violence of building deadly walls; why, 27 years after *L'Autre cap*, it is more difficult than ever to revive Europe's tradition of openness ... *if* it ever existed.

So what does it mean to hit the wall? Hitting the wall means that all possibilities are petrified, arrested in a perverse twist that one could name as the revenge of an unaddressed *aporia*. The wall turns human and non-human animals equally into walls themselves. By that I mean that everyone is walled up, walled in, "wallified." Europe becomes a penitentiary concept in which all Europeans are incarcerated. What the wall petrifies as possibilities of the future is also what it allows, as thinking, as writing, as acting and acting out, back against the wall. Whenever there are walls, there are artists and thinkers. Artists like Jacques Derrida, who, not by chance, knows a lot about what it means to be incarcerated both physically and conceptually (Derrida himself was incarcerated behind the "communist" wall-iron curtain when, in late 1981, he was arrested by the Czechoslovakian government upon leading a conference in Prague). Artists like Hélène Cixous, whose mother was incarcerated in Algeria and in whose work the figure of the prison is omnipresent. Derrida taught and wrote about the death penalty and the incarceration of African Americans in the United States, and about the long incarceration of Nelson Mandela in South Africa during apartheid. One of the very first plays that Cixous wrote with Ariane Mnouchkine was a four-minute piece performed at the foot of the walls of the Prison de la Santé in Paris in the context of political actions led by the Groupe d'Information sur les Prisons founded by Michel Foucault. A wall is the artist's condition and wake. The artist awakens at the wall (*au pied du mur*). All artistic moves would be digressions on the wall, from the wall, against the wall in all of the ambiguous meanings of the expressions as art transcends, crosses, and surmounts the wall. Art, the artists, would be the ones who make us aware, not just of the visible, absurd, deadly physical walls that surround us, but of the vicious abstract notion that is created by walls, an abstraction that is always correlated to sovereign, authoritarian, dominant powers, to ideological apparatuses and other phallic institutions for which denying the evilness of the wall—turning it into a necessity, a protection— operates as a denial of the transposition. Which is why the idea of an *obsidional complex* shows that it is impossible to bring down a wall without engaging a deconstruction of the logics of dominations—which means, in other words, that there is no abolition of walls, and not only physical ones, without art, without transpositions.

I. First Digression: Walls of Crystal
(Hélène Cixous, *Gare D'Osnabrück à Jérusalem*, 2016)

Crystal. November 9, 1938. Silence.

> Quand ma grand-mère a obtenu son expulsion inespérée, Osnabrück est
> arrivé à Oran comme l'exotisme incarné. Je résume:
> Ma grand-mère a obtenu son expulsion à la fin de 1938. Elle n'a parlé
> à personne de la *Kristallnacht*. Le mot de *Kristall* est arrivé à Oran
> pour désigner les verres de Bohême. Ces verres étaient trop beaux pour
> être vrais. On n'a jamais bu dans ces verres. C'était impossible. Les
> verres sont toujours debout sur leur étagère. Ils sont pleins de silence.
> Personne n'a jamais osé avoir poussé la curiosité d'entamer le silence venu
> d'Osnabrück.
> Omi était à Osnabrück le 9 Novembre 1938?
> Omi est composée des traits suivants: 1) les robes de soie luisantes 2) le
> mot de Kristall qu'elle utilisait pour désigner les verres de Bohême, arrivés
> avec elle à Oran. Des verres élevés comme des cloches d'église, mélodieux
> lumineux. On les regardait. On les désirait. Ils montraient hauts comme
> des tiges de roses métamorphosées sur leur étagère. On n'osait pas. Une
> fois par an—non, on ne s'en servait pas—on leur présentait un peu de vin
> par respect. Ils étaient plein d'un silence enchanté 3) à cela s'ajoute son
> style allemand, un idiome animé d'un grand nombre de modalisateurs
> se rapportant aux affects d'horreur, terreur, répugnance, indignation,
> courroux, en sonates passionnées, qui me transportaient d'excitation. Je
> répétais ces phonèmes furieux comme autant de synonymes de l'orage
> logé dans ma grand-mère. J'en étais fière. Moi aussi je voulais jouir de
> ces fureurs *furchtbar, ekelhaft, widerlich, dreckig, hässlich, grässlich,*
> *entsetzlich, schauderhaft und so weiter.* Il y en avait des centaines.
> C'était à la fin de novembre 1938.
> —Omi était à Osnabrück le 9 Novembre 1938? demande ma fille.
> —Sans aucun doute, dis-je. D'une manière ou d'une autre. Entre
> Osnabrück et Jérusalem. (Cixous 2016, 53–54)

Wall of crystal: wall of silence. Omi, Hélène Cixous's grandmother
arrives as a political refugee in Algeria after November 9, 1938. And
what arrives with her is "silence." What arrives is silent. Silence is the
legacy. Silent is the legacy. What we find when we open the folder, what
lies here when we consult the record of this story, *is* silence, it is silent.
It is the archive of "silence" and the silent archive; it is silence instead of
an archive: "[Les verres] sont pleins de silence." (53). Silent story, silent
film or, to be more precise, silence built in, built by a talking movie.
"Silence" is contained by the bohemian crystal glasses Omi brought

with her. They are full of silence. This silence is a silence of crystal. It replaces the horror; it is the other side of the cry. The cry is kept mute behind the wall of silence. The silence of the impossible, the impossibility of drinking in those glasses echoes the horror, the terror of the German language that Omi brought to Oran, in Algeria, to the house on Philippe Street, to the parks where baby Hélène Cixous used to go with her Omi, to the beach in Oran ... The Mediterranean Sea also encrypts this silence. The thunder that Omi brought with her was contained by the intact crystal of the glasses and by the furious German names voiced by Omi, with which the artist Pierre Alechinsky drew-wrote in and around Cixous's text: "furchtbar, ekelhaft, widerlich, dreckig, hässlich, grässlich, entsetzlich, schauderhaft und so weiter ..." (54). Omi doesn't speak, what she leaves as a present, as a legacy to Hélène, is the poetry of a few crystal glasses brought by the refugee. And words. This poetry is made of both silence and horror. Poetry is what Cixous receives as a tragic gift. The glasses remain silent until, in 2016, more than 70 years having collapsed on the scene and nearly all (but one) of the survivors having passed away, Cixous takes back the glasses of *Kristall* with this haunting question: how come Omi, Rosie, Rosalie Klein, her German–Jewish grandmother, was allowed to leave Germany, and not just "leave" but leave with *all of her belongings*? There were no miracles in Nazi Germany at the time, as it was completely forbidden for Jews to leave the country and, furthermore, leave with their belongings. All this took place after the infamous *Kristallnacht*. Why, how? The silent glasses are the answer: Omi never spoke of it. Silence is the answer, silent is the answer, but poetry was the most important thing that was then saved. The wall remains as a wall of silence. The other name of this silence is: *Gare d'Osnabrück à Jérusalem* by Hélène Cixous. Poetry. Poetry: a silence of horror turned into the miraculous silent poetic appearance of a few ageless colorful bohemian glasses.

And of course, this structure is a part of what it means to be not only a refugee, but also to be born of a refugee mother in June 1937, and then after November 1938, born of another refugee, her grandmother Rosie (Rosalie) Klein. This is what the glasses "say." What the wall of silence inflicts on the refugee is the *impossibility of the story*, the denial of the story, and its unending redemption as an impossible, possible poem. Unlike the wall, or to be more precise, the wall "itself," *aporia* is a poetic notion. Aporia asks what the "wall itself" could mean. It claims that there is no such thing as the wall itself. The glasses say to Cixous: you are a born-refugee. The poem says: we are all born refugees. But we keep this silent as a secret for ourselves that either dies in our heart if it is not revealed or gets lost as a secret if it is shared … unless it becomes a poem. A poem: it keeps everything secret while revealing everything. A daughter of silence under this deconstructive law of the secret, Cixous is the poet, and the poem is this never-ending, non-monogenealogical identification that crosses all of the walls, deconstructs them (it deconstructs the "wall itself"), is smuggled through the bars of the prison. The poem is what goes through the bars and the walls of the prison when it allows Derrida and Cixous's mother to feel light and free while in prison. "Voyez Jacques Derrida," Cixous writes,

> il n'aura jamais été aussi étrangement heureux qu'une fois cueilli par la police pragoise et incarcéré pour de bon sans l'avoir espéré … C'est qu'on ne peut pas être heureux de bonheur, mais seulement par frottement du cœur avec l'impuissance et la disparition. …
>
> C'est comme pour ma mère Ève Cixous sage-femme arrêtée sous un prétexte, tandis qu'elle déclarait à la mairie d'Alger l'enfant né le 9 novembre 1962 en sa clinique d'accouchements, et menée menottée à la célèbre prison de Barberousse. Ce qui la gêne, c'est que pendant cette captivité, elle ne s'était jamais sentie aussi libre et sans soucis. Aux autres dehors les ennuis et les inquiétudes, elle, *derrière les murailles* avait tout le temps de se faire une mise en plis avec des carottes pour bigoudis. (Cixous 2000, 109–10, emphasis added)

"elle, *derrière les murailles*" … The cycle of violence never ends until the poem reminds us that, after all, the wall is just a wall, the *Muraglia* is nothing but a stupid, stubborn, mute wall, until the cry of literature rises. Until silence becomes literature, theater, film, a manifesto, a newspaper investigation by *Der Tagesspiegel*, or by *Il Manifesto*. Literature arises as a cry for justice when the poem deconstructs the wall itself; and it starts at the foot of the wall when the poem reminds us that the unjust wall is just a wall. We hear that voice. The voice says: it does not resurrect the dead. That is tragically true. Like the walls of Troy, the tragedy is pierced by the wall, it survives the wall. Like the baby of November 9, 1962 in Algiers, like Omi who fled Germany after November 9, 1938, Hélène Cixous of Troy was born in it.

II. Second Digression: Calais, the Wall
(*Le Dernier Caravansérail*, 2006)

Recording the persistence of the wall

The first wall faced by the refugee on his/her journey is a wall of silence. Silence, here, means: wall of fallacies, wall of indifference. A wall of ignorance. A wall: the proper name of which does not suffer transpositions. Or to be more specific, built by sovereign powers who do not want to deal with transpositions.

> Évidemment, je m'appelle "Mnouchkine," je ne m'appelle pas "Dupont," mon père est venu en exil, il avait quinze ans, mes grands-parents étaient arrêtés en Russie, ils n'ont pas pu venir, ils sont venus quelques années après, mais … en travaillant avec ces gens-là [*les réfugiés nda*], on sait bien que c'est leurs enfants qui vont trouver la solidité totale, ou leurs petits-enfants quand ça se passe pas très bien … en France. … Les gens qui ont vécu des choses très dramatiques, parlent très peu. Heureusement, sa sœur, ma tante, me parlait plus. Mais quand même, je découvre maintenant à quel point y'a des gens que je retrouve, qui savent plus sur mon père, que même moi, que moi-même. C'est souvent comme ça. … J'ai fait ce que vous, vous ne devez pas faire, j'ai pas pensé mon père mortel. C'est-à-dire que, un jour il me parlerait. Moi ce que je vous conseille de faire, vous, c'est que si vous avez une grand-mère, des grands-parents, prenez un petit magnétophone et enregistrez, faites-les parler! Ce sont des trésors, ce sont des trésors. Vos propres parents, ont vécu des choses que vous ne connaissez pas, qui sont parfois des révélations. Et ils ont souvent des scrupules à vous en parler parce qu'ils pensent, et ils n'ont pas tort, que ça ne vous intéresse pas. Et c'est qu'au fond, pour l'instant, ça ne vous intéresse pas. Et quand ça vous intéresse vraiment, parfois c'est trop tard. Donc, faites-le. (Mnouchkine and Théâtre du Soleil 2006)

This is what Ariane Mnouchkine says to a group of high school students in 2006 on the day after the screening of the film *Le Dernier Caravansérail* in Avignon. "Take a tape recorder and record your parents' stories" (ibid.), is her advice. And what triggers this injunction is the fact that she was, like Cixous, born of refugees, that her father came to France as a teenager. What is remarkable, here, for Mnouchkine, is the fact that being born of this refugee meant that what she inherited from her father was the relative silence that he kept regarding what had happened to the family. He had kept silent his stories of horror, "Les gens qui ont vécu des choses très dramatiques, parlent très peu" (ibid.). In a way, silence is this wall that is being built between the refugee and his/her story, while the quintessential experience faced by the refugee in

Figure 7.2 Ariane Mnouchkine and Mansour, from Sangatte to Paris
(screen capture of *Le Dernier Caravansérail*).

his/her flight is the moment when he/she hits the wall. The wall seems
never to disappear. There would be no *exile* without this structure,
without facing a certain wall, either in the country or region that forces
the refugee to take the risky road of exile, or in the country or region
in which he/she attempts to take refuge. The purpose of the wall would
be to imply the concrete and metaphysical experience of a non-response
that is typical of what happens when one faces or hits the wall. In more
than one way, Mnouchkine and Cixous's play and film *Le Dernier
Caravansérail* are, like Cixous's crystal glasses, full of silence. This
silence is a region of Cixous's mind, of her upbringing as a born-of-
refugee. Silence–silent is the legacy of the crystal glasses; they contain
the story of the refugee, and they are the archive of the originary lack
of archive that any archive encrypts and attempts to conjure. Walls of
silence could be the most insurmountable dimension of the wall. But
those walls are also the ones from which Mnouchkine and Cixous, since
1983 and *L'Histoire terrible mais inachevée* ..., have created marvels in
which walls of indifference, ignorance, of fallacies, fall in their dreams
of theater, as well as in their cinematic dreams.

The screenshot in Figure 7.2 shows a scene from *Le Dernier
Caravansérail* (the film). It shows Ariane Mnouchkine herself staging

the work that she did at a time that might have been when she was still developing, writing, and conceiving the play. The character of Mnouchkine collecting the stories of refugees in order to create a play is a part of the play. This *is* the play; this is the film. The film is also notably about how it is made possible. Mnouchkine is the one in the driver's seat, holding a small recorder.

In light of what Mnouchkine tells the students after the screening of *Le Dernier Caravansérail* in Avignon in 2006, the fact that Mnouchkine features herself in the play and the film amounts to more than a depiction on stage of the concrete conditions by which the play was made possible. This indicates that those works are more than a collection of fragmented "stories," big and small, of exile from Afghanistan, Africa, Russia, the Balkan region and more ... they are about the inspiration, about the reasons why a play and film can outlive the wall and deconstruct it, they are about the *act of recording* that lies at the core of the story itself as a conjuration of silence. This scene of recording is a critical component of what we usually do not know, even in families like Mnouchkine's own family, like Cixous's own family where they apparently did not record, did not pay attention to silences, or at least, did not have the feeling that they had recorded enough. Cixous, who, after almost all the witnesses have disappeared, notices that there are still enigmas, crucial enigmas that she still, in 2016, has not been able to decipher. Her book *Gare d'Osnabrück à Jérusalem* revolves around the crystal silence of these enigmas. Transparent and full of shades, of haze, of nights, of *Nacht und Nebel*, night and fog. In a way, it is, of course, a matter, for Mnouchkine, of dealing herself with her father's silent story of immigration and exile that is also at stake in Cixous's 2016 text and many others. But it is more than an attempt to "compensate" or exorcise the fact that they might feel guilty for not having recorded, or not having recorded "enough." It would be utter naïveté to believe that the story can ever be "fully" recorded and told. The wall remains. What remains is the wall. The act of creation occurs at the specific spot where the enigma of exile faces the wall long after the actual move of exile took place. The fact that, no matter what, something will always be missing defies any attempt to record. There is a resistant, unsurmountable remainder embedded in the exile story that will always be silent, unknown, undecipherable. Another name for this mystery is: language, writing. Poetry as a process, as a performance, as an invisible act of recording.

The Performance

Cixous and Mnouchkine, co-writers, with the "troupe" of *Le Dernier Caravansérail* are *performing* something with those stories. Something that lies precisely in what could be tracked as a definition of the phenomenon of "transposition." They are *performing the silence* that is carried out, in their works, in their bodies, by their literary texts, plays and films understood as sublime conjurations of silence that can never be fully subsumed in the creation (play, film) itself. In a way, *Le Dernier Caravansérail* invents "silence" like the filmmaker Robert Bresson once claimed that "LE CINÉMA SONORE A INVENTÉ LE SILENCE." (Bresson 1975, 50). Along those lines, Bresson also creates a fruitful concept of "silence obtenu" (ibid.). *Le Dernier Caravansérail* achieves more than just "giving a voice" to the refugees. It confronts the ways by which refugees are silenced by the wall(s). The play and the film transpose the irreducible silence that silences the refugees, into the realm of creation. Mnouchkine collects and connects the stories, and the play shows the act of recording (the tape recorder) in a moving car that travels from the past of the migrant to the future of the arrival of the refugee. This work is a genuine political gesture that implies that a powerful *act of transposition* is an *act of translation*. Most of the dialogues in the play–film *Le Dernier Caravansérail* are in Farsi, Pashto, Kurd, Russian, German, etc. Giving a voice to the refugees through a choir of voices and a symphony of languages reveals the dynamics at stake when refugees are silenced. Staging this process for Mnouchkine, Cixous, and the Théâtre du Soleil, is a way to shed light on the ways by which the dominant, mainstream "story" of immigration in our societies always steals the refugees' narrative from them—and often begins with the lack of translation, mistranslations, with the refusal to translate. When the transposition takes place, something that the *Tagesspiegel* attempted to do happens: grace. "They" are no longer unknown, "they" are no longer the forgotten NN (*nomen nescio*), "they" are no longer numbers. They are not even "words" applied to them like the countless word-labels, word-walls, word-bars, word-prisons, and other word-poison that the common, trivial daily use of language generates. Poisonous word-labels create prefabricated "ideas" on "immigration," on the "undocumented," as Mnouchkine explains:

> Je pense que l'inspiration est contenue dans le spectacle. C'est la vie de ces gens-là. Comme toujours, c'est le concret. C'est-à-dire, vous, moi, *on*

a des idées sur l'immigration, sur qu'est-ce que c'est qu'un sans-papier ou ce que c'est que quelqu'un qui essaie de rentrer dans un pays qui ne le veut pas ... *on a des idées là-dessus.* On a des compassions, plus ou moins responsables, ou, ou ... *mais au fond on ne sait pas* et je pense que c'est venu d'un jour où j'ai voulu aller voir Sangatte, tout simplement. Comprendre ce que c'était. Sans savoir du tout pourquoi. C'était par curiosité civique. Et puis *tout d'un coup on rencontre des gens qui ont des yeux, une voix, un bonnet, un foulard*, qu'on invite à déjeuner dans un petit restau à Calais et qui, pendant qu'ils mangent vous racontent des instants de leur vie, enfin ... à qui on demande qu'ils racontent des instants de leurs vies, et qui, une fois qu'ils commencent à vous faire confiance et qu'ils, surtout, une fois qu'ils comprennent que entre guillemets, vous ne pouvez rien pour eux, vous n'êtes ni journaliste, ni flic, ni ministre, ni ... ils commencent ... *ils nous parlent* ... (Mnouchkine and Théâtre du Soleil 2006, emphases added)

"Ils nous parlent." No longer "they" of the abstract numbers, of the unknown, but "nous," us. This "us" as a "nous," as a "we" that they want to address, to question, to make responsible instead of pointing at them. Their words, their languages reverse the terms (transposition) of the common (mis)use of the language; they replace the projections of the journalist, of the cop, of the minister, all those who have "ideas" and produce dominant representations of who "they," "these people," are. And they become human, real, in place of what, in the vast majority of cases, is a society that has *no idea* (Mnouchkine highlights that), precisely, of who "they" are because society does not speak their languages and never attempts to do so ... The play–film is conceived in face of a society that is for the most part trapped, imprisoned in its platonic cave of what Derrida calls the "monogenealogical thought." All of a sudden, Mnouchkine, Cixous, the entire "troupe" not only give them words, but allow them to express themselves in their own words/ languages. They do not just speak, they come alive, they cross the wall of death, the "leather of our indifference," as Mnouchkine puts it.[3] And

---

3   The Théâtre du Soleil has been open as a place of refuge to (literally) hundreds of undocumented refugees and exiles. The examples are numerous, but one could mention the fact that Mnouchkine housed hundreds of undocumented expelled from the St Ambroise Church in the summer of 1996 and hosted them in the Cartoucherie in the trailers of the Théâtre du Soleil. At that time, Mnouchkine had started a hunger strike. I have personally met with many members of the company who found refuge in the Cartoucherie and are now a part of the company.

this transposition defines theater in Mnouchkine's own words. She is still talking to the high school students:

> Il y a quelque chose qui traverse le cuir de notre indifférence. Vous voyez, par exemple, on dit "les déportés." Sortons du *Caravansérail*, on dit "les déportés' "les camps de concentrations ..." vous pouvez dire ce terme comme ça, hein, "camp de concentration" sans rien ressentir! Ces mots-là sont froids. Et puis tout d'un coup, vous, vous zoomer, enfin, vous choisissez quelqu'un. Une femme. De quarante-huit ans. Rousse. Très belle. Qui tente de passer par la fenêtre pour échapper à la Gestapo qui est en train de venir l'arrêter. Vous ... vous voyez? Tout d'un coup: ah, tiens ... c'est moins froid! Et, elle a été dénoncée par sa concierge. C'est moins froid. Rue Claude Matrat à Issy-les-Moulineaux. C'est moins froid. Et la concierge n'a jamais été inquiétée ensuite. Et cette femme, elle est arrivée à Auschwitz; et elle a été gazée immédiatement. Parce qu'elle a quarante-huit ans, et donc, elle est déjà vieille, alors qu'elle est jeune. Et elle a été séparée de son mari, qui lui, est parti ... Bon, au fond c'est ça. Parce que tout le monde, on peut rester, on peut rester à "camps de concentration," "deportation," "antisémitisme" ... vous voyez ce que je veux dire? "Racisme" tous ces noms, qu'est-ce que c'est? C'est quelques signes noirs sur un papier blanc. Qu'est-ce que fait le théâtre? Il fait voler ces lettres, et il met à côté un teint, un portrait, une broche, un souvenir, de la souffrance, du caca, dans le train, vous voyez? Et petit à petit, on se voit. On imagine et on compatit, c'est-à-dire, on souffre avec. Et c'est ça le théâtre. Donc, moi c'est pas que je veux "vous montrer la misère" ... c'est moi qui veut la voir *vraiment* enfin! Parce que je ne la vois pas! Parce que je suis trop encombrée de ma vie quotidienne, de ... parce que je sais que si je la vois pas j'irai en enfer! Quel que soit l'enfer. Que mon rôle, enfin, mon rôle d'être humain, c'est de voir. Donc, au fond, c'est ça, c'est l'incarnation, c'est la vraie incarnation. L'incarnation des états, des corps en souffrance. (Mnouchkine and Théâtre du Soleil 2006, emphases added)

This could well define the notion of transposition:

> "Racisme" tous ces noms, qu'est-ce que c'est? C'est quelques signes noirs sur un papier blanc. Qu'est-ce que fait le théâtre? Il fait voler ces lettres, et il met à côté un teint, un portrait, une broche, un souvenir, de la souffrance, du caca, dans le train, vous voyez? Et petit à petit, on se voit. (Mnouchkine and Théâtre du Soleil 2006)

As it is explained by Mnouchkine, theater is this art of restoring the exhausted meaning of words while turning them into flesh and persona. Mnouchkine points at the discrepancy between what she calls the *signes noirs*, the dark, cold signifiers, and the flesh of the refugees in her play. Transposing means embodying, literally, and theater engages the physical embodiment of this "incarnation." In doing so, creating *Le Dernier Caravansérail* also re-enchants and reinvents the signifier in order to break the *Muraglia, la muraille*, the wall, in order to restore a poetic freedom. This is what protects us from hell (*l'enfer*) according to Mnouchkine. Hell is what happens when there is no transposition. Mnouchkine's theatrical, artistic liberation, is a transposition *by definition*. Transposition is the other name of theater for Mnouchkine and it is a *praxis*. Practicing the transposition would be the art of liberating, of emancipating oneself. There would be no liberation, no escape from hell, without a transposition *at work*. Mnouchkine incarnates the words, she is a "transposer," she transports the words to what they mean practically while turning them into concrete human beings. We can no longer say the word "refugee," the word "undocumented," the word "exile" or the word "wall" without seeing Mansour, without hearing Azadeh's lover Fawad scream, without thinking about the daughter who does not want to cross to England without her parents, without the cry of those who have died, without facing the wall, the fence, the barbed wire, ourselves.

Transposing the "Ficelles du Théâtre": *Le Dernier Caravansérail*, a Film-play

Within this logic of transposition, the work that we are considering here is not by accident both a play *and* a film (Picon-Vallin 2007, 46–76), Making this play available for a larger television audience (on the European TV channel ARTE) required this translation from the stage to the screen. It also created a physical archive (film) of what is, in theater, condemned to vanish as a physical trace. This transposition is critical for us, not only because of the "grammatical" transposition that occurs between theater and cinema, but also because the themes of the play and film are specifically rooted in what happens when people's stories are rewritten by migration processes. In this work, Mnouchkine and Cixous highlight the fact that a migration process is in relation, is in dialogue with silence, but that it also lies at the origin of stories, it is the idea that *any story* would tell of a migration understood as a transposition, the idea that, for them, art is transposition. The vocation of this transposition process is to be diffracted through a multiplicity of stories that happen on multiple continents. The play–film takes us to a vertiginous number of countries and languages. Transpositions[4] and translations are at play everywhere. Both the play *and* the film deal with translations, crossings, passages, borders, at the edge of what is considered comprehensible.

When the play, for example, features the risky crossing of the river, it is entirely rewritten and reconfigured for its cinematic transposition. This does more than just change the way we watch as it creates a different (cinematic) story out of the "same" (theatrical) story. This is something that Cixous often indicates when she refers to the fact that each story tells a story in *lieu of another one*. This comment by Cixous is triggered by a reflection on biography[5] and, interestingly, in the transposition from the theater play to the film, the focus of the film is more on faces than on scenes (tableaux), on individual challenges rather than broader interactions. It is not incidental that the "tableaux" of the plays used to be called "operas" by the *troupe* of the Théâtre du Soleil company as Ariane Mnouchkine indicates in the scenes of the play that she comments on in the bonus features of the DVD of *Le Dernier Caravansérail*. Theater, music, cinema in multiple languages—this is the symphony of migration, of exile, of pain and tears; this opera offers a symphony of transpositions.

But there is more. Another transposition is operated at the core of what "recounting" the stories of migrations implies for Mnouchkine, Cixous, and the company. It is related to the fact that the "inspiration" for this play–film is, of course, the subject: the migrants in Calais and Sangatte, and their stories of exile are what triggers this "voyage toward their future," as Mnouchkine puts it. But it is also about staging and

4 "Transposition" is the word used by scholar Béatrice Picon-Vallin in her book on the Théâtre du Soleil about what many of the plays of the post-2001 period have in common: "On connaît le nouveau visage du Soleil au XXIe siècle par les 'films de théâtre' réalisés à la Cartoucherie, dont chaque tournage a pu influencer le spectacle qui suit. Pourtant, les films ne sont pas des spectacles, ils en sont la recréation cinématographique, pour laquelle Mnouchkine a cherché des procédés permettant de les faire passer à l'écran. Ainsi, pour *Tambour sur la digue*, elle accuse l'aspect très théâtral du spectacle pour pouvoir le filmer et réinjecte le théâtre dans le cinéma par des opérations purement cinématographiques. Difficile de traiter ici de cet important travail de transposition qu'ont nécessité ces 'films de théâtre'" (Picon-Vallin 2014, 254).

5 "Toutes les biographies comme toutes les autobiographies comme tous les récits racontent une histoire à la place d'une autre histoire." (Cixous and Calle-Grüber 1994, 179. [This sentence is from Hélène Cixous]).

featuring this inspiration itself. So in a way it is about featuring the transposition. What if this entire *œuvre*—also subtitled "Odyssée" in reference to the greatest Mediterranean poem ever written, that of Homer—was a transposition? Theater, and especially theater in Mnouchkine's understanding, shows its inspiration: it displays and stages the origin of its songs, of its "operas," it shows its "making of." Its trivial machinery is *in* the play because *it is* the play, its actors and actresses making the play and acting it/in it is the true history of the wall that Ulysses faces in his long journey across the Mediterranean. It shows itself as theater, as an "artifactuality" (Derrida), and it is a transposition. As a reminder, many of the protagonists of this Odysseus are refugees, are exiles who took refuge in the Théâtre du Soleil, like the Afghan Azizullah Hamra, like the Iraqi Kurd Sarkaw Gorany, like the Iranian refugee Gholam Reza Hosseini or the 17-year-old (at the time) Chinese refugee Xian Rong Chen. Mnouchkine met most of them in Sangatte (Mnouchkine and Théâtre du Soleil 2006, 8). Interestingly, here, this mindset is not only a conception of theater, but it is also a conception of cinema, as the cinematic transposition will also show the "ficelles," the machinery, the stage management. Mnouchkine reminds us, in her discussion with the students in Avignon, that this characteristic is not in fact at odds with cinema, but is the very etymology of cinema. Of a cinema that has kept its father figure intact, here, in terms that recall how, for Mnouchkine, recording the refugees' stories and putting this moment of recording in the play as a scene, was an art of compensation and sublimation for the fact that she never really got to ask her father about his family's experiences as refugees. So this cinematic projection of the play consists of retrieving and redeeming, while taking it farther. Building the scar tissue that is needed between cinema and its repressed origin is at the core of the concept of theater-cinema. It is also what happens between Mnouchkine and her silent father, as well as between Cixous and her silent Omi (her grandmother). In a way, one could hear an attempt by Mnouchkine, the filmmaker of *Le Dernier Caravansérail*, to save the film's repressed memory from having been invented and performed as a theater play:

> Soit nous décidions qu'on sortait, qu'on allait sur une vraie rivière … soit nous gardions dans le film, —comme le cinéma le faisait à ses débuts—, *les ficelles du théâtre*. C'est-à-dire du plastique pour faire une rivière la nuit, de la soie pour faire la mer le jour, ou le fleuve, un oiseau de papier … Nous avions nos outils de théâtre et nous faisions avec nos

outils de théâtre, mais dans des cadres cinématographiques. Mais quand j'ai vu certains résultats, certaines scènes, c'est vrai que ça me fait penser au début du cinéma, quand le cinéma ne mettait pas un point d'honneur à surtout tuer le père, c'est-à-dire tuer le théâtre! Je pense que là, c'est un film qui est, qui est content de son père ou de sa mère, qui utilise les artefacts, les petits bouts de ficelles très humbles du théâtre. (Mnouchkine and Théâtre du Soleil 2006)

"Un film qui est content de son père ou de sa mère," "a film that is at ease with its father or mother" says Mnouchkine, whose father Alexandre Mnouchkine was a renowned film producer. The key part here is that, in building this scar tissue, Mnouchkine, Cixous, the *troupe* of the Soleil (among whom there are many refugees, historically), give a site and bodies to what Mnouchkine characterizes as "dark signifiers" (*signes noirs*), to the silence that lies at the core of the representation, of the performance, and of history—and also, at the core of the silent relationship to the shared past that Mnouchkine has with her father, film producer, refugee. She creates a theater play that is "contente," at ease with her father film producer, through the lens of exile, through a transposition that takes her peacefully from the realm of theater-the-father-of-cinema back to cinema. Here lies the paradox of the wall in the film-play. If the wall is removed from this play, if the impassable river, if the insurmountable furious waves of the sea do not exist, there is no longer a play, a film. A film at ease with itself, with its theatrical origin, is still a film, and a play, about the horror of migration in today's Europe (and world), as a path toward what Mnouchkine's father and family has been through, while mostly remaining silent, like the wall on which she projects her vision of a film-play, of a play-film. But the way refugees hit this wall is less unknown and disembodied after *Le Dernier Caravansérail*. A new signifier, incarnated by "true" humans, re-enchanted by Homer–Mnouchkine–Cixous–Théâtre du Soleil, makes the wall what it "is," beyond the emptied signifiers secreted by the repressive, trivial daily languages in use, beyond the daily routine of the current ecosystem created by our dominant opinion leaders and a largely hostile and criminal political spectrum and mainstream media, that is well accommodated with the indifferent killings of the refugees. In *Obstétriques cruelles*, Cixous writes:

Ce qui est arrivé à la victime, l'horreur, la faute de la victime, car elle a été jetée dans l'inhumanité, l'Enfer dont on doit garder l'horreur intacte: le dire c'est l'évanouir, l'apaiser, cela elle le sent elle veut garder la souffrance vivante enrubannée de silence et d'épouvante. Et cependant elle veut léguer l'horreur. Elle veut que je livre le secret. (Cixous 2000, 116)

This passage of *Obstétriques cruelles*, published in 2000, echoes what takes place when Cixous, Mnouchkine and the company of the Soleil are confronted with when they work on the *Odyssées* of *Le Dernier Caravansérail*: keep the horror intact while saying it, embodying it; reveal the secret while keeping it secret, intact, keeping everything silent at its place while unveiling and circulating it. This work of art "appeases," it "faints" the [intact] horror, the wall. The horror becomes our treasure. "Treasure" is the word used by Mnouchkine when she incites the students to question their parents and listen to their stories …

More than one decade later, this is also what Cixous writes about Adel Abdessemed's art. Another transposition. Theater, cinema, and now the fine arts, are all languages that are multiplied *ad infinitum*; they represent constant attempts to deal with the elementary paradox of the secret pain. Of the wall. Its silence of suffering is impossible to decipher, while at the same time the need to record, to keep, to write and document, is generated by the horror it contains, like that of Omi's crystal glasses. And the need to transmit it. To transpose. "Un écrivain est tout nourri d'horreur" writes Cixous in *Obstétriques cruelles* (Cixous 2000, 112).

III. Third Digression: Algeria, Internal Exclusion, Originary Exile

The history of exile is inseparable from the history of denying its essence. Refugees, Mnouchkine points out, have a hard time talking about their horror story of exile. They do not tend to transmit it to their children. Double denial, on one side self-imposed by the refugees because of the need to survive and move on; on the other side, for drastically different reasons, generated by the host country, which tends to silence the refugees. Exile is usually denied by history. The history of exile is indistinguishable from its denial by history, which triggers the exile of most refugees. We know it but rarely acknowledge it until artists like Mnouchkine, Cixous, and the Théâtre du Soleil point it out: the camps, whether Sangatte, Calais, the Calais Jungle, Lampedusa, or Lesbos, the camps of the Porte de la Chapelle, of the Porte d'Aubervilliers (known as "campement du millénaire") or elsewhere, those unfortunate tents and barracks draw maps of the world at war (often wars created by the Western nations that deny legal entry to refugees), maps of a suffering that is endured by the Kurds, the Afghans, the Iraqis, the Somalians, the Eritreans, the Libyans, the Algerians. Algerians like Adel Abdessemed who once declared that "[Algeria] had attempted to eliminate him" (Morel 2018, Time Code 00:32:42). But that we do not know, we do not want to know. This double an-archiving of the event, double denial, double layer of silence applied to the refugee, is at stake in Cixous's work on/with Adel Abdessemed:

> S'il n'y a pas un projet, politique, philosophique, explicite, tout l'élan d'Adel, son essor belliqueux et joyeux, son énergie créatrice inépuisable sont orientés vers le désir et l'espoir intrépides de soustraire les sans-défense au triomphalisme de la violence ordinaire, à la la cruauté des pouvoirs individuels et collectifs politiques et métaphysiques, marchandisants et religieusement dictatoriaux. Il est le chantre des opprimés, des balayeurs, des femmes menacées de voile, des animaux otages ou pourchassés, le camarade de l'enfant immolé, du juif persécuté, de l'ouvrier du bâtiment, des peuples naufragés qui confient aux flots sans pitié leurs existences déracinées.
>
> En ce siècle où c'est tous les jours déluges ... il n'y a pas d'Arche. À la place du bateau hôtelier, de calamiteux copeaux de la *Méduse*. Au lieu du Déluge décidé par l'Artiste divin qui s'autocritique, c'est de toutes parts la pulsion de mort, le désir déchaîné d'expulser, de chier l'autre, de le jeter par-dessus bord dans la cuvette infinie du Néant. (Cixous 2018, 77).

Adel Abdessemed—like Cixous and Mnouchkine with *Le Dernier Caravansérail*—is "saving himself," as the French language allows (*il se sauve*); he is a fugitive. And in a sense, we will see that Cixous is also a fugitive and that this flight was there at the origin of Cixous and of Abdessemed. Abdessemed is safeguarding himself in France after having been threatened with death in 1994, prompting him to flee Algeria, a country, as Cixous puts it in *L'Insurrection de la poussière* (2014), that cultivates chains and censorship in all kinds of ways. In the passage of *Les Sans Arches* quoted above, the double denial takes the form of the destruction of not only the "pourchassés" (the hunted), the "persécutés" (the persecuted), and the "naufragés" (the shipwrecked), but also of the biblical "arche" (ark), of the *radeau de la Méduse*. Not only has this era destroyed the oppressed, the persecuted, the shipwrecked, but it has also destroyed *the very notion of salvation*: "la pulsion de mort, le désir déchaîné d'expulser, de chier l'autre, de le jeter par-dessus bord dans la

cuvette infinie du Néant." Double destruction, of the shipwrecked and of
the notion of rescue, of salvation: The intense creative dialogue engaged
by Cixous with Abdessemed allows us to refine something that lies as
a possibility in the Théâtre du Soleil's *Odyssées* of the play-film. The
time lapse that separates those two creations, *Le Dernier Caravansérail*
and *Les Sans Arches*, is about the same as what I pointed out at the
beginning of this chapter between discovering the outrageous number of
1,652 migrants killed in the Mediterranean Sea between 1995–1998 and
today. Between *Le Dernier Caravansérail* (2000–2006) and *Les Sans
Arches* (2018), something happens. The total "defecation" of the other
("de *toutes* parts la pulsion de mort, le désir déchaîné d'expulser, de *chier
l'autre*") named by Cixous in her text on Abdessemed's work notably
revolves around the question of what art can do, what art consists of in
this era of destruction. It is not only that art can help retrieve the stories
of individuals like in the play–film of the Théâtre du Soleil, it is about
asking if the very *act* of safeguarding, of rescuing, but also of the *idea*
of "salvation" itself is still there. It's not just that this era is no longer
helping, rescuing—it is that it seems to consider it no longer necessary
to rescue what is—no matter what—taken as "shit," considered trash
(see Adel Abdessemed's *Hope* installation). The ruin of salvation is now
complete, declare the poet Cixous and the artist Abdessemed. We've
already mentioned that the artistic work starts when our backs are
against the wall: "L'artiste en lui [Adel Abdessemed] s'éveille *à l'instant
même où le mal est fait*" as Cixous writes in *Les Sans Arches* (Cixous
2018, 12). What immediately follows is not by accident a reflection on "la
barque des migrants":

> Lorsqu'il n'y a plus rien à faire, il est trop tard pour sauver la victime, la
> vie se rend, la mort est prête, reste.
>   C'est là, entre les deux instants, quand dans la barque les migrants
> flottent au-dessus du temps, quand sous la masse le faon flageole et ses
> genoux fléchissent vers la fin, quand on n'entend plus du dernier cri que
> l'écho qui se perd, qu'Adel saisit ce qui (se) passe. (Cixous 2018, 12)

What remains is artists like Abdessemed, playwrights and directors like
Mnouchkine, and poets like Cixous who remind us of this. Differently
and similarly, through all of the subtle transpositions that their works
engage, they are saving, not only the refugees, the shipwrecked, the
"Sans Arches," but also, more importantly today than ever, the rescue
and the rescuer, saving the act of safeguarding and the narrator, who are
the same:

Qu'est-ce qui nous lie, pensais-je? Ça, pensais-je, le goût du lien, l'instinct de *sauvegarde* et aussi cette chose mystérieuse qui se perd à notre époque: la commémorialité maternelle. L'instinct de raconter aux descendants, afin de donner le passé au futur, au passé le futur, de *sauver* la grand-mère dans l'enfant. (Cixous 2000, 115)

Sauver, to save. This is my emphasis. It entails saving salvation. Safeguarding, recording—the tape recorder, the saving-machine, is on in the play—is the salvation of writing, it is writing the salvation. It is not about conservation as a funeral or the museographic act of freezing the past, it is about saving the future, about promising, about *safeguarding the possibility of a future*, that is the possibility of justice as the indeconstructible justice that lies to the wall, where the artist awakens, because it is late, way too late, always too late.

Works Cited

Alighieri, Dante. 1829. *La Divine Comédie: Le Paradis, Chant XVII*. Translated by Antoni Deschamps. Paris: Imprimerie de la Chevardière.

Audisio, Gabriel. 1935. *Jeunesse de la Méditerranée*. Paris: Gallimard.

Bresson, Robert. 1975. *Notes sur le cinématographe*. Paris: Gallimard.

Cennetoğlu, Banu. 2017. "Liste von 33.293 registrierten Asylsuchenden, Geflüchteten und MigrantInnen, die aufgrund der restriktiven Politik der Festung Europas zu Tode kamen Dokumentation von UNITED for Intercultural Action; Stand vom 15. Juni 2017," *UNITED for Intercultural Action; europäisches Netzwerk gegen Nationalismus, Rassismus, Faschismus und für die Unterstützung von MigrantInnen und Geflüchteten*. https://www.tagesspiegel.de/downloads/20560202/3/listeentireberlinccbanu.pdf. Accessed December 11, 2019.

Cixous, Hélène. 2000. "Obstétriques cruelles." In *Autodafé*, Anagrama, Agra, Denoël, Feltrinelli, Seven Stories Press: Milan, Barcelona, Athens, Paris, New York City.

——. 2014. *Insurrection de la Poussière*. Paris: Galilée.

——. 2016. *Gare d'Osnabrück à Jérusalem*. Paris: Galilée.

——. 2018. *Les Sans Arches*. Paris: Gallimard.

Cixous, Hélène, and Théâtre du Soleil. 2006. "*Le Dernier Caravansérail*, Ceux qui nous ont parlé: ce qu'ils sont devenus." In *Le Dernier Caravansérail* [DVD booklet]. Paris: Bel Air Classique, ARTE France Développement, CANOPÉ. A.

——, and Mireille Calle-Grüber. 1994. *Hélène Cixous, Photos de Racines*. Paris: Des Femmes.

Derrida, Jacques. 1991. *L'Autre cap*. Paris: Minuit.

European Parliament. 2019. "Which languages are in use in the Parliament?" *News European Parliament*. https://www.europarl.europa.eu/news/en/faq/21/which-languages-are-in-use-in-the-parliament.   Accessed December 11, 2019.

International Organization for Migration (IOM). 2018. "Mediterranean Migrant Arrivals Reach 15,289 in 2018; Deaths Reach 517." In UN IOM. https://www.iom.int/news/mediterranean-migrant-arrivals-reach-15289-2018-deaths-reach-517. Accessed December 9, 2019.

International Organization for Migration (IOM). 2020. "Missing Migrants." UN IOM Data Analysis Center. http://missingmigrants.iom.int. Accessed February 2, 2020.

International Organization for Migration (IOM). n.d. "Flow Monitoring Europe." International Organization for Migration (IOM). http://migration.iom.int/europe/. Accessed December 9, 2019.

Le Monde. November 12, 2017. "Un journal allemand établit une liste de 33 293 migrants morts en essayant de rejoindre l'Europe." https://www.lemonde.fr/europe/article/2017/11/12/un-journal-allemand-etablit-une-liste-de-33-293-migrants-morts-en-essayant-de-rejoindre-l-europe_5213876_3214.html#iJw477oCBaXyiA5s.99. Accessed December 9, 2019.

Mnouchkine, Ariane, and Théâtre du Soleil. 2006. "Entretien à l'école du Petit Mistral dans le cadre de l'opération 'Lycéens à Avignon.'" In *Le Dernier Caravansérail, Interview by Jean-Claude Lallias, Catherine Goupil, Manuela Marques, Catherine Goupil*, DVD 1 supplements, Scérén-CNDP, 2006. B.

Morel, Olivier, dir. 2018. *Ever, Rêve, Hélène Cixous* [Film]. Paris, Notre Dame: Zadig Productions, University of Notre Dame.

Picon-Vallin, Béatrice. 2007. "Parler du monde, parler au monde. *Le Dernier Caravansérail* et le 'ciné-théâtre' d'Ariane Mnouchkine," *Théâtre d'aujourd'hui n° 11: De la scène à l'écran* Paris: CNDP.

———. 2014. *Le Théâtre du Soleil, les cinquante premières années*. Arles: Actes Sud.

PART IV

Screen Cultures

CHAPTER EIGHT

Lessons in Adaptation

The Postcolonial Classroom in *Entre les murs* and *L'Esquive*

Nicholas Harrison

In French colonial debates about education, "adaptation" meant tailoring the curriculum to different localities and different student bodies.[1] Today, colonial education is often associated with radical *non*-adaptation: something as out of place as history lessons on "nos ancêtres les Gaulois" delivered to young Senegalese children who had quite different ancestry, and different ancestral myths. Yet adaptation could also be a colonial policy. In its simplest form it could mean attempting to engage pupils by connecting teaching materials with local cultures, identities, and circumstances, for example when a teacher in rural Algeria got young French learners to chant "Aomar pompe l'eau," or "Mohand emplit le bidon." More drastically, adaptation could be about readying students for their inferior place in the colonial hierarchy. "[D]ans un État républicain ou simplement libéral," writes one colonial commentator in 1899, "il est naturel qu'on habitue les esprits à l'examen et à l'analyse de toutes choses et, par conséquent, que l'instruction soit fortement imprégnée de littérature, d'histoire et de philosophie." Things are different in the colonies, he says: what is needed for the colonized is schooling "[d'] un caractère purement pratique et professionnel." When

1   I am grateful to Emma Wilson for the opportunity to share a very early version of this material with colleagues and students in Cambridge, and to Lia Brozgal, Emily Butterworth, Elizabeth Eger, Ros Murray, and Vinay Swamy as well as to participants in the French research seminar at King's College London for their responses to later versions.

it comes to the colonial underclass, "il importe d'éviter tout ce qui peut faire naître ou développer l'esprit de discussion."[2]

The term adaptation is not much used in such senses now, but occasionally one can still hear echoes of that colonial-era rhetoric. When, in 2003, the French education ministry organized a "Débat national sur l'avenir de l'Ecole," one of the questions posed was: "Comment l'Ecole doit-elle s'adapter à la diversité des élèves?" That question was incorporated verbatim into François Bégaudeau's autobiographically-inspired novel *Entre les murs* about life in a school in contemporary Paris (Bégaudeau 2006, 61, 64), and then into the filmscript based on the novel (Stoppel 2010, 62–63). In Laurent Cantet's version (2008), one of the films on which this chapter will focus, the ministry's wording did not make the final cut, but the question remained central.[3] Issues around the "fit" between diverse students and a particular curriculum are also at the heart of Abdellatif Kechiche's *L'Esquive* (2003), the other film on which I will focus, which includes scenes, and takes inspiration, from Marivaux's play *Le Jeu de l'amour et du hasard* of 1730. At points in both films, questions about educational fit, in the context of postcolonial migrations, relocations, and reinventions, intersect with issues around adaptation in its other, cinematic sense: issues, that is, around the relative, shifting prestige of words and images, and the ideological work done by—and/or expected of—different genres and media. But in Kechiche's case, given the film's radical transformations of its literary source material—an eighteenth-century play rather than a contemporary novel—"transposition" may be a better word; and although this chapter will touch on questions of cinematic adaptation as such, it is the colonial echoes of "adaptation" that are more important to my discussion. My hope is that there will be something productively disorientating

---

2   These brief remarks on colonial education draw on my book *Our Civilizing Mission: The Lessons of Colonial Education* (Liverpool: Liverpool University Press, 2019). The examples come respectively from Besserve-Bernollin (1981, 135) and Billiard (1899, 33–34).

3   Responses to Cantet's film, which I do not have space to discuss, are also relevant here: they evinced widespread willingness to express anxiety—some of it fundamentally racist—about education in a multicultural society. See Debril 2008, an interview with Xavier Darcos, then Minister of Education; Vincendeau 2009; and Christopher 2009. I consider Christopher a possible winner, from a strong field, of the prize for the most offensive comment in the first wave of reception: Cantet's film, he wrote in *The Times*, should be shown to all MPs because of the light it cast on "one of the most toxic ethnic stews in Paris."

about keeping in mind that idea, and the clashing perspectives around it, including colonial suspicion of the capacity of literary education to promote "l'esprit de discussion," as I respond to the films' encouragement to think again about who should study what, and where we expect it to lead.

Both films raise questions about the place of student identities in the classroom, especially in French lessons (or their equivalents in other societies); about the educational uses of a literary tradition, including a theatrical tradition, characterized both by inherited meanings and by the possibility of reinterpretation and change; and about the socio-cultural function of education. I want to suggest that on all these issues we can learn something from Cantet's and Kechiche's films. Whatever "lessons" they offer are, however, exploratory and ambivalent, and this chapter will follow the films' lead in that regard too, on the assumption—which I will address directly in the final section—that much of the value of the films as such, as of teaching that makes film or literature its object, lies in that exploratory quality.

It is not by chance that the lessons we see in *Entre les murs*, as in *L'Esquive*, are French lessons rather than, say, chemistry classes. French as an academic subject has various historical foundations, among the most important of which is, or has been, a sense of alignment between a language, "a literature," and a "national identity." That sense is partly imaginary, but institutions of education have helped make it self-fulfilling, to some extent.[4] In that tradition the French language and the literature of France have been taken to encapsulate Frenchness, itself a notion that has always been somewhat racialized; and French educationalists have worked on the basis that to teach the language and the literature together is at once to give insights into that identity and, more pragmatically, to help cement it, binding students together—in the first instance, male students in metropolitan France—as future citizens.

4   Another foundation (see Steiner 1967) is the relationship, again partly imaginary, of modern European literatures to the literatures of Rome and Greece. In *Entre les murs* when we, along with François, discover that Esméralda has been reading Plato's *Republic* in her spare time, the intended effect hinges on the high cultural status that such texts continue, to some degree, to enjoy, but also on their loss of (imagined) centrality and their restricted currency among different sectors of the population.

In Cantet's *Entre les murs* the protagonist, François, a French teacher in a *collège* in Paris's 20th *arrondissement*, could be said to "adapt" his teaching in various ways, and with varying degrees of success, in response to the identities or the "diversity" of the students in his classroom. In one small instance the issue arises in the form of a sample sentence, as it did for the teacher in French Algeria who came up with "Aomar pompe l'eau." François wants his students to understand the word "succulent" and writes on the blackboard: "Bill déguste un succulent cheeseburger." The sentence draws on everyday life and nods toward a US-dominated popular culture with which, François may assume, all his students are familiar. But one of them, Khoumba, challenges him, asking why he always chooses names like Bill rather than Aïssata, say, or Rachid, or Ahmed; and her friend Esméralda chimes in: yes, he always chooses "Des noms de babtou." They are winding him up, of course, but at the same time making some sort of assertion about their identities: "babtou" is an inversion of the word *toubab* sometimes used in central and West Africa to designate white people, and is an example of the *verlan* or back slang that François keeps asking them not to use in the classroom. When François asks what they mean, Esméralda says: "noms de Français" then, with an ironic smirk, "de céfrans" (*verlan* for *Français*). "So you're not French," says François, with his own characteristic ironic look. Esméralda answers "no," then, "En fait je suis française, mais pas fière de l'être." And with this he, as a good liberal, can of course agree. (It's the sort of thing I might say about being British, or English.) He adds: "si je choisis à chaque fois les prénoms en fonction des origines diverses qu'il y a dans cette classe, je vais pas m'en sortir." They respond, reasonably enough, that he could introduce some more variety; and they clearly want his examples to bear some relation to who they are. As ever, the fundamental, prior issue raised by any question of educational "adaptation" is how the norm is defined—who defines it, who or what it excludes, and how far it is open to change.

François's phrase "origines diverses" is carefully chosen; more carefully chosen, anyway, than the words of Bégaudeau in the book, who says: "Si je commence à vouloir représenter toutes les *nationalités* au niveau des prénoms, j'vais pas m'en sortir" (33, emphasis added). Both versions of his assertion point toward the ethnic composition of the classroom, which bears some relation to the contours of the French empire;[5] and in that

---

5   When an interviewer remarked to Cantet that France's social make-up is "a direct result of [its] imperial ambitions of centuries before," Cantet appeared

classroom, in contrast with the staff common room, he is in a smallish minority as a white person (a disparity discussed in Gueye 2010). In the book this is signaled first—and perhaps primarily—by characters' names: in his opening description of the common room Bégaudeau writes (13): "Nous nous prénommions Bastien, Chantal, Claude, Danièle"—and so on, in alphabetical order, through to Valérie. The relatively unusual usage of *se prénommer* adds a kind of emphasis, and makes his sentence sound a little like part of a grammar drill, which one might connect with Khoumba's point about the cultural norms carried in language teaching. Not all readers will think to themselves that these are *noms de céfrans*, however. In the film the corresponding "information" is primarily visual, a matter of different skin colors and different ethnic "types," but that still leaves much room for interpretation. All spectators, in our racialized societies, will see the differences in the racial composition of the staff and student bodies, but not all will register those differences consciously, or think about them critically. In any case, the idea of *nationalités* sits uncomfortably here: visual traits, like first names, may be a sign of "origins" in a broad, vague sense, but they certainly don't give any information on nationality.[6]

Nonetheless, nationality does come up in both book and film, in the classroom and in the school yard, and also, in relation to questions of expulsion and deportation, in the staff common room; and in both book and film, as in the world outside, notions of nationality are ensnarled with notions of race. In the first classroom sequence when François asks his students to write themselves a nameplate, we see that Chérif has drawn an Algerian flag next to his name. Several of the boys

reluctant to pursue the issue (Harris 2008, 102). In Bégaudeau's book colonialism as such comes up in passing. A teacher complains that when a student called Djibril stated that the Spanish are racist, and she responded that the Spanish are no worse than anyone else, all the other students started yelling their agreement with Djibril. This prompts her to describe the students to her colleague as "des vrais sauvages" and to say "Ils ont une espèce de racisme anti-Blanc," then: "Le colonialisme, OK, mais là ça va y a prescription" (105). In both the film and the book there are more echoes of imperialist/racist language in the speech made by a teacher who complains that the students "m'ont fait un souk," are "en rut," and sound like "animaux sauvages" (Bégaudeau 2006, 213–14; the equivalent scene is about 26 minutes into the film).

6   One student, Wei, whose family is at risk of being deported, describes himself as Chinese, and in his case that presumably *is* a description of nationality, but one can assume that most if not all of the other students are French.

are obsessed with the *Coupe d'Afrique des Nations* and support the team of the nation from which members of their family once came—Morocco, for example, or Mali. Those boys ridicule Carl, whose family background lies in the West Indies (that is, in a *département d'outre-mer*), when he says that the national team that he supports is France. In his "self-portrait" he says he hates racists, and also hates Materazzi, an Italian footballer who in the 2006 World Cup final was memorably headbutted by Zinedine Zidane. (Materazzi had insulted him, and it was widely believed that the insult was racist; Zidane was sent off; and France lost.[7]) Carl's support for the French team does not mean, however, that his perspective is one of republican color-blindness; the players he is most interested in, and pretends to be when playing football in the yard, are Black.[8]

Distinctions of social class are, of course, caught up with these racial distinctions in many scenes. At one point a question from Esméralda prompts François to start teaching the imperfect subjunctive, an exercise greeted with skepticism by his students. The obvious justification for doing so is that it is a feature of some literary texts, especially older ones. François alludes to this in the novel, albeit half-heartedly as a teacher, and with self-referential irony as a novelist: "vous le trouverez dans des romans, et encore, pas très souvent" (189). In the film he does not offer any sort of literary justification: the students assert that the standard by which French should be judged is contemporary spoken language, and François gets drawn onto that ground, claiming, unconvincingly, that he and his friends use the imperfect subjunctive regularly in conversation—after which he is forced to admit that to do so is rare in speech, and that the students may be right when they label it "bourgeois." François's principal argument in the end is that the students need to distinguish between different registers, the informal and the formal, "l'oral et l'écrit." That seems like sound advice, but the distinctions are unclear to them. In the book (92) one of the boys makes a telling confusion between "l'intuition" and "la tuition"; what someone like François—middle-class and well educated—has come to experience as intuition regarding the nature and usage of different

7   The incident was commemorated in a sculpture by the Algerian artist Adel Abdessemed, which was shown in Paris then briefly in Qatar; see https://www.adelabdessemed.com/oeuvres/coup-de-tete/, accessed April 2, 2021.

8   See Brozgal 2019 for more analysis of the film's handling of issues of race and "color-blindness."

registers needs to be learned.[9] As François suggests, that is one of the purposes of French lessons, and would be in any school, with any group of students. Here again one might challenge the origin and nature of the norm, but the questions of principle are complicated by pragmatic questions about social cohesion and the prospect of social mobility: those with "non-standard" French, or a poor command of the norms of written French, may be disadvantaged socially if they are not made aware of, and given a command of, certain norms of speech and writing, whatever the socio-historical foundations of those norms may be.[10]

The lack of clarity about the difference between, and relative status of, the "spoken" and the "written" lies partly in the distinction itself, of course; and inevitably this plays out differently in the book and the film. In the book there is a moment of irony—irony about linguistic norms in writing, and about teaching—when François says to the class: "c'est pas parce qu'on vous demande d'écrire un dialogue qu'il faut écrire comme on parle, vous voyez?" (257). His concern, only partially hidden behind the shifting use of *on* (and the joke), may be more about how *they* speak than how he speaks, as the exchange over *verlan* suggested; again, hierarchical identities are in play. In both book and film, François's speech is different from that of his students; for example, the film, where speech was only semi-scripted, captures a moment when Bégaudeau interjected an ironic "certes," an expression that the students, and the people playing the students, were unlikely to use, especially in speech. (Cantet points this out humorously to Bégaudeau in one of the "extra" videos on the DVD.) At the same time, however, his writing, as well as his own speech, differs from the style of writing he advocates. Things get complicated at this point: in the book, the words Bégaudeau *writes* are presented as speech, and he goes on to write, about the "ne" of negation, "à l'écrit, on le met. [...] Toujours le faire, même si soi-même on trouve pas ça important" (258). This is nicely self-reflexive: he's just omitted the "ne" in writing, contradicting the advice offered in that very sentence, as well as the advice in the previous sentence about not transcribing one's own speech directly. We see and "hear" that writing and speech are different; but at the same time, we are reminded that literary writing often includes

9   For an analysis of this sequence inspired by Pierre Bourdieu's educational theories, see O'Shaughnessy 2015, 138–39.

10   An argument along these lines was made by Antonio Gramsci in the Italian context, even though he saw that the very notion of a national language reflected a privileged group's hegemony (see Mayo 2014).

speech, and is not always, and need not be, characterized by elevated or so-called "written" language. Any trained teacher or critic of literature would recognize this, of course.

Bégaudeau's book is enriched by the various strands of irony and reflexivity here, and, without wanting to exaggerate its originality or other merits as a literary work, I would say that it develops a fruitful relationship with the long and ever-evolving written tradition that it evokes, and that it joins. I am thinking also of a moment toward the end when the students (including two called Abdelkrimo and Fatih, perhaps a nod toward *L'Esquive*) are involved in a public performance of a nineteenth-century play, Musset's *On ne badine pas avec l'amour.* For me, at least, the dated but beautiful language that is quoted from Perdican's speech was a highlight of Bégaudeau's novel (286–87: a speech about the universal importance of love), partly because it was given renewed resonance when it was juxtaposed with, and erupted into, Bégaudeau's differently spoken/written French, and its different socio-cultural context. When Bégaudeau's book turned into Cantet's film, however, Musset did not survive the transposition. Indeed, in the film, French literary tradition disappears almost entirely.

That shift and that near-absence seem to me to have something to do with adaptation in the postcolonial sense (here, the attempt by François, and by Cantet, to respond to a particular student body, whose particularity is understood partly in ethnic/racial terms) as well as the cinematic sense. When the history teacher, who appears rather traditional and inflexible compared with François, suggests to him that they make thematic links across classes around the *ancien régime* and the Enlightenment, François, although he has not yet decided what to study with his group, brushes him off, saying that Voltaire is too hard for them. When, in one of the closing scenes, they discuss what they have learned that year, the only book mentioned is Plato's *Republic* (which was not on the curriculum—see note 4); the script had suggested a positive mention of Boris Vian's *L'Ecume des jours* (214), but that did not make it into the film, where Esméralda comments that all the books chosen by François are terrible. On the board in the background during a lesson on versification there is a very brief glimpse of three lines from Arthur Rimbaud's poem "Les Effarés," but you could easily miss it, and that particular lesson soon disintegrates catastrophically, with François calling two of his students "pétasses," and Souleymane, one of the most difficult students, storming out and accidentally injuring Khoumba. The only book we see them studying is Anne Frank's *The Diary of a Young*

Girl. That is a good thing to study, I would say, and indeed its almost incontrovertible value could be the reason it was chosen, by the fictional teacher or by Cantet. What is more, the choice may also, as Guiney points out (2017, Chapter 6), reflect educational policy at the time. But it is a choice that raises—or, to put it another way, avoids—important questions about what in the tradition of (French) literary study is worth preserving, for François's particular students or for other students.

What is striking about the choice of Anne Frank's text from that perspective is its significant distance from the traditional foundations of French as an academic subject: it was not written in French, and it is not a "literary" text in the sense that has been central to that tradition, which associates literariness strongly with fictionality as well as a particular creative relationship to language. What is more, there is little sign that the students find the text engaging. Nobody in the class, François complains, has read the extract they were asked to read; and they don't really discuss it. Instead, it comes to serve as a kind of pretext to do something else. This suggests that if the curriculum is being "adapted" here, it is not only through the choice of text but also in terms of critical/ pedagogical methodology. François uses Anne Frank's diary to launch an exercise in self-portraiture—a move that may seem a little inapt, if you feel that more attention is due to the specificities of the text and its context. The students' objections are different: one, Lucie, protests that her own life is uninteresting in comparison; and Souleymane refuses to take part on the grounds that François's interest in their personal lives is intrusive. Yet despite the students' misgivings François persists, and in the end the student who is seen to get most out of the exercise is Souleymane. Cantet, it seems, wants us to view the exercise as a success; but in some ways his film seems to have other ideas, or at least to make room for a skeptical response.

The scene where the self-portrait exercise is seen to take flight is filmed not in the usual classroom but the computer room, and the different space is the first of a series of visual shifts marking François's move into a realm of greater pedagogical success. This is not to deny that in the main classroom scenes too there is much that feels positive. There Cantet shot with three cameras, one trained constantly on François, the other two on students as they answered questions or messed around.[11] The

---

11 The mode of filming is described by Cantet in interviews and commentaries on the "Extras" disc in the Artificial Eye DVD set, and is analyzed by critics including Williams (2012).

way the camera loses focus and pans belatedly to catch up with a student who suddenly speaks, or draws attention in some other way, makes the classroom feel full of energy. It helps give the images their "documentary" feel, which is an aesthetic choice and partly a matter of artifice, but also reflects a degree of improvisation in those scenes. As well as connoting authenticity, then, Cantet's technique captures something authentic about the kind of improvised and somewhat theatrical performance required of teachers as they respond to students' interventions and interruptions (another small, and usually positive, form of adaptation), and their testing out of different roles. But, especially in the film's cinemascope format, the space also feels crowded; and the camerawork, as well as the narrative, conveys the sense that some energy is being wasted. François tries to exercise the level of control needed to maintain a sense of direction; and in scenes such as the exchange over the subjunctive, his position of authority is suggested by the way he stands at the front while the students are seated in rows facing him, looking up at him. Shots and counter-shots establish a sense of complicity at moments, for example when François teases Khoumba, but this setup can also suggest an opposi-tional relationship, and we also see conflict. In the computer room, by contrast, everything appears calmer and more purposeful: all the students are focused, the camera is less twitchy, and when François approaches Souleymane, he stoops down to look closely at the computer screen, turning his head to look at Souleymane from quite an intimate distance, sharing the shot with Souleymane, Boubacar, and other students. Soon after this we see Souleymane standing alongside François, smiling with pride and embarrassment as François acclaims his self-portrait, a series of photos that François pins up for all to see.

One of the implications of this sequence is that the students respond positively, in personal and educational terms, when they feel that lessons speak to their identities and when they have opportunities to express themselves. As I have already emphasized, there are long-standing aspects of the French literary/linguistic pedagogical tradition in play here, but we are also seeing a successful adaptation of some sort. Although Souleymane initially objected to the self-portrait exercise as intrusive, he overcomes his misgivings and takes the chance to represent something of his personal life. One photo shows his Koranic tattoo, another his multiracial group of friends, all drawn from his class. His shift of attitude is connected above all, however, with his most arresting image, a photo of his mother. We see it first at the beginning of the sequence, in a close-up on the viewfinder of Souleymane's camera, and it gains in significance because we see it a couple more times as he works on the computer, before Cantet's camera lingers over it, again in close-up, when the photos are put on display. Souleymane's mother holds up a defensive hand toward the camera, and we can see (and we are also told) that she dislikes photos; so *she* still finds the exercise intrusive. This reinforces our impression that there is a gap between her and the world of the school (and of the film): we were introduced to her in the sequence immediately before this one, when she was François's last appointment at the parents' evening, an encounter that left him looking deflated. She can neither speak nor read French, and is unaware of her son's difficulties in the classroom. We hear her talking quite a lot, but many of her comments go untranslated by Souleymane's brother, who is serving as interpreter. What is more, none of her speech is translated for the film audience. Her lack of French is disempowering, and disadvantageous to her son. When the photo brings her, and his personal world, into the school for the second time, Souleymane shows he is willing to override her sense of intrusion, and perhaps a certain sense of difference; the implication is that the image (along with the photo of his classmates) represents a successful move away from her and toward the school's own social and educational cultures.

The apparent success of the self-portrait exercise in the eyes of the students and of Cantet is reconfirmed when, at the end of the school year, and the end of the film, François unexpectedly gives all his students bound copies of their collected work. The delight they express seems real, and plausible. By that time, however, Souleymane has been kicked out of school, after his mother has appeared for the third and final time, accompanying him at the *conseil disciplinaire*—a scene whose implications I will examine further in the final section. For now, I want simply to note that Souleymane's fate represents one significant limit on the achievements of the self-portrait exercise, irrespective of the exercise's merits in itself. Another limit, if one is looking for ways to adapt and renew, rather than reasons to discard, the French/literary curriculum and its role in developing "l'esprit de discussion," is that Souleymane's experience of educational success depends not on writing but on photography. This is a medium with which he is already familiar, and with which he feels relatively comfortable. Although François asks his students to *write* a self-portrait, he greets Souleymane's switch of medium with enthusiasm. (He subsequently asks Souleymane to add brief captions, but we barely see them and they do not seem essential to his work.) Within the diegetic world François's openness to the switch is understandable in terms of Souleymane's prior disengagement, as well as the inherent interest of photography as a medium of self-portraiture.[12] It may also be understandable, if one looks at things from Cantet's perspective and with cinematic adaptation in mind, in terms of photography's close relationship with cinema. Be that as it may, the upshot is that the French lesson is seen to work best when François proves willing to move away from both language and literature.

Compared with François, the French teacher in *L'Esquive* comes across as relatively conventional in her approach. She has some success in drawing students into an "unadapted" curriculum, in the form of Marivaux's play *Le Jeu de l'amour et du hasard* of 1730. This presumably reflects something of Kechiche's own education (he was born in Tunisia, but grew up and went to school in France), and an interest in French literary tradition. In most respects the double encounter of Kechiche and of the students with Marivaux appears to be a triumph. The students carry the Marivaux beyond the classroom both as characters—that is, voluntarily, in the film's internal universe—and as facets of Kechiche's highly accomplished transposition of the play into film form. So while the literary source material is unadapted within the diegetic world in the classroom, rehearsals, and a performance, it is at the same time radically adapted cinematically, shaping plot, theme, and dynamics in playful and thought-provoking ways. To a significant extent, the film's meanings emerge through the counterpoint and interpenetration of the narratives, genres, and historically specific languages—worlds—of the play and the film.

One of the effects of this juxtaposition/incorporation is that we are constantly reminded that the teenagers' way of talking to each other, and interacting with one another, involves a kind of performance in which the everyday is infused with the theatrical. It is possible to think of their interactions as a kind of modern *marivaudage*, an idea pursued by critics including Swamy (2007) and Gomot (2014). Seeing things that way need not imply that the characters' speech lacks real emotion, or that the film lacks authenticity.[13] On one level, this modern *marivaudage* is simply the way these characters speak, and the way they are; but the

---

12   It is worth remembering that the high era of selfies, and of disapproving pronouncements on selfies, had not arrived when the film was made.

13   Osman Elkharraz, the actor who played the protagonist Krimo, has suggested,

quotidian theatricality of their way of being means that even a relatively inflexible character like Fathi proves capable of switching codes and stepping in and out of different roles, as must the four main characters in Marivaux's play. When Krimo's mother comes to the window after Fathi has barked Krimo's name outside their block of flats, Fathi immediately shifts tone and register. The abruptness of the change makes it quite funny—it's almost as if he's a language learner doing his oral exam ("Bonjour Madame … Comment allez-vous?")—but as in the play, the stagey and the real are intertwined. The switch of register is at once a performance of politeness that seems slightly artificial, and a genuine form of politeness. In such ways the film's high cultural underpinning, which could be taken to reveal a gulf between Marivaux's world and the world of these young people, can also suggest that their "sub"culture should indeed be thought of as a culture, not a lack of culture; and it allows the circulation of value between the two worlds: a certain sense of dignity, say, or, at the level of representation, a certain sense of "relevance." This also raises questions about any assumption that "mainstream"/literary culture, or bourgeois culture, is the true, direct, or sole inheritor, or prolongation, of the now distant culture of Marivaux.[14]

The culmination of the students' work on Marivaux is the performance of the play just before the end of the film, an event that brings together the students, the teacher, and a whole community of friends and families. Krimo, however, is a notable absence, or a presence only on the margins. His attempts to take part, and so to give himself a way of courting Lydia, have not necessarily got him any further with her, and have been disastrous from the teacher's perspective. His failure has a deep effect on the whole tone of the film as well as its plot, and this complicates any sense that the unadapted curriculum in the diegetic world, in the form of Marivaux's play, has proved an unequivocal success. Nevertheless, the fact that some of Krimo's friends have embraced the play suggests that some of the difficulties he faces are his own. What is it, then, that holds Krimo back, and what in the Marivaux, besides *marivaudage*, works for the others? And might Krimo's particular case, along with that of

however, that Sara Forestier's delivery did not sound authentic to him; Elkharraz 2016, 65.

14 Shea argues that, today, "Marivaux's language is as foreign to the well-to-do Parisian as it is to the banlieusard: as such, it belongs more readily to all" (2012, 1145).

Souleymane, have any general implications for the curriculum and the educational system in which he never seems to feel at home?

Gender is one factor that shapes and seems to inhibit Krimo's participation, and another area in which the adaptation or transposition of the play's world into the film's world is deft and illuminating. Across both film and play the spheres of masculine and feminine behavior are in constant interaction and dialogue, but also somewhat distinct. At moments the interaction involves male dominance, both indirect—manifested for example in a kind of machismo that is internalized to some degree by the girls but is more marked among the boys—and direct, for example in Fathi's sometimes violent interventions in the girls' lives. (At different moments, when he isn't acting/being polite to Krimo's mother, Fathi acts as a marriage broker, a bully, and some kind of would-be theater or film director.) These unequal gender codes may help explain why in general the girls seem more comfortable with theater than do the boys: the codes of femininity seem to allow greater awareness of—and greater comfort with—the performance of gender *as* performance. That appears to soften the boundary between theater and reality, making it easier for them to step into theatrical roles. Lydia seems simultaneously self-conscious and unselfconscious (without seeming fake or "not herself") when she keeps using her fan, a prop from the play, even when she is not, or not fully, "in character." All of this may also help explain why the girls, in this film as in *Entre les murs*, often appear more comfortable in the theatrical space of the classroom.

Other issues faced by Krimo are more individual. Whereas Cantet's film is set almost entirely within the walls of the school, never showing us the students in any other context, Kechiche's camera spends most of its time in public spaces, where the young people hang out when not at home or at school. In *Entre les murs*, as we have seen, the little we learn of the students' wider lives surfaces—along with our sense of how little we know about them, and how little the school knows—through snatches of dialogue, through the self-portrait exercise, and through the walk-on parts of family members who attend meetings. In the case of Krimo, by contrast, not only do we see and learn something about his mother (the only parental figure with a substantial role); we also go inside his home. Throughout the film, and especially in the classroom, Krimo's expression is often emotionally blank, but his relationship with his mother is visibly warm; and the intimate scenes when he is with her or alone in his room are important to our sense that he has a complex inner life. What is more, the scenes in his flat lead into the first two classroom scenes, inviting us to make connections between his home life and his experience of school. In the classroom scenes his inner life is crucial, in fact, although to the teacher it is invisible, or visible only as a kind of blockage.

The first classroom sequence follows an evening scene in Krimo's flat. He returns home to find his mother asleep on the sofa, exhausted after a visit to her partner, his father, in prison. When she tells Krimo there is a picture for him in her bag, we don't get to see it properly, or not at first: a side shot shows Krimo looking at it, but we are not offered the point of view shot we might expect. Then, expressing sympathy for how worn out his mother is, he says "Vivement le voilier!" and goes into his bedroom. The remark makes sense when we see him in close-up, from behind, pinning the picture to the wall. It is a painting of a sailing boat, and the next shot, from the same angle but further back, reveals several similar paintings already attached to the wall—three of which are then emphasized in a series of extreme close-ups. They seem to be connected with notions of escape or transformation, and hopes for a better future. (The fantasy behind "Vivement le voilier!" is echoed in a remark—slightly implausible, or non-naturalistic—made later by Fathi when expressing regret that Krimo has split up with Magali; he had imagined them all, he says, sailing around the world, with Krimo and Magali's children.) The paintings that Krimo's father sends him, in which at least some of the boats look like dhows, may also suggest something about art's relationship with origins, and certainly something about its role in both self-expression and communication.

When we move into the classroom the sound of the teacher's voice precedes fractionally the cut away from the bedroom; but what we see first is not the teacher but Krimo again. This transition, with its overlapping sound, suggests that the different spaces are leaching into each other. The last close-up of a sailing ship, some kind of point of view shot (emotionally if not necessarily formally), leads to another close-up: a slightly out-of-focus Krimo with his head down, making his own drawings. The whole classroom scene, like many in this film and in Cantet's film, is shot with a highly mobile, often unstable camera, frequently so intimately or even intrusively close to individual characters that they break the frame. After a few shots of the teacher and then some other students we get an extreme close-up of Krimo's downturned face, then, very briefly, his drawings, a tangle of schoolboy doodles. What we hear during these shots are some instructions for French homework, as the teacher dictates an essay question about how Marivaux could be said to privilege emotion over action. One could say the same about Kechiche's work in this scene. Krimo, wrapped up in his thoughts, fails to act as he should (he appears not to be writing down the homework task), and all this establishes another link, and another contrast, with the action—or inaction—in Krimo's flat, where the understated emotional currents between Krimo, his mother, and his absent father found some sort of expression in spaces that were low-key, darkly lit, and relatively static.

Krimo perks up when three of his classmates—including Lydia—are called on to rehearse in front of the others. We see them in a shot over Krimo's shoulder, close to his point of view. Lydia/Lisette, now in close-up, launches in, and when Rachid/Arlequin responds, the camera pans belatedly across to his face, as if reacting to spontaneous dialogue. As in *Entre les murs* this technique gives the sequence a "documentary" feel in a loose sense, and here it associates the play more closely with the diegetic "real"; but at other moments—for example when we cut to Frida/Silvia just before her entry—we can see that the camera knows what will happen next. Whereas Cantet's technique, and Bégaudeau's diverse roles, may blur the boundaries between fiction and reality in *Entre les murs* (making it easier, perhaps, for some commentators to treat it as a documentary, or as a pretext to express their personal anxieties about contemporary education), it remains clear that Kechiche in his film, like Marivaux in his play, is constructing in an exploratory way, for his audience, the fictional world of his characters.

At the same time, as I have noted already, the film points to theatrical aspects both of everyday behavior and of teachers' and students' roles in the classroom; and the play within the film, for all its theatricality and overt fictionality, acts as a bridge between the classroom and the world outside. The film shuttles between the two spheres as it investigates Krimo's inner life. Another dimension, more overtly political, opens up when the rehearsal of the scene from Marivaux is interrupted by Lydia asking the teacher a question about their roles, about how best to play rich people playing poor people and vice versa. The question has additional emotional weight for the audience because we have already seen it prompt an argument between Lydia and Frida when they were rehearsing on their own. Beyond the immediate issue of dramatic technique lie questions about the relationship between the rich and the poor and about the relationship between theater and reality. The teacher responds with a forceful critical analysis:

la question qu'elle [Lydia] pose, elle nous amène vraiment au cœur de la pièce. Ce que Marivaux nous dit, là, les riches jouent les pauvres, les pauvres jouent les riches, et personne n'y arrive … Personne n'y arrive, bien, ce qu'il nous montre c'est qu'on est complètement prisonnier de notre condition sociale, et que, quand on est riche pendant 20 ans, pauvre(s) pendant 20 ans, on peut toujours se mettre en haillons quand on est riche, et puis en robe de haute couture quand on est pauvre, on se débarrasse pas d'un langage, d'un certain type de sujet de conversation, d'une manière de s'exprimer, de se tenir, qui indiquent d'où on vient. [...] On est conditionné, complètement conditionné par son milieu d'origine, et on reste entre soi. Et on peut toujours se déguiser, on n'échappe pas à sa condition d'origine. Donc, quand vous devez jouer les riches et les pauvres qui jouent les pauvres et les riches, il y a des moments où ils y arrivent—mais pas vraiment, il reste toujours des traces de cette condition—puis des moments ils y arrivent pas du tout; il y a les vieux réflexes qui viennent.

The camera stays close to the teacher's face for most of this speech but cuts occasionally to the students, notably when they chorus "des pauvres" in response to her question about who the poor fall in love with. This speech and its echoes through the subsequent classroom sequences have complex implications for questions about the fit between the students and the curriculum—and more specifically here about the place in their education of this old play, and of her analysis.

The teacher's generalizations, which pass through the play and into the world, are quite compelling, and are articulated from a critical perspective that may be understood to be, or intended to be, politically progressive and egalitarian; but in their context, they may also sound quite brutal. Again here, as in François's classroom, the would-be general, impersonal pronoun *on* proves not to be entirely impersonal; it keeps fissuring, or getting stuck to one person or another, losing some of its generality, and eventually giving way to an awkward alternation between *vous* and *ils*. The teacher's own position in relation to the generalizations is (again) very different from that of the students— which casts doubt on the general validity of the generalizations, and more specifically here on the supposed universality of the play and/or its "message." Along with her age and position, the teacher's way of speaking French already marks her, for us as for her students, as someone different, from a relatively privileged background; and everyone can see that she, like François, and unlike most of her students, is white. Perhaps in some sense she too is "prisonni[ère] de [sa] condition sociale," but the constraints on her are quite dissimilar to those faced by someone like Krimo. "[O]n n'échappe pas à sa condition d'origine" is advice more pertinent, and more aptly connoted, for Krimo than for the teacher; she probably has no particular reason to want to "escape." For *his* family, as we have just been reminded, imprisonment is not just a metaphor. Similarly, when Lydia talks about putting on a "robe de haute couture quand on est pauvre," the film has primed us for the remark to take on particular emotional and socio-cultural weight. We have seen her, with a subsidy from Krimo, haggling her way into the posh frock she is wearing in the classroom, and it impresses her friends ("on dirait Miss France," says Zina) but will not necessarily appear posh to everyone who watches the film. The scene ends with another close-up of Krimo's face, slightly dreamy but attentive as the teacher explains that even love, reputedly a pure sentiment, is "influencé par l'origine sociale."

In the second classroom scene Krimo, who has bribed a friend to allow him to take the role of Arlequin in the play, has achieved a limited sort of transformation: he is now wearing a costume, and gets to be on stage with Lydia. This scene, like the earlier one, is preceded by a short sequence in his bedroom. Krimo is already in the harlequin costume, and has the possibility of some sort of success ahead of him, though he looks less than confident. He has managed, more or less, to learn his lines. But in class he mumbles them in a monotone, unable to bring them to life. The teacher could be talking about the film as well as the play, and to us as well as him, when she asks: "tu te rends compte de l'importance du langage dans cette pièce et dans cette scène?" Understandably she becomes increasingly frustrated. When she says to him: "il est déguisé, il s'amuse, il imite un maître—tu sais ce que ça veut dire? Ça veut dire quelqu'un qui a du pouvoir, donc essaie de … essaie de jouer quelqu'un qui a du pouvoir," the different socio-cultural positions of the teacher and the students again make themselves felt a little awkwardly (to us, and to the students). She, the "maître(sse)" in the classroom, has some power; he can only try to pretend.

We return, very briefly, to Krimo's bedroom, and to his often-hidden emotional life, after that second classroom sequence: we see him slumped in a chair, sniffing and passing his hand over his face, perhaps wiping away tears. The medium shot, from slightly above, shows details from his room that suggest more of his inner world, if you look closely: another sailing ship or two; a surprisingly neat desk; the corner of a poster commemorating Muhammad Ali's knock-out of Sonny Liston. Some discreet extra-diegetic music rises up, for the first time in the film, carrying us through the next brief side-shot of Krimo smoking (perhaps somewhere different, perhaps at a different time), and into the beginning of the sequence where Krimo tries to kiss Lydia when rehearsing with her outside school. The music creates another bridge between his private thoughts and the world of drama. We do not hear music again until near the end of the film, when the Marivaux performance is preceded by a play performed by young children, also a moment of heightened emotion. In that final theater scene music is heard twice, in different forms, when the children pretend to be birds. Its uncertain trans-diegetic status suggests it is about the audience's emotions as much as it is part of the performance; and again art—music this time— becomes associated with imagined escape and/or transformation.

The sense of joy in that generally upbeat final theater scene, to which I will return in the closing section, is poles apart from the third and final classroom scene, which is typical of Kechiche in its use of precarious close-ups and lots of shouting, and the way it goes on and on long after you start to hope that it might stop. As in earlier scenes, the camera tends to move gradually nearer to the characters' faces to ramp up the emotional tension. It reaches its peak when the teacher, ever more exasperated by Krimo, yells at him:

> Il y a du plaisir à faire ça, il doit y avoir du plaisir à sortir un peu de soi. Sors de toi! D'accord? Amuse-toi! Aie du plaisir à ça. Change de langage, change de manière de parler, change de manière de bouger, amuse-toi! [...] Amuse-toi, libère-toi, tu comprends ce que je veux dire? [...] AMUSE-TOI! DONNE-TOI!

The experience—and the uncomfortable pleasure—of watching this involves a complex layering of perception. In this sequence as in others we know the whole thing is a fiction (albeit one that relies on and captures many facets of reality), with another fiction inside it; and we see the characters simultaneously succeed and fail in their attempts to transform themselves, verbally and otherwise. It is clear why the teacher reacts to Krimo's performance by saying: "il n'y a pas de cœur, il n'y a pas de conviction, il n'y a rien," but there is dramatic irony here: as we know, and most of Krimo's immediate audience in the classroom knows, his inhibitions stem partly from the fact that his heart really is involved. He is genuinely attracted to Lydia, in the same way that Arlequin is attracted to Lisette, and does not need to be told: "elle est belle, tu touches sa main, c'est merveilleux." In one of the few overt signs of emotion in his performance as Arlequin he discreetly caresses the back of

Lydia's hand, a gesture shown to us in close-up, but presumably invisible to the teacher. He has already given of himself by taking on the role; and by disguising himself—not as Arlequin, but as someone who wants to take on the role of Arlequin in a play—he has done what the characters in the play have done. He has adapted, in his way, to the material he is being asked to study, however inflexible he appears to his teacher. There is a further dimension of irony for the film audience: we can enjoy how well all the *real* actors here are playing their roles, including Osman Elkharraz in the role of Krimo, made into a "real" actor at least for the duration of this film, and acting as someone who cannot act.

There are a couple more layers of possible irony here, and perhaps some further implications for how teachers should choose their material, how they should approach it with their students, and what they should expect to come of it. The first emerges if one recalls that Marivaux worked with the "Comédie-Italienne," whose acting and staging were non-naturalistic. According to Sermain (2013, 116), Marivaux, like other playwrights of the era, "ne compte pas produire sur scène une illusion de réalité ou de présence." Migé makes the same kind of point (2006, 16): "Marivaux apprécie le jeu collectif, distancié et dépourvu de naturel : ils [les comédiens] jouent et montrent qu'ils jouent sans jamais faire corps avec leurs personnages. Le masque qu'ils portent interdit d'ailleurs toute identification et accentue la théâtralité." I don't mean to suggest that Marivaux would have admired Krimo's technique; even in the different context described by these critics, Krimo's performance would, I imagine, have appeared less than riveting. This literary-historical backdrop is a reminder, nonetheless, that actors have not always been expected to "inhabit" their role, and that being a member of a theater audience did not always mean, and does not have to mean, finding the characters convincing or seeking any simple form of identification.[15]

Finally, a certain sense of irony may arise from the apparent disjuncture between the theoretical, political analysis of the play that Krimo's teacher has offered her students, and her expectations of them as students. As we have seen, before bellowing at Krimo: "Change de langage, change de manière de parler, change de manière de bouger," she had told her class that they were "complètement prisonnier[s] de [leur] condition sociale" and explained: "on se débarrasse pas d'un langage […] d'une manière

---

15   For those (like me) with little knowledge of that tradition there are helpful entries on Comédie-Italienne, *commedia dell'arte* and Arlechinno in Hartnoll and Found 1993.

de s'exprimer, de se tenir, qui indiquent d'où on vient." If you put those comments together, it is tempting to think that she has no right to be surprised if Krimo cannot change.

In her introduction to the 1991 anthology *La République et l'école* Elisabeth Badinter wrote: "Grâce à l'école, des générations d'enfants pauvres ou immigrés se sont intégrés à la société française et ont pu y faire leur chemin, en respectant les valeurs de la République" (cited by Guiney 2004, 184). Both *Entre les murs* and *L'Esquive* capture some of the positive energies implied by Badinter's assertion, but also cast light on its internal tensions, and the way it makes light of the difficulties faced by a Krimo or a Souleymane. The films may help us detect a whiff of racialization in Badinter's phrase "enfants immigrés"; that sort of label is often attached to children born in France who have not themselves immigrated, children who are—like Esméralda and virtually all of the other students in these films—French, whatever the complexities of their identities and affiliations, and who are in any case already part of French society. The films can also help us see something crude, and revealing, in the way Badinter places immigrants and the "poor" in the same relationship to education. There is of course significant overlap between the two categories, but it is simply wrong to imply that the poor are not members of French society until school takes charge of them; the phrasing suggests unselfconsciously that true French society—the norm into which others may be assimilated, or that they may seek to challenge or adapt—is to be identified with "les bourges," as Lydia puts it to her friends, or "les riches," as she puts it to the teacher, and *their* "values" or culture—or subculture. On another level, as the films also suggest, Badinter's remark may implicitly exaggerate schools' success in allowing children to "make their way" in society and to achieve "integration"—another word with colonial echoes—when some of those children start out disadvantaged economically and/or by ambient racial discrimination, or other forms of discrimination. Integration or assimilation, into an unequal order, may not really be on offer to an underclass, even if, as under a colonial regime, a few individuals may "escape" their original social conditions.

What is more, educational institutions, with or without a veneer of "meritocracy," can serve to perpetuate social hierarchy. Both films are tinged with pessimism about that aspect of education's social function or effect, even if they also envisage other, more positive capacities and outcomes. In an interview, Cantet remarked: "Schools in France create a lot of exclusion. They enable a kind of sorting process—there are those who will attend university, others will be sent to vocational schools, and then there are others who fail or are expelled" (Goodman 2008).[16] In *Entre les murs* the apparent socio-cultural distinctions between the teachers' common room and the classroom could be read as a sign of that dynamic, and it is evident later in the film. The school year closes with François asking his students what they have learned, and one, Henriette, approaches François timidly, looking crushed, and says she has learned nothing all year, but does not want to go to a *lycée professionnel*—that is, a school "adapted" to less academic students, oriented toward sectors of employment for which more academic education is not required. Cantet's film also ends up conveying a general sense that François's classroom, relaxed and accommodating though it may be in some respects, is part of a more rigid hierarchical structure, both educational and social. When Souleymane is expelled—the French verb in this context is *exclure*—it is arguably not for any very good reason; and in any case, the process through which the decision is taken is distorted by the ultimate impulse toward solidarity among the *maîtres*. There may be a vote in the *conseil disciplinaire* but it involves a pantomime of democracy, with a "ludicrously oversized" ballot box whose capaciousness and transparency appear ironic (Strand 2009, 268). As François himself points out (in a spirit of criticism, because his instincts are liberal, and because he has reason to feel guilty about his own behavior as well as his role in this structure), the outcome of these meetings is always *exclusion définitive*. In Souleymane's case, his mother's lack of French again makes things more difficult—for him, for François and for (most) spectators of the film. Souleymane is called upon to translate but is reluctant to do so, suggesting—and enacting—a gulf of communication between the school and the diverse cultures that lie intermingled beyond its walls, and that are woven inextricably into students' experiences of education. In Souleymane's case, as Khoumba explains to François, expulsion from school will also mean "exclusion" from France. The symbolism linking educational failure or rejection with a wider failure of social integration

---

16   In the same interview Cantet made the (problematic) remark: "People have the notion that school is like a sanctuary, sheltered from the world, where children are taught wonderful things. But unfortunately—or fortunately—these kids don't have simple lives. They're all different races, with different backgrounds. In some homes, the French language is never even spoken."

was chosen by Cantet, who was particularly invested in the Souleymane storyline; but it could have been chosen by Badinter.[17]

L'Esquive also hints at the limits on what schools can achieve in promoting opportunity, social mobility, and equality, and not only through the figure of Krimo. Toward the end of the film Krimo, Lydia, Zina, Frida, and Fathi are stopped and searched by the police. A copy of *Les Jeux de l'amour et du hasard*, crumpled through extensive use, is found in Frida's pocket, and a police officer flicks through to check if she is hiding something. Perhaps it seems implausible that Frida is interested in her schoolwork, or in that sort of play; and the officer, when she finds nothing compromising inside, tosses it away. The sequence ends with a close-up of the book stranded on a car bonnet, a shot that surely invites a symbolic interpretation. Frida's serious-minded involvement with the play and by extension her engagement with school are made to appear irrelevant at this moment—to her, and to the representatives and enforcers of social order. It seems these "enfants pauvres ou immigrés" are being kept in their place.[18]

We do not get to see what happens next, however. We may assume that at least some of the group would have been taken off to the police station, but Kechiche cuts abruptly to an image of a child peeking out from behind a theater curtain, which leads into the sequence where the small children are pretending to be birds, which then leads into the final Marivaux performance. Marivaux, it turns out, is on the same bill as an adaptation of Farid al-din Attar's Sufi poem *Conference of the Birds* (though this is not named), and this staging too is a great success.[19] Kechiche shows a contented audience, including Fathi, then a happy

---

17   On the Souleymane storyline see Harris 2008. Vincendeau remarks (2009, 36) that the film made itself a "hostage to fortune" in showing Black and "Beur" students as the most disruptive. Wood, in a thought-provoking discussion of the film (2009), writes that we are supposed to think that for Souleymane to be sent to Africa is "a fate worse than death."

18   Kechiche sometimes places emphasis on class where spectators might expect emphasis on race. In the police sequence there is no sign that Lydia is treated any better than the other girls, and we have just discovered that Fathi did not actually know who Lydia was, or that she was white—something that has of course been visible throughout to the other characters and to spectators, but that never gains any explicit or unequivocal relevance.

19   The incorporation of this material, according to Sachs's pleasingly counter-intuitive argument (2014, 144), may even be "the film's quintessential republican gesture."

community after-party. Magali, we suddenly see, has a new boyfriend, and, although other characters show that they—like us—are surprised by that turn of events, we may have the disconcerting feeling that there are gaps in the narrative logic as well as the chronology. It is almost as if the film is toying with alternative endings, in different registers, and with very different levels of optimism about the transformative powers of theater/film and education. The violent *dénouement*, something of a cliché for a film about the *banlieue*, may appear more plausible;[20] but the joy of the theater scene, implausible or not, leaves us with a generally positive feeling about these students' encounter with the traditional French curriculum in the form of Marivaux.

I suggested earlier that it is tempting to conclude, in light of the critical/political analysis drawn by the teacher from Marivaux, that she has no right to be surprised if Krimo fails to throw himself into the play, and if in some deeper sense he seems unable to change. But that would not be a satisfactory conclusion. The restrictive wider social circumstances evoked in the police scene make her work more difficult, and limit her success, as do the particular problems faced by Krimo; but there would be no point, unless from a deliberately reactionary perspective, in teaching *this* play to *this* group of students, or for that matter to any group of students, if its ultimate and incontrovertible "message"—perhaps the message one might expect from an author from a noble background, and from a play written under the *ancien régime*—was that their identities and life trajectories were essentially fixed.[21] There is bathos here, not only because we can see limits to the change the teacher can expect, but also because when she yells at Krimo she mainly just wants him to be a better actor. Yet when she says "Sors de toi! […] Change de langage […] libère-toi," her vocabulary resonates with the highest political ambitions of both art and

20 Swamy (2007, 63) discusses the police scene as an "eminently recognizable trope," arguing that Kechiche's ellipsis "emphasizes the very quotidian nature of such violent encounters."

21 Tarr 2007 discusses this tension, linking the teacher's confidence in the play with Kechiche's assumption that the young amateur actors in his film would also benefit from access to the "means of expression" (139). Tarr worries that the film "runs the danger of allowing a white professional actress to outperform the non-professional beur actors" (139). I am not sure how far that amounts to a criticism of the film, but it is true that Forestier's subsequent career has been the most successful, for reasons that may be linked to race as well as class. See also Elkharraz 2016.

education. Fundamentally, her educational practice must work against the deterministic view that she attributes to Marivaux's play.

This is not to say that her political "reading" of the play is illegitimate, but it gives insufficient weight to the complex and diverse reactions that the play can produce—and in this way misrepresents both how the play "delivers" and the nature of her own work. The close relationship between reality and representation is crucial to both, but so too is the gap between reality and representation. As I emphasized in my discussion of the many-layered and sometimes uncomfortable experience of watching Krimo suffer in the classroom, making sense of film or theater always involves an understanding of the differences between theater/film and reality. Learning from plays, films and literature should involve, and hone, that same understanding, and the complex pleasures and insights it can support. In that creative/pedagogical space, Marivaux's play does not necessarily endorse the idea that "on est complètement prisonnier de notre condition sociale" (as something generalizable, across time and place, from these fictional characters), and certainly cannot require its audiences to do so. One of the markers of a "successful" play, book, or film, according to most critics and teachers, is its ability to generate multiple meanings, perhaps to mean different things to different people at different moments, and to hold different meanings in tension. Kechiche's inventive transposition of Marivaux into film and into the suburbs is, to my mind, a particularly good illustration of this sort of polysemy and plasticity. And part of the teacher's job when dealing with something like Marivaux's play—or Kechiche's film—is to allow the students to test out their own varied reactions and interpretations. A text's politics, which is not determined by authorial origin or intention, cannot be inferred from immanent critical analysis alone; it must be considered as a matter of "impact," through the experiences as well as the meanings the text offers, in whatever broad and shifting realms of reception it reaches. Those realms are shaped and mediated in significant ways by critics and teachers, but not ruled by them. And it is in those realms, where reactions reach far beyond any simple process of recognition or identification, that any play carries significance, and that its meanings take substance. Some of the students in *L'Esquive*, irrespective of what the teacher says, and despite the obstacles that their society puts in their way, adapt to her unadapted curriculum, throw themselves into it, and take something positive from it.

All of this implies that the formal or aesthetic dimensions of Marivaux's play, or anything comparable that we may study—the way it offers a layered experience of affective complexity and allows a proliferation of possible meanings—have a close and positive relationship with how democratic education can work at its best, fostering participation and the "esprit de discussion." That sort of positive emphasis on artistic forms has shaped my own discussions of the films in this chapter, and how I envisage its possible interest to other critics/teachers/students, just as it shapes what I (and many others in the "humanities") do in the classroom when teaching film or literature. This sort of idea of "form" also helps us see, and articulate, the value of something like Souleymane's photographic self-portrait, despite what I described earlier as the limits of François's attempts to help Souleymane: the fact that the opportunity for self-representation was somewhat formalized and creative (to a degree that it is not in incidental speech, say, or choice of clothing) was a precondition of whatever educational success the exercise had as well as whatever aesthetic success he achieved, helping him to come out of himself a little, and communicate better with those around him.

This leaves us with many questions about how we choose what we teach, the norms that, as teachers, we may seek to sustain, adapt or overturn, and how we factor in what we know or assume about the identities of our students. The context of our choices today is not only the current "decolonial" scrutiny of the origins and identities of writers and filmmakers, students, and teachers, but the educational and critical history that this chapter has both evoked negatively and drawn on. I have depicted that history as compromised by its entanglements with a racialized, gendered nationalism, but it has also helped create spaces, methodologies, and vocabularies allowing people in schools and universities to teach and write about literature, theater, and film. I have emphasized in this final section that those spaces are opened up and sustained partly through careful attention to the "aesthetic" dimensions of medium, form, narrative construction, and so on; but it must also be emphasized that nobody has ever constructed a curriculum according to purely formal or aesthetic criteria, and that aesthetic criteria have never been pure. Within this history, to which film is a latecomer, anyone with aspirations as the author or creator of the kind of work that other people might take seriously, and might even study, has been disadvantaged by being a woman, by having skin that isn't (categorized as) white, and even, in a sense, by being alive.

If I have chosen, in this chapter and sometimes in the classroom, to talk about *Entre les murs* and *L'Esquive*, the reasons include the fact that those films have helped me think again, and encouraged me to think harder, both about what is worth keeping from a certain literary/ pedagogical tradition, aesthetically and pedagogically, and about how and why it might be "adapted"—questioned, extended, and altered.[22] It is also because, after all this, I am still not entirely sure what to make of them. In writing about these films, and in discussing them with colleagues and students, my mind has kept changing. It has mattered to me that both films treat the endless renegotiation of identities as an ongoing part of the work of cinema and of education alike; and—or but— it has mattered to me too that both, in their different ways, seem to draw on and sustain the assumption that an encounter and negotiation with alterity is among the things making literature, theater, and film valuable, in themselves and in the classroom. In Kechiche's film, of course, this includes the alterity of the past and of older forms. The real and imagined distance between Marivaux and the students in *L'Esquive*, an aesthetic matter as well as a matter of history and identity, is part of what allows their array of responses, and brings pleasure to them, or some of them; and the interplay it stimulates between identity and alterity allows them a kind of distance on themselves—and so, perhaps, indirectly, insight into themselves. The artistic forms that allow people to "express" themselves, and that allow writers and filmmakers to speak to other people across significant cultural distances, also take us outside ourselves; and those forms and their languages are never just, and never quite, our own.

Works Cited

Bégaudeau, François. 2006. *Entre les murs*. Paris: Gallimard.

Besserve-Bernollin, Lucette. 1981. "Adaptation de l'idéalisme des textes aux réalités algériennes." In *1830–1962: des enseignants d'Algérie se souviennent … de ce qu'y fut l'enseignement primaire*, edited by Émile Hazan, Henri Saurier et al. 131–47. Toulouse: Éditions Privat.

Billiard, Auguste. 1899. *Politique et organisation coloniales: principes généraux*. Paris: Giard & Brière.

Brozgal, Lia. 2019. "Seeing Through Race in Contemporary French Cinema." *L'Esprit créateur* 59.2 (Summer), special issue: *Race and the Aesthetic in French and Francophone Cultures*, edited by Cécile Bishop and Zoë Roth: 12–24.

22   One interesting pedagogical/critical response to this complex landscape is the anthology *Entre-Textes: Dialogues littéraires et culturels* edited by Panaïté and Klekovkina (2018).

Cantet, Laurent, dir. 2008. *Entre les murs/The Class*. London: Artificial Eye, 2009. DVD.

Christopher, James. 2009. "The Class." *The Times*, February 26. https://www.thetimes.co.uk/article/the-class-8rkwtwh87x6. Accessed April 2, 2021.

Debril, Laurence. 2008. "Pour Xavier Darcos, *Entre les murs* est 'l'histoire d'un échec pédagogique.'" *L'Express*, September 26, 2008. https://www.lexpress.fr/education/pour-xavier-darcos-entre-les-murs-est-l-histoire-d-un-echec-pedagogique_576469.html. Accessed April 2, 2021.

Elkharraz, Osman, with Raymond Dikoumé. 2016. *Confessions d'un acteur déchu: De* L'Esquive *à la rue*. Paris: Stock.

Gomot, Guillaume. 2014. "Lisette en Seine-Saint-Denis: le marivaudage en jeu dans *L'Esquive* d'Abdellatif Kechiche." In *Marivaudage: théories et pratiques d'un discours*, edited by Catherine Gallouët with Yolande G. Schutter, 227–40. Oxford: Voltaire Foundation.

Goodman, Lanie. 2008. "Top of the Class." *The Guardian*, May 27: 28.

Gueye, Abdoulaye. 2010. "The Color of Unworthiness: Understanding Blacks in France and the French Visual Media through Laurent Cantet's *The Class* (2008)." *Transition* 102: 158–71.

Guiney, M. Martin. 2004. *Teaching the Cult of Literature in the French Third Republic*. London: Palgrave Macmillan.

——. 2017. *Literature, Pedagogy, and Curriculum in Secondary Education: Examples from France*. Cham: Palgrave Macmillan.

Harris, Brandon. 2008. "Social Studies." *Filmmaker* 17.1 (Fall): 100–03, 127–28.

Harrison, Nicholas. 2019. *Our Civilizing Mission: The Lessons of Colonial Education*. Liverpool: Liverpool University Press.

Hartnoll, Phyllis, and Peter Found, eds. 1993. *The Concise Oxford Companion to the Theatre*. First edition 1972; new edition. Oxford: Oxford University Press.

Kechiche, Abdellatif. 2003. *L'Esquive/Games of Love and Chance*. New York: New Yorker Video, 2006. DVD.

Mayo, Peter. 2014. "Gramsci and the Politics of Education." *Capital and Class* 38: 2: 385–98.

Migé, Alain, ed. 2006. Marivaux, *Le Jeu de l'amour et du hasard*. Paris: Petits Classiques Larousse.

O'Shaughnessy, Martin. 2015. *Laurent Cantet*. Manchester: Manchester University Press.

Panaïté, Oana, and Vera A. Klekovkina, eds. 2018. *Entre-Textes: Dialogues littéraires et culturels*. Abingdon and New York: Routledge.

Sachs, Leon. 2014. *The Pedagogical Imagination: The Republican Legacy in Twenty-First-Century French Literature and Film*. Lincoln: University of Nebraska Press.

Sermain, Jean-Paul. 2013. *Marivaux et la mise en scène*. Paris: Desjonquères.

Shea, Louisa. 2012. "Exit Voltaire, Enter Marivaux: Abdellatif Kechiche on the Legacy of the Enlightenment." *The French Review* 86:6 (May): 1136–48.

Steiner, George. 1967. "To Civilize Our Gentlemen." In *Language and Silence: Essays 1958–66*, 75–88. London: Faber & Faber.

Stoppel, Karl, ed. 2010. *Entre les murs: scénario de François Bégaudeau, Laurent Cantet et Robin Campillo*. Stuttgart: Reclam.

Strand, Dana. 2009. "Etre et Parler: Being and Speaking French in Abdellatif Kechiche's *L'Esquive* (2004) and Laurent Cantet's *Entre les murs* (2008)." *Studies in French Cinema* 9:3: 259–72.

Swamy, Vinay. 2007. "Marivaux in the Suburbs: Reframing Language in Kechiche's *L'Esquive* (2003)." *Studies in French Cinema* 7:1: 57–68.

Tarr, Carrie. 2007. "Reassessing French Popular Culture: *L'Esquive*." In *France at the Flicks*, edited by Darren Waldron and Isabelle Vanderschelden, 130–41. Newcastle: Cambridge Scholars Publishing.

Vincendeau, Ginette. 2009. "The Rules of the Game." *Sight & Sound* 19.3 (March): 34–36.

Williams, James. 2012. *Space and Being in Contemporary French Cinema*. Manchester: Manchester University Press.

Wood, Michael. 2009. "At the Movies." *London Review of Books* 31:5 (March 12): 8.

CHAPTER NINE

Cinematic Transpositions of the "Republic"?

Fatima and *D'une pierre deux coups*

Vinay Swamy

I. Prelude: Transposition and the Tempered Scale

Transpose: Write or play (music) in a different key from the original: "the basses are transposed down an octave"

Oxford English Dictionary

The sensibilities of Western music, I am told, were different, when Johann Sebastian Bach (1685–1750) first composed his now classic music for *The Well-Tempered Clavier* (BWV 846–93). At the cutting edge of new soundscapes in an otherwise untempered world of music, Bach's work for the keyboard showcased his prowess in the new musical space, made available since the advent of the concept of tempering—the alteration of musical distance between each semitone in a musical scale, rather than following the strict harmonic progression that produces notes in a particular key—allowed, for the first time, by approximating the same ratio in the intervals between notes, the possibility of transposition[1] and

---

1   Transposition is a concept that is intimately linked to Western music, given that musical notes in this system have been conventionally linked to a fixed pitch (440 Hz is a concert A). As a point of comparison, in other musical systems, such as in Indian classical music, for instance, the fundamental note (Do in the Western solfege system, or Sa in most Indian languages) does not have a fixed pitch. Rather, the entire scale is dependent only on the tonic (Sa) chosen by the musician based on

modulation[2] from one key to another with relative ease. Prior to the use of a tempered scale, modulating from say the key of C major to G# minor was not practically possible given that those keys are not related to each other in the harmonic series that form them, and because the musical distance between the notes in each key varies according to their specific harmonic relationship. For instance, though the triads CEG (C major) and E♭ G B♭ indicate major chords, the intervals between these notes would not be identical in the untempered scale, making them sound slightly different. Bach's brilliance and musicality allowed him to tap into the newly tempered keyboard to transport his public from the home key of C (for instance) through clever cadences and modulations to various other keys, creating surprises and unexpected shifts and transpositions, before bringing us back home to C, for a final and satisfying resolution, all with mathematical precision. Even in this new well-tempered context, transposition, and modulation, though much more feasible, still brought out the different colors of each key (due to the slight but audibly different ratios between intervals) through which the music traveled.

At the turn of the twentieth century the revolution of the tempered clavier took a new turn. With the introduction of equal temperament, the distance between each of the 12 semitones in the octave was rendered equal (to the twelfth root of 2).[3] This further innovation made available to the musician (and their audience)—through further approximation— a larger palate of sounds. Composers such as Debussy and Schoenberg among others capitalized upon this expanded palate, and paved the way for others, who have since explored atonal relationships, thus, at the outset, affording a richer understanding of the musical possibilities, with no "home" key. Even with a home key, unlike in an untempered scale based purely on harmonic progression, or even with the tempered scale first championed by Bach and in vogue in the eighteenth and nineteenth centuries, one can now transpose a piece to a key of choice, without changing the relationship between the various notes. However,

---

their voice or the instrument's timbre. Thus, the question of transposition does not arise in the same way. For more see T. M. Krishna (2013, 49–51).

2   Bach often uses the "circle of fifths"—CGDAEBF—to modulate from one key to its relative a fifth apart.

3   For more on the physics of this temperament, see the Reading Feynman Blog entry on the twelfth root of 2 at https://readingfeynman.org/tag/12th-root-of-2/, accessed November 4, 2020.

on further exploration, it becomes clear that this form, now ubiquitous in modern Western music, produces a certain homogenization of sound. Thus, if the possibility of transposition, in Western music, has become much more flexible within an equal-tempered environment, such transpositions retain a certain homogeneity of color that has been key to the auditive (un)learning process and expectations in the twentieth and twenty-first centuries.

In other words, though the modern ear has become accustomed to the additional transposition—from Bach's well-tempered clavier to an equally tempered modern piano—what is gained in the flexibility of transposition championed by the Baroque composer comes at the expense of the flattening of the color of a well-tempered scale.[4]

II. Theme and Variation: Cinema and Nation

Cultural studies in particular underscores cinema as a medium that expresses the specificities of a culture, a society, a nation, but also as one that plays a significant role in shaping those very institutions. I'd like to borrow some cogent propositions from Susan Hayward's influential 1993 tome *French National Cinema* to reflect on this give and take, on how cinema partakes in the construction of the myth of the nation. Going back to Benedict Anderson (1983), Hayward reads the nation as that imagined community that is born of the interplay of the tension between difference and continuity. The first because even the most revolutionary universalist thought needed to be harnessed by recognizing and acknowledging the limits of such universalism

---

4 As Michael Rubenstein clearly explains, on a well-tempered piano, "major chords in the keys of C or F are very stable compared to in the keys of C# or F#. This is a result of the former having major thirds that are more in tune. One can hear this without being an expert. For instance, playing a C and an E two octaves higher, one gets a major third that sings for a long time. However, doing the same thing with F# and A#, the major third does not sing as richly. Rather, one gets a wavy texture, with the third pulsating in a manner that gives it a feeling of instability and excitability. Further, in Thomas Young's temperament, because there are several perfectly tuned 5ths and 4ths, and depending on which key, some other very close intervals, the piano resonates like a gorgeous chime when the sustain pedal is pressed thus freeing the other strings to resonate in sympathy with whatever sounds are present." http://www.math.uwaterloo.ca/~mrubinst/tuning/tuning.html, accessed November 4, 2020.

through difference—linguistic, ethnic, or other.[5] The second, through the invocation of a so-called continuous history—such as the daily plebiscite that Ernest Renan famously discussed in 1882—that gives us a myth of unbroken lineage, into which we, as individuals, are meant to insert ourselves in the present. In considering cinema, Hayward suggests seven typologies that might help us articulate how the "National" is enunciated and projected (1993, 6–16). Of particular interest here are the last two, concerning questions of framing—cinema of the center and cinema of the periphery—and dialectical construction—cinema as the mobilizer of the nation's myths and of the myth of the nation. In what follows, I will return to both these productive categories. I hope to show how pursuing the last two Hawyardian categories might be helpful for us to understand how such films interpellate the national and in so doing, foreground questions of belonging. In particular, my goal is to trace the short but hopefully revealing genealogy of a certain kind of cinema, that has strived to make place for Maghrebi immigrants and their descendants in France, a population that long remained invisible in various representations of the French nation.

In his edited volume *French Cinema in the 1990s*, Phil Powrie (2000) takes up Hayward's development of continuity and difference and situates the relationship between cinema and the nation in a discussion of the major political and economic changes that were afoot in that decade: the French cultural exception rule was invoked for cinema in the 1993 round of the General Agreement on Tariffs and Trade (GATT) negotiations (GATT evolved soon afterwards into the World Trade Organization), the nascent political power of the European Union,[6] and the rise of the historical film or *film de patrimoine* (which goes back to the idea of Hayward's first category of narrative). With the political organization of many directors (especially around the crisis of the refugee evacuation from the Saint Bernard Church in August 1996),[7] there was a parallel rise of the social-realist mode of cinematic expression. Thus,

---

5   This dependence on such specific tools is convincingly explored by Etienne Balibar in "The Nation Form: History and Ideology" (1991).

6   This growing political union was most notable with the Schengen agreement (1985), which dismantled internal borders over the next decade, as well as the Maastricht (1992) and Lisbon (2007) treaties, which further consolidated the political union.

7   For a cogent analysis of the Saint Bernard crisis, see Mireille Rosello's *Postcolonial Hospitality* (2001).

cinema, as other cultural political institutions are wont to do, can also function as a *projection nationale*, to use the 1998 formulation by the *Cahiers du cinéma* critic, Jean-Michel Frodon.

All these developments are equally important for us to consider when discussing a corpus of films that has foregrounded the relationship between Maghrebi migrants (and their descendants) and the French Republic, and have slowly but surely made their mark on the world of cinema since the mid-1980s, while, as I have argued elsewhere (2011), sometimes upholding certain conventional interpretations of the Republic. As such, these films have been partaking in constructing, as much as being mobilized by, the myth of the nation.

Since the mid-1980s, *Beur* and *banlieue* filmmaking, to use terms first proffered by Carrie Tarr (2005), have traced the particular histories of immigrant and marginalized populations that have otherwise gone largely underrepresented in French cinema. As the terms *Beur* and *banlieue* indicate, this cinema has often been characterized by the way in which it privileges representations of the mostly unequal relationship between mainstream France and those in the margins of French society, both quite literally—given the peripheral locations of the suburbs or *banlieues*—and culturally speaking, as indicated by the adjective *beur* (a qualifier for descendants of Maghrebi immigrants to France), which, as contested as it might be, has nevertheless gained currency and has been frequently used by the media since the last decade of the twentieth century.

Early adaptations such as Mehdi Charef's 1985 film *Thé au harem d'Archimède* clearly foregrounded not only the spatial separation between urban metropolitan France and the *banlieue*, but also, and crucially, the geo-cultural divide that it had come to connote. The title of the novel-turned-film is of course a reference not only to the lack of (access to) cultural capital for the principal characters, but also to the failure of the state to integrate these marginalized youths through its principal institutional tool that is the Republican school.

In this still (Figure 9.1), we have that moment clearly enacted as Balou (Charly Chemouny) struggles to spell "théorème" at school. This moment poignantly foregrounds the fundamental failure of Republican education in fulfilling its integrative mission. By screening how such myths are mobilized, the film puts pressure on hegemonic production of the myth of the nation. Also, in situating this critique within a framework of center versus periphery—both quite literally with the *banlieue*, and through the film's own peripheral position within the French cultural

Figure 9.1 Balou (Charly Chemouny) struggles to spell "théorème"
in *Thé au harem d'Archimède*. Mehdi Charef 1985.

landscape, Charef's film reveals the unquestioned assumptions that prop up the construction of the nation's myths. The film privileges spaces akin to what Marc Augé (1992) has described as *non-lieux*, or transient spaces, in which human beings remain anonymous, spaces in which do not hold enough significance to be regarded as *lieux*.[8] In this context, films such as Charef's critique the impression that the *banlieue*, for many intramuros Parisians, doubles up as *non-lieu*. Throughout Charef's film, Balou and his friends hang out in the garbage-ridden "terrain vague" in the liminal areas between *banlieues*, thus foregrounding that the supposed *non-lieu* that is the banlieue is in fact not only inhabited, but also very much a *lieu* that matters.

Skipping ahead a decade, perhaps the most cited example that represents in explicit terms the tension resulting from the imbalance in

8   Augé includes spaces such as airports, hotel rooms, freeways, or shopping centers, as exemplars, as no individual inhabits such spaces, and for most (except those who work there), the transitory nature of their interaction with the space renders them different in our minds from *lieux*, or places, which are imbued with significance. Thus, our interactions with space are very much colored by the status accorded to them. Of course, the perception of space as *non-lieu* or *lieu* is subjective, depending on the individual's perspective.

power dynamics between the "center" and the "periphery" is Mathieu Kassovitz's 1995 film, *La Haine*. Much has been written about the film. So, I'll just note that although the film depicts 24 hours in the lives of three young men from the *banlieue*, on a very particular day after riots, this film was taken by many as having documentary value. President Chirac held a screening to allow his cabinet to "understand" the *banlieue* (in the singular).[9] The film pays little attention to women's perspectives, nor does it foreground intergenerational relationships. Yet, ironically, this film about the periphery and the marginalized came to command cultural capital that Hayward would characterize as the privilege of a cinema of the center. The protagonists turned into the iconic "black, blanc, beur" trio, mirroring and indeed evoking that other ur-symbol of the French nation, the "bleu, blanc, rouge" or the tricolor flag of the Republic. Of course, many have shown the myopic nature of such an analogy (Konstantarakos 2000; Vincendeau 2005), and exposed the problematic—to say the least—stereotyping that such an appellation engendered.

Evidently, several other contemporaneous films were more nuanced in their portrayal of the life of Maghrebi immigrants and their descendants in France (Tarr 2005; Durmelat and Swamy 2015). As I have stated elsewhere (Swamy 2015), while Malik Chibane's trilogy (*Hexagone* (1994), *Douce France* (1995), *Voisins voisines* (2005)), for instance, did not receive popular endorsement to the same degree as *La Haine*, or enjoy the same critical acclaim as later films that depict so-called *banlieue* life, they nevertheless present a more coherent retrospective view and underscore both temporal links and spatial continuities in their representation of integration in France. Abdellatif Kechiche, for his part, began his career by presenting a complex and nuanced approach to the question of the center versus the periphery. His second film, *L'Esquive* (2004), which depicts high school students from the *banlieue* preparing to enact a play by Marivaux, won four Césars, including best picture, director, screenplay, and upcoming actress, Sara Forestier, whose career was launched by this film. In staging the seventeenth-century classical playwright's work, and its critique on-screen, Kechiche sets up an elaborate rhetorical device that allows us to compare at several levels the

9 In light of the cinematic celebration of *non-lieux*, the reductive if not irreducible, nature of the singular ought to be eschewed, especially since banlieues—in the plural—are marked by class and ethnic, not to mention political and cultural, diversity.

structures of both the film and the play on the one hand and the contemporary social debate on the place of the *banlieue* in the imaginary of the French nation on the other. In its diegesis, the film presents for consideration a new narrative of national belonging—after all, the so-called marginalized teenagers of the *banlieue* are not only able to code-switch adeptly between argot and classical French; their play production clearly puts the question of whose cultural capital Marivaux has turned into, and thus, who can be considered French. In addition, with its success, the film—as consecrated cultural object—forged its way into Hayward's center, through legitimization with its Césars, that is to say, and became an icon of French Cinema. Kechiche's own star rose, as he went on to make other award-winning features.

Sketching this short cinematic genealogy allows us to observe that since the early 2000s, there has been a qualitative shift: filmmakers of Maghrebi descent are no longer limiting themselves to foregrounding subjects related to the migratory experience of their families. For instance, Rabah Ameur-Zaïmèche—whose first feature *Wesh wesh qu'est-ce qui se passe* (2002) was celebrated for highlighting *Beur* and *banlieue* filmmaking—and Kechiche have turned their focus to other contexts and subjects.[10] Similarly, many *Beur* actors have gone on to fashion successful careers as stars in films in which they are no longer just being cast as characters of Maghrebi origin: Roschdy Zem (*Happy Few*, 2010), Sami Bouajila (*De vrais mensonges*, 2010) or Sabrina Ouazani (various TV appearances), to name but three. Thus, as scholars (Higbee 2013; Durmelat and Swamy 2015) have observed in the more recent past, as categories, neither *Beur* nor *Banlieue* filmmaking can any longer fully encompass the large variety of films that might be loosely identified in this corpus, nor can they solely account for a noticeable shift that began a few years after the turn of the millennium. Even with those films that do foreground Maghrebi presence in France, their approach to questions of integration has changed. This shift—a transposition, if you will—has to do with the way the films position their observations on integration, and what *a prioris* their critiques unveil.

Thinking in terms of Bach and his music for the well-tempered clavier helps clarify this observation. For contemporary interpretations of French republicanism have tended to operate in an environment analogous to the equal-tempered scale on which most twenty-first-century musicians

---

10   See for instance *Vénus noire* (2010) and *La vie d'Adèle* (2013) by Kechiche or *Les chants de mandarin* (2011) and *Histoire de Judas* (2015) by Ameur-Zaïmeche.

play Bach's preludes and fugues. The flexibility being able to transpose Bach's music is akin to the French nation's stated egalitarianism and blindness to difference (*la logique universaliste oblige*). However, although transpositions in such spaces are smooth, and the prelude in C can be played in D or F, and the large majority of people would not tell the difference (not having absolute pitch), what is flattened in this equal-tempered environment is the loss of the color of the music that Bach's well-tempered scale still preserved. Perhaps, then, creating and operating within a well-tempered environment—as these films seem to do—would allow us to appreciate color and difference within a Republican framework. I would like to offer two examples, to illustrate my point.

III. Fugue in Two Parts: Of Maids and Mothers

D'une pierre deux coups (2016), a first feature-length film by Fejria Deliba, is the site of productive transposition of several long-standing dialogues and debates about France's history with respect to Maghrebi immigration and the face of the present-day French nation. Deliba, who herself is of Maghrebi origin, acts in a new (transposed) capacity, moving from being the object of the camera as Zouina—the intrepid young immigrant in Yamina Benguigui's *Inch'Allah dimanche* (2001)—to the auteur of a film that presents a very different face of the Republican family. The nagging question of the legitimacy or the tenuous nature of belonging to a French space that has plagued descendants of Maghrebi immigrants in France is transposed in this film into an act of recognizing in a matter-of-fact manner the complex ways in which immigration has contributed to creating a new, if transposed (in the well-tempered environment) variation that we still recognize as the French nation.

Origin does not matter to Zayane—played by the exuberant Milouda Chaqiq (also known as Tata Milouda), the popular slam artist who began to engage in this artform later in life—the feisty 76-year-old mother of 11 and the long-term resident of a *cité* close to Paris. In fact, when her younger friend Amel (Brigitte Roüan) suggests that they take a trip to celebrate her birthday, noting that the older woman has not "dépassé les frontières de la cité" except to visit her daughter's hair salon, Zayane quickly retorts: "J'ai pas besoin de déplacer [*sic*] la frontière ... pourquoi faire?" thus pushing back on Amel's light critique! This charming malapropism is indeed not a Freudian slip, which might be attributed to an immigrant unsure of their place in French society. Rather, Zayane's seemingly dismissive statement in fact transposes the debate around the policing of external (national) and its internal (cultural, class) borders in order to bring our attention to a space that is delineated as one of Zayane's own making, and one in which she is eminently comfortable. In this moment, Zayane's emphatic statement reveals an underlying comfort about her social belonging (and thus citizenship, even if not meant in the legal sense of the term) such that the tenuous position of the immigrant is no longer open for debate, despite our discovering that she does not know how to read or write. Although this is retrospectively unsurprising, given that it is not altogether uncommon for Maghrebi immigrants for her generation to be illiterate, Zayane's strong-willed character and ability to reach out for help when needed,[11] indeed show that the narrative of integration as one that necessarily includes *éducation à la française* has been transposed in Deliba's film and can be played out in a different key, as it were: in the variation that Zayane plays out, integration is certainly not dependent on the twin pillars of literacy and public education that have upheld the Republic since the late nineteenth century.

The world and life for Zayane, then, centers around her apartment. Although her children have left the familial nest, they are nevertheless still very much in touch with, and depend on, their mother (if not each other). The arrival of the death notice of her former employer, Michel Chevalier—for whom she had worked as a maid in pre-independence Algeria prior to migrating as a newly-wed to metropolitan France—upsets the fine equilibrium that Zayane has achieved in her life, having settled in a Parisian suburb for over 50 years. Chevalier's widow, Christine, adds in the obituary notice that there is a box of Zayane's belongings waiting for her in the Chevaliers' home in Cheverny.

Thus begins an adventure in time and space for Zayane who sets out on a quest to recuperate her mysterious belongings. Not having seen Christine since she married and left her job as maid to move to France brings up various emotions for Zayane, and she reveals—to Amel— for the first time that she had a secret love interest, Michel's photo

---

11   We are privy to at least three instances of Zayane asking for help: from a young man by the bus stop who reads a death announcement that she receives; from a neighbor who writes a note that Zayane leaves for her children on her refrigerator door; and from a couple at a station who help Zayane to call Amel after she has lost her way.

Figure 9.2 Amel (Brigitte Roüan) and Zayane (Milouda Chaqiq) on the road in *D'une pierre deux coups*. Deliba 2016.

studio assistant, whom she had to forego as her marriage had already been arranged by her family. The two star-crossed lovers respect their families, but keep in touch through the silent super 8 movies that Zayane makes and sends in exchange for passionate audio cassette recordings from her lover. Years later, when the erstwhile assistant decides to return to Algeria, he entrusts the films he received to Michel Chevalier.

The drama that unfolds takes place in parallel (hence the title, *D'une Pierre deux coups*) as we follow Zayane on her road trip to recoup her belongings, while her adult offspring, frantic that their mother has gone "missing," congregate in her apartment and discover some of the secret (but chaste!) super 8 movies of a young Zayane and her love interest from their days as maid and intern in the Chevaliers' Algerian home and photo studio respectively.

The unveiling of Zayane's unspoken *histoire d'amour* is a drama that could take place in any family in France. Many in her generation had connections with Algeria, as Christine Chevalier acknowledges in a matter-of-fact manner. And Zayane's family too could be "any" French family. While the film seems aware of the portrayal of the family as a French family, it proffers a perspective on integration with more self-assured confidence than seen in films from previous decades about descendants of Maghrebi immigrants to France: her children are professionals (whether they are in the medical field, run businesses, or are employees in the service sector); they dress much like the rest of France,

Figure 9.3 Zayane's children discover their mother's romantic past
in *D'une Pierre deux coups*. Deliba 2016.

whether or not they are veiled; they smoke (or not), drink wine, and
have different religious and political persuasions. As Anne Diatkine
(2016) puts it, "Voilées, pas voilées, mariés ou pas, avec enfants et
statuts sociaux divers: ce pourrait être lourd, mais là encore, lors de cette
réunion familiale, Fejria Deliba déjoue les clichés."[12]

That several critics and reviews (Avoir-alire.com 2016; Diatkine 2016;
Lesinrocks.com 2016; Sotinel 2016) all remark on this last aspect—that
the film does not fall into the trap of clichés—signals that it avoids the
expectation of a certain portrayal of immigrants and their descendants
as maladjusted or struggling to integrate into French society. Moreover,
and perhaps more importantly, it is also an indication of the successful
transposition carried out by Deliba in the film in order to focus our
attention on difference not as a stereotype (or one that needs to be
"declined," to use Rosello's 1997 term), but as an integral part of the
(Republican) family. As such, Zayane's road trip and the revelation of
her secret also offers us a rich metaphor for France's own rediscovery

---

12 Louna (Linda Prevot Chaïb), for instance, speaks almost no Arabic, and
has married a non-Maghrebi French person, and wears blond wigs and "figure-
enhancing" pads, while her sister Leyla (Myriam Bella) wears a hijab. Sofiane
(Farid Bouzenad), their brother, has married a white Frenchwoman—Marilyne—
who has converted to Islam and wears a burka.

of its past. As the author of the review in Slate.com (2016) eloquently phrases it, Deliba transposes Zayane into a space "qui la mène moins vers la province que vers le passé, territoire enfoui, à la fois passé affectif d'une femme et passé colonial de deux pays." I note here that the reviewer foregrounds not just a migrant's history (*territoire enfoui*) or that of the country of origin, but one that is shared by both nations—Algeria and France. It is this recognition of shared (post)colonial history, and thus shared memory that *D'une pierre deux coups* is successful at staging in parallel (the mother never shares a cinematic frame with her children, as they discover their mother's romantic—and the nation's colonial—past), giving us a renewed appreciation of the polyphonic harmonies (and discords) in the French Republic of the twenty-first century.

A remarkable fugal exploration in its own right, the work of Philippe Faucon—whose many films (*Samia* (2001), *Dans la vie* (2006), *La trahison* (2008), *La désintégration* (2012)) offer nuanced, non-dramatic readings of the on-the-ground workings and realities of postcolonial France—is a rich source for productively transposed understandings of the Republic. *Fatima* (2015), the film which won three Césars in 2016, and its title character are *remarquables*—in the French sense of the word—for there are many significant shifts and transpositions at play.[13] The film won the most coveted awards for best film, best adaptation, and most promising actress (Zita Hanrot). This recognition, much like that of Kechiche's films, moved Faucon's work from the margins of French cinema, focused on immigrant culture, to epicenter French high culture (much to the chagrin of some), and thus pushed that society to consider what constitutes art, and Frenchness, and indeed, to revisit Hayward, the interplay between the one and the other.

What is rare in Faucon's focus on a single middle-aged mother of Maghrebi origin is that the film makes the challenges of integrating Fatima's daughters ancillary to our understanding of the mother's own struggle to find a place in French society. Of course, Yamina Benguigui's 2001 film *Inch'Allah dimanche* had presented a young immigrant woman's struggles to establish a new life in the north of France in the mid-1970s. Yet, in this instance of Faucon's socio-realist filmmaking, 12 years after Benguigui's, and a good 40 years in diegetic terms, the major questions on the continued inequities related to class,

---

13   Adapted from Fatima Elayoubi's *Prière à la lune* (2006) and *Enfin, je peux marcher seule* (2011).

ethnic stereotyping and gender are all raised through the eponymous character Fatima played by a non-professional actress, Soria Zeroual. It is by identifying with her person that we, the viewing public, are led not only through a journey of understanding the obstacles associated with integration, but are also perhaps led to consider whether the notion of integration is truly and wholly dependent on assimilating language or partaking in so-called shared customs.

If Fatima's younger daughter is deeply entrenched in the now-familiar issues of rejection in a society that eschews difference, the elder daughter strives to improve her lot by submitting to that cruel but opportune mythical Republican equalizer, public education. Nevertheless, what we observe is not the same narrative of assimilation or integration that has now been told in many ways over the last three decades. Instead, Faucon, not for the first time (see his *Dans la vie* (2006)), focuses on the challenges that a middle-aged mother has to overcome for the benefit of her children.

In a key sequence (see Figure 9.4), which in my view is the veritable climax of the film, Fatima makes a breakthrough after months of suffering from a lingering but undiagnosable debilitating pain after a workplace accident. The film's viewers are presented with Fatima reading aloud to her sympathetic doctor a thought-provoking and indeed poetic rumination on her status as a maid and immigrant mother. The invisibility of her work and the dignity with which she carries out her responsibilities are thus rendered visible both to herself, and most importantly to the film's (French) audience.

Fatima's poetic production doesn't just relieve her from her phantom psychosomatic injury. In this moment, she becomes Faucon's challenge to the public and the nation to engage in a critical thought process about the meaning of integration. Thinking back to the still from Charef's 1985 film (Figure 9.1), the frame for such a discussion seems to have been transposed to another register. Apart from the simplicity of the camera work (a static close-up shot), I would like to signal some avenues for further exploration.

First, this is a 44-year-old woman in a hijab who speaks, and she reads out her composition in Arabic.[14] Thus the emphasis of the primacy of the French language as a vehicle for inclusion in the nation is put into question; and sartorial choice, though not made as a defiant

14   Many on the (far) right in France were quick to critique both these aspects as further indication of the erosion of so-called French values. See for instance Labbé 2016; Louyehi 2016.

Figure 9.4 Fatima (Soria Zeroual) explains her difficulties as a quasi-invisible immigrant worker and mother in *Fatima*. Philippe Faucon 2015.

activist statement, visibly challenges interpretations of the public (secular Republican) space as necessarily devoid of religious or cultural expression. In this sense, Faucon transposes the long-standing and acrimonious debate on headscarves and inclusion in France to simply demonstrate in a non-threatening manner the very real existence of people such as Fatima, and the integral nature of their contributions to the national fabric of today's France.

Furthermore, Fatima is able to foreground her struggles not only in terms of personal gain—one of her daughters is able to afford a professional education—she is also able to present most eloquently a critique of how the privileged render invisible the labor of innumerable Fatimas of the world, who are truly essential to the success, especially, of women of higher classes and society in general.[15] Thus, Faucon is able to transpose a potential discussion of the de facto basis of inclusion within the Republic based on perceived ethnic or cultural difference to one that reflexively centers around questions of class and gender inequities that are extant in French society today. The repetition of the words "Min doun Fatima"—without (some) Fatima—which creates a clearly audible poetic alliteration, does not just reduce the title character's first name to a

15 In this, an extended analysis might juxtapose Cherrie Moraga and Gloria Anzaldúa's *The Bridge Called My Back* (Persephone Press, 1981).

common noun. Here, I suggest it also presents an instance of "declining" the stereotype, to recall Mireille Rosello's 1997 formulation, with which the stigmatized, colonial connotation of Fatima, as a nameless domestic worker, is reappropriated by this Fatima—the Fatima with whom we now identify, our Fatima—to expose the normally hidden workings of labor relations in a neoliberal economy.

It is also worth noting that unlike in many other films of the 1980s and 1990s,[16] it is possible for Fatima to deliver her critique in a safe space within a Republican public institution that is the *Santé publique*, with a non-judgmental, if not encouraging, interlocutor. I would like to suggest that this is indeed a significant transposition in the framework of public discourse, which allows for Faucon to focus on aspects of the Republic and its goal of integration that would have otherwise fallen into the shadows of a narrow interpretation of *laïcité* using universalist logic.

Finally, there is another transposition worth noting. For Faucon, the context in which casting *Fatima* occurred was entirely different from that in first major film:

> Pour jouer les deux filles, c'était plus simple qu'à l'époque où j'ai tourné *Samia* [2001], il y a quinze ans, puisqu'aujourd'hui, ces jeunes femmes existent en agence, et se destinent à être comédiennes, ce qui n'était pas le cas alors … (Gester 2015)

I take these remarks as a bellwether for off-screen integration at work in French society. Casting Fatima's teenage daughters is now possible through professional agencies that maintain young Maghrebi actors on file, when even at the turn of the millennium, filmmakers had recourse to "*casting sauvage*" for there was no existing palette to choose from in commercial casting agencies. In referring to his previous film, *La désintégration* (2012), about the making of a terrorist, Faucon's statement perhaps is most eloquently revealing and a sign of the times as well:

> Quand on a présenté le film *Désintégration*, on a utilisé cette image: un arbre qui tombe fait plus de bruit qu'une forêt qui pousse. Avec *Fatima*, j'ai filmé la forêt qui pousse. (Develey 2016).

---

16   See for instance the literal and cinematic dénouement in *Douce France* (Malik Chibane, 1995), in which Farida, who had fought to keep her hijab on throughout the film, including in a feisty exchange at a cultural center in defense of an alternative interpretation of *laïcité*, decides to forego her hijab and thus implies a more integrated future (Swamy 2015).

This possibility of a silently growing forest explains why Sylvie Durmelat and I wondered if we could even talk of a cinema *Beur ou de banlieue* anymore (Durmelat and Swamy 2015). Furthermore, we suggested that perhaps there would be no more cinema about Maghrebi immigration per se. Rather, the French public now has access to films with directors and actors of Maghrebi origin who have acquired the legitimacy to narrate and act not only their own stories, but also, increasingly, those of others. These observations are not an expression of naive optimism about a society that has become more inclusive, far from it. Rather, this cinema continues to engage with Republican ideology in creative and critical ways that increasingly escape classification, and thus indicate that the questions of discrimination and social coercion, as they are posed both by the characters of the films and the directors and actors who make them, are more difficult to attach solely to (post)colonial migration. To think along with Faucon, perhaps we need to begin to pay more attention to the growing cinematic forest. In this, the question of belonging and place within society has been transposed from one that weighed heavily on "proof" (to be) provided by migrants and their descendants, to a phase in which such questions revolve more around the discords and new chromatic harmonies created by relationships now presented as entirely integral to the national space.

Coda

Since 1968, of the handful of women who have served as models for Marianne, the well-known allegory for liberty who serves as the most popular symbolic incarnation of the French Republic, a majority have been icons of French cinema.[17] While sculptures and other iconic representations of these women are not officially sanctioned by legislation, it is significant that the mayors' association of France votes regularly for a well-known personality in the public sphere and, more often than not, has chosen a cinema star to represent France as Marianne. In many ways, the election of these feminine matinée idols is not only the clearest instantiation of the direct rapport drawn between cinema and the French Republic but is also indicative of the

---

17 The following film stars were all elected as models for Marianne: Brigitte Bardot (1968), Michèle Morgan (1972), Catherine Deneuve (1985), Lætitia Casta (2000), Sophie Marceau (2012).

rich, multilayered and interdependent, if transposed, relationship that binds the two institutions. Soria Zeroual and Milouda Chaqiq—the actors who incarnated Deliba and Faucon's protagonists Zayane and Fatima—will probably never attain the status needed to be elected as the next Marianne—the Republican idol—by the mayors of France. Yet, in enacting the lives of everyday women (*non-remarquables*), as maids and mothers, Zayane and Fatima transpose their characters from being *figures absentes* into unlikely cinematic icons who not only shed light on those living in a perpetual peripheral social penumbra, but also lay bare some of the myths of the nation. In so doing, the performances by Chaqiq and Zeroual signal that Faucon and Deliba were right to spotlight new timbres and voices in the complex fugue that is the French Republic.

With their cinematic transpositions, filmmakers such as Faucon and Deliba allow us to rethink the role that films play in cultural discourse and their relationship with the (construction of the myth of the) nation. Like Bach's well-tempered explorations, their films too remind us that color and variation are part of a tempered Republic. These are interpretations that deliberately move away from an equally-tempered model, in which the French motto of *liberté, égalité, fraternité* is often narrowly interpreted as eschewing difference. If Deliba and Faucon are able to bring their French public to recognize difference as indeed inherent to the Republic, they can do so thanks in part to the three decades of filmmakers of Maghrebi descent, who worked to enrich the well-tempered environment.

Works Cited

Anderson, Benedict. 1983. *Imagined Communities: Reflections on the Origin and the Spread of Nationalism*. New York: Verso.

Augé, Marc. 1992. *Non-lieux, Introduction à une anthropologie de la surmodernité*. Paris: Seuil.

Avoir-alire.com. 2016. "D'une pierre deux coups—La critique du film." April 18. https://bit.ly/2kBxLs2. Accessed May 23, 2019.

Balibar, Etienne. 1991. "The Nation Form: History and Ideology." In *Race, Nation, Class: Ambiguous Identities*, 86–106. New York: Verso.

Develey, Alice. 2016. "Philippe Faucon: 'Réaliser *Fatima* a été une nécessité.'" *Le Figaro*. February 27. https://bit.ly/2LHK3LW. Accessed April 23, 2019.

Diatkine, Anne. 2016. "'D'une pierre deux coups,' voyage au centre de la mère." *Libération*. April 19. https://bit.ly/2kF8M7a. Accessed April 2, 2019.

Durmelat, Sylvie, and Vinay Swamy. 2015. "Postface." In *Les Ecrans de l'intégration: immigration maghrébine dans le cinéma français*, edited by Sylvie Durmelat and Vinay Swamy, 285–301. Saint Denis: Presses Universitaires de Vincennes.

Elayoubi, Fatima. 2006. *Prière à la lune*. Paris: Éditions Bachari.

——. 2011. *Enfin, je peux marcher seule*. Paris: Éditions Bachari.

Frodon, Jean-Michel. 1998. *La projection nationale: Cinéma et nation*. Paris: Odile Jacob.

Gester, Julien. 2015. "Philippe Faucon: 'je voulais mettre en avant des figures absentes à l'écran.'" *Libération*. October 6. https://bit.ly/2GscZ6T. Accessed April 23, 2019.

Hayward, Susan. 1993. *French National Cinema*. London and New York: Routledge.

Higbee, Will. 2013. *Post-beur Cinema: North African Émigré and Maghrebi-French Filmmaking in France since 2000*. Edinburgh: Edinburgh University Press.

Konstantarakos, Myrto. 2000. "Which Mapping of the City? *La Haine* (Kassovitz, 1995) and the *cinema de banlieue*." In *French Cinema in the 1990s: Continuity and Difference*, edited by Phil Powrie, 160–71. Oxford: Oxford University Press.

Krishna, T. M. 2013. *A Southern Music: The Karnatik Story*. New Delhi: Harper Collins.

Labbé, Florence. 2018. "Fatima aux César: le cinéma français célèbre le voile." *Riposte Laïque*. February 27. https://bit.ly/2kzBg2k. Accessed May 1, 2019.

Lesinrocks.com. 2016. "D'une pierre deux coups—Critique et avis par Les Inrocks." *Les Inrockuptibles*. April 15. https://bit.ly/2LcS62h. Accessed April 30, 2019.

Louyehi. 2016. "Le film 'Fatima' ou le politiquement correct en action, qui plaît tant aux bobos!" February 28. https://bit.ly/2J2RL1m. Accessed May 1, 2019.

Renan, Ernest. 1947–1961 "Qu'est-ce qu'une nation?" 1882 lecture. In *Œuvres complètes*, edited by Henriette Psichari, 887–906. Paris: Calmann-Lévy.

Rosello, Mireille. 1997. *Declining the Stereotype: Ethnicity and Representation in French Cultures*. Hanover, NH: University Press of New England Press.

——. 2001. *Postcolonial Hospitality: Immigrant as Guest*, Palo Alto: Stanford University.

Powrie, Phil. 2000. "Introduction." In *French Cinema in the 1990s: Continuity and Difference*, edited by Phil Powrie, 2–22. Oxford: Oxford University Press.

Slate.com. 2016. "'D'une pierre deux coups,' la malle aux trésors." April 19. https://bit.ly/2L9nq1S. Accessed May 2, 2019.

Sotinel, Thomas. 2016. "'D'une pierre deux coups': une saga familiale transmé-diterranéenne." *Le Monde*. April 19. https://bit.ly/2sumehV. Accessed February 2, 2020.

Swamy, Vinay. 2011. *Interpreting the Republic: Marginalization and Belonging in Contemporary French Novels and Films*. Lanham, MD: Lexington Books.

——. 2015. "Re-présenter les banlieues: *La Trilogie urbaine* de Malik Chibane." In *Les Ecrans de l'intégration: immigration maghrébine dans le cinéma français*, edited by Sylvie Durmelat and Vinay Swamy, 265–83. Saint Denis: Presses Universitaires de Vincennes.

Tarr, Carrie. 2005. *Reframing Difference: Beur and Banlieue Filmmaking in France*. Manchester: Manchester University Press.

Vincendeau, Ginette. 2005. *La Haine*. Urbana, IL: University of Illinois Press.

Films Cited

Ameur-Zaïmèche, Rabah. 2002. *Wesh wesh qu'est-ce qui se passe*. Haut et Court.

——. 2011. *Les chants de mandarin*. MK2.

——. 2015. *Histoire de Judas*. Potemkine Films.

Benguigui, Yamina. 2001. *Inch'Allah dimanche*. ARP Sélection.

Charef, Mehdi. 1985. *Thé au harem d'Archimède*. KG Production.

——. 1994. *Hexagone*. Studio Canal.

——. 1995. *Douce France*. Ciné Classic.

——. 1995. *Voisins voisines*. Noé.

Cordier, Anthony. 2010. *Happy Few*. Le Pacte.

Deliba, Fejria. 2016. *D'une pierre deux coups*. Haut et Court.

Faucon, Philippe. 2001. *Samia*. Pyramide.

——. 2006. *Dans la vie*. Pyramide.

——. 2008. *La trahison*. Pyramide.

——. 2012. *La désintégration*. Pyramide.

——. 2015. *Fatima*. Pyramide.

Kassovitz, Mathieu. 1995. *La Haine*. Studio Canal.

Kechiche, Abdellatif. 2004. *L'Esquive*. Rézo films.

——. 2010. *Vénus noire*. MK2.

——. 2013. *La vie d'Adèle*. Wild Bunch.

Salvadori, Pierre. 2010. *De vrais mensonges*. Pathé.

PART V

Musical Movements

CHAPTER TEN

"Sound" Tracks and Soundtracks

Clandestine Crossings, Film Aesthetics, Ethics, and Politics

Hakim Abderrezak

In this chapter, I examine the importance of sound in films that narrate migrants' and refugees' failed crossings of the Mediterranean Sea, and the space that sound *occupies* in these narratives.[1] It is not innocently that I use the term "occupy," because the addition of asynchronous sound can be out of place or take up unwarranted space. In short, this gesture has the potential to be a violent act. For instance, I consider the possible harm in placing extra-diegetic sound, such as music, over intradiegetic sound, such as voice. This exploration seems all the more critical when the narrative evokes the personal histories of those who have perished at sea or of those who retell the stories of the departed in an attempt to restitute their muffled voices or invoke memories of the deceased.

The cinematic treatment of clandestine migrations presents new challenges. One of them is how to reproduce the hurdles faced by harragas; namely, their plights and fights.[2] Among the challenges that

1   In order to not have to use both "migrants" and "refugees" to differentiate between two categories of people who cross the same sea in same types of modes of transport, hope to reach the same continent, and refer to themselves by way of Arabic terms, such as *harragas*, which convey more effectively the nature of their experience, from now on I will employ this Arabic term (*harragas* in the plural form and *harrag* in the singular), which is currently in circulation in various European languages.

2   As indicated in the previous note, *harragas* is the Arabic term used in the Maghreb to refer to individuals who migrate clandestinely.

the filmmakers face is how to express the dying process at the core of these films and sometimes to explain precisely what prompted them to take on the daunting topic of migration. Their dilemmas include how to depict death objectively when a film can also be made to raise awareness and to provide a platform for condemning the policies that police the sea. External aural material risks covering instead of unveiling. If perceived as noise, it might distract from awareness rather than attract responsiveness. This leads me to my main query: What is a "sound" soundtrack? Put differently: What, in the auditory components of a film, has restorative or non-destructive qualities? The dearth of studies concerned with sound in films dealing with clandestine sea-crossings and related themes justifies posing such questions. This chapter could have been titled "Toward a Theorization of Sound in Film about Clandestine Migration." Indeed, it lays down questions aimed to help build a theoretical apparatus for thinking about clandestine migration in cinema through one of its main components: the aural material that composes its fabric. The treatment of sound that "tracks" is essential in analyses of films depicting death and documenting harragas' lack of voice—figuratively and literally speaking. It invites us to think about how to treat the subject without falling prey to excessive pathos, especially in the works of directors who acknowledge their objective of soliciting empathy in their audience.

As Will Higbee rightly remarks, "This primacy of the image as the site of representation (and thus signification) of identity construction in film has meant that in the study of diasporic, postcolonial, and ethnic minority cinemas there has been relatively little space for a discussion of sound (and even less of film music)" (2009, 225). Film speaks, and it begs us to hear it too, as is suggested in the title of a text published by Oxford University Press, *Hearing the Movies: Music and Sound in Film History* (Buhler et al. 2010). What does film music narrate? Or what (part of the) story does it tell in "diasporic, postcolonial, and ethnic minority cinemas"? Films such as Chus Gutiérrez's *Retorno a Hansala* [*Return to Hansala*, 2008]—which will be briefly discussed here—and Merzak Allouache's *Harragas* (2009)—which I analyze toward the end—provide an excellent opportunity to tackle the issue of the foreign Other and the Other's foreign language as a probable second-time or second-hand invader. Indeed, productions whose scripts feature an inclusion—or intrusion—of a notable amount of language associated with a colonial past can be the ground—or battleground—for the return of the colonizer. The foreign language lands in the film armed with its own codes that presumably inflict the cross-cultural encounter with a hierarchy and an agenda. Foreign language is itself a sound, one that is sound or not, depending on whether it cohabits with the local vernacular or inhibits it. It would be wrong to think of sound as merely "an extra"—to use a cinematic term, in other words an element that has no significant role, for often it plays a crucial role in the narrative. Many recent works are based on real stories or real people, while others strive to reflect upon a real phenomenon through fiction. My attempt at hearing what sound has to say will be undertaken in the largest sense of the term, including what Will Higbee coined as "displaced voice," namely "multi-linguality and multi-vocality and heteroglossia" (2009, 226). In this chapter, sound will be understood to also mean film music and silence. The choice of post-production elements may constitute an important factor in revealing or burying elements of information about whom the soundtrack speaks. One could ask if sound replaces, rearranges, or restores the voices that characters/individuals never had, as their lives were characterized by adversity and their deaths shrouded in anonymity. My investigations, questions, and conclusions apply to a wide range of cinemas (e.g., Maghrebi, Middle Eastern, African, postcolonial, binational, multinational, global South, exilic, diasporic, "accented," etc.).[3]

Seeing and hearing go hand in hand in the experience of film watching, which is why an unraveling of underlying layers of meaning can be better achieved when an examination of sound accompanies that of sight. The study of sound has been marginalized in "diasporic, postcolonial, and ethnic minority cinemas." Yet this medium constitutes a key avenue in apprehending image and, in subtitled films, how sound appears or disappears is another important aspect in tracking the various practices employed to pass along or by-pass the original message. To this end, special attention will be paid to subtitles in foreign films and in particular the encounter between local image and foreign sound. The term "foreign" is to be tackled in its French sense, namely as both "foreign" and "stranger." The two words connote the common denominator "strange." I look at both the act of inserting external material in post-production, and the incorporation of unexpected, deterritorialized, or uncalled-for matter within the dialogue. Additional considerations arise from the

---

3 For an explanation of "accented cinema" and an excellent explanation of differences between several categories of world cinemas, see Hamid Naficy's *An Accented Cinema: Exilic and Diasporic Filmmaking* (2001).

choices and acts of injecting sound (understood here to cover a vast spectrum, from music to voice, language, and background noise). When material is added, is it layered on top of music that is performed *in situ*? Is it devised to tease out, enhance, supersede, or magnify? Does it burden or bury all elements instead? Do diegetic and non-diegetic non-visual elements work in alliance with or defiance of one another? Post-production editing is a valuable and necessary aspect of film production. While I recognize its importance and benefits, this chapter draws attention mainly to the possible shortcomings and hazards of certain add-ons, such as film music and subtitling that renders only a select amount of dialogue, for example. In this study my goal is to point at some of the questions that one has the right to ask when confronted with the association of image and sound, in particular when the latter is added in post-production that is influenced by exterior, external, and extensive forces—such as anti-immigration policies, deportation and detention practices. Thus, this short piece does not seek to answer the myriad questions posed but rather to assist in refocusing discussions of meaning by bringing sound into the picture and to demonstrate that sound, too, carries ethical inquiries worthy of concern for scholars of postcolonial and world cinema. In fact, film analysis ought to give more weight to sound—sound that is not always illustrative and decorative, but is more often than not the vector of various multifaceted dynamics, including geopolitical, ideological, neocolonial, and economic. These are all at the core of the phenomenon of clandestine cross-continental human movements, which—the scholarship argues and agrees—derives significantly from colonial, postcolonial, and neocolonial situations.

Elsie M. Walker aptly warns us,

> Though some soundtracks do not call attention to their own construction, we must be aware that they are all designed to create affective impact—to pretend otherwise is to assume the possibility of neutrality or unmediated authenticity. When it comes to approaching film from a postcolonial point of view, this can in itself be an insidious form of threats. (2015, 91)

This important reminder points at notions of intentionality and positionality. When one says "soundtrack," one thinks primarily of music, which is one of the mediums used to "create affective impact." It is not the only one, and many elements are regularly mobilized to direct or dictate our reading of the composite work commonly called "a film," which we say "we watch" but which in fact we watch *and listen to*. Then, is a soundtrack able to soothe the pain and sorrow of those who are reminded of their loved ones dying in the Mediterranean when watching/listening to a film that treats the perilous journey? What function does select music—intended to trigger our sympathy—play for the perished harragas, since they are no longer around to hear it? One could argue that it is a first attempt at building a memorial for them. It might be considered a gift for their loved ones and a contribution from the filmmaker to honor the memory of those whose lives were lost at sea. In fact, quite a few features contain a dedication "To the memory of ..." displayed on the screen in tandem with a song, a score, or silence. One "insidious form of threats" includes the failure to provide an alternative narrative to dehumanizing portrayals of harragas in media and politics where they are mentioned by way of numbers and statistics, or in images of masses and hordes that draw an impression of mobilized foreigners coming to invade European nations as they pour in—uninvited—on the southern countries' beaches. This threat is heightened by the widely accepted notion that dead bodies should not be shown. Yet distancing risks dissociation. Directors who made the decision to shoot the last moments of harragas' lives continue to be a minority. Chus Gutiérrez, for instance, in *Return to Hansala* made the choice to personalize the maritime journey in order to un-dehumanize harragas. Her project is clear and stated from the very beginning, in the first scene—well before the opening credits start appearing on the screen. Her method is a deferential one in that it enables harragas to take center stage in her film, before the identity of actors. The real identity of harragas is her focus and concern. The Spanish director not only zooms in on the dying process but purposefully lingers on it, accompanying the horrid visual depiction with the sound of gasping for air and suffocation underwater. In this production, the film score does not interrupt. It accompanies the individual as he exhales his last breath, in an effort to pay homage and to attempt to make the extra-diegetic viewers catch a glimpse of the horror of drowning by pulling them under the surface as the handheld camera shot reproduces the downward movement of the struggling body.

The practice of handling, choosing, and editing sound imposes its own commentary, be it personal, social, political, ideological, or economic. As a result, it has implications that provoke an interrogation of motivations. Other scholars have raised direct questions with regard to the relation of sound and image. Elsie Walker lists bullet-pointed questions in her article to show that this topic triggers more questions than provides answers. Among them are: "What forms of colonial and/or postcolonial reality does the sound track represent?" and "How does the sound track position the perceiver in relation to the characters? In particular, whose perspectives are we encouraged to hear most strongly?" (Walker 2015, 11). Asking questions about sound in cinema is all the more legitimate as colonial, postcolonial, neocolonial, (geo)political, ideological, institutional, and subliminal workings can be invisible to the spectator, or inaudible for that matter. Kevin J. Donnelly argues that in this mode of artistic production there are "occult aesthetics," to be understood as "hidden workings or processes that are unable to be observed" (2014, 1). Although a foreign language is not a hidden working, per se, it risks being easily perceived as an occult entity that escapes understanding in the best-case scenario, or must be remediated heavily by an abundance of subtitles, or obliterated altogether by dubbing. Conversely, it is possible for an outsider to perform hidden workings through a manipulation of the original work by adding material that does not belong to the culture or resonate with it. Before the opening credits appear in *Return to Hansala*, while the character drowns, the aforementioned soundtrack features an austere score meant to reproduce wailing as well as the pitiless nature of the sea in an attempt to solicit virtual empathy by proxy in the absence of physical proximity. Film scores are effective in eliciting emotion across national and cultural boundaries. Should foreign bodies always be conveyed in their foreign tongues? Certainly not, for the message must be grasped and this implies a translation. Then, must foreign sound be erased completely to only allow Western references? Certainly not, for sound encompasses more than words, and thus a Western audience can be receptive to messages in a foreign tongue—albeit incompletely—by means of the emotional power of music. Aware of the soundtrack's potential to exclude and essentialize, Gutiérrez weaves together the score with the Moroccan migrant's heavy breathing and the names of Spanish and Moroccan actors. Additionally, when she employs a song, she chooses one in Arabic, precisely to emphasize the local in order to better re-enact and personify the native experience, and to shy away from the pitfalls of colonial, postcolonial, neocolonial, (geo)political, ideological, institutional, and subliminal workings. The Arabic song plays while the final credits scroll on the screen and numbers (of dead harragas, capsized boats, drowned pregnant women, unaccompanied children, etc.) pop in and out until the final number 36.7—the body temperature of healthy individuals, regardless of nationality, ethnicity, gender, class, religion, language—closes the long list of figures. From the first scene characterized by the harrag's suffocating voice, to the last, where a man and a woman sing in Arabic to fluctuating and unreliable statistics and data superseded by a scientific fact, Gutiérrez gives voice to subjects who constantly turn into the objects of Western discourse, not only through image but also through sound.

Let me segue into a reflection on the key term around which this volume pivots, namely "transposition," and explain how I employ it and how it plays out in the context of films about clandestine passages across the Mediterranean and/or the burning desire to cross the sea.[4] *Trans-position* is a term that wholly applies to a discussion of clandestine *trans*-marine crossings, which stem from and tease out old and new powers that assign people and countries their *positions* on geopolitical and global maps betraying sharp divides along the lines of wealth, race, ethnicity, and religion. The act of transposing entails the process of translating, which equates to transforming, making something into something else, which can imply taking a sentence, a thought, someone, etc. somewhere else. For harragas, it is a dream, a goal, a promise—that of being taken to another place, ultimately physical but first imaginary by way of "leavism" and second-hand images, stories, and sounds of the West recounted by harragas and seen on TV screens.[5] But what happens when the transition or transmutation falls flat; in other words, when the transportation embedded in the frail mode of transference fails? Transposition is tightly tied to the notion of positionality in relation to the power relationships that demand that global South citizens stay home and by the same token paradoxically prompt them to seek a way out of their forced confinement. Transposition contains both the idea of a movement and the means that carries out the move (the fishing boat, called *bote, patera, cayuco, pirogue* in the sending or receiving countries). This concept is synonymous with the idea of a shifting positionality on the map, across borders, and across the sea, as harragas navigate between immigration policies and legal statuses. Accompanying soundtrack can be used to convey the changing positionality and personality of characters as they pass from one place to another (from country to country or from life to death).

The category of Mediterranean films treating failed crossings of the sea begin with, focus on, or end with death. The soundtrack is called

---

4 For an extensive study of clandestine crossings of the Mediterranean Sea in cinema, literature and music, see Abderrezak 2016.

5 "Leavism" is the strong desire to leave one's country clandestinely. For a complete definition of the term, see *Ex-Centric Migrations: Europe and the Maghreb in Cinema, Literature, and Music* (Abderrezak 2016).

bande originale in French, the literal translation of which is "original track." What is original (as in, organic) about a *bande* in a film about failed clandestine human movements when the depiction of death is obliterated? If the sound in a track is original, then theoretically it should be genuine and not synchronized. Yet ironically, repeatedly, the technical work done to construct the *bande originale* is made of countless ultra-sophisticated sound effects in an attempt to render the original material (more?) original. Is that sound or a trap? The organicity of the soundtrack in a film like *Return to Hansala* resides in the commitment to make the euphonic report without much artifice upon the euphoric (leavism, anticipation, suspense, and the departure) and the tragic (drowning, distress, or death). Post-production editing, which is always secondary, chronologically speaking—and arguably secondary in the sense of less time having been invested in the process—contributes unevenly to shaping the final object. Consequently, one could easily imagine that the "combined" voices of characters, actors, directors, editors, and other decision-makers who have a stake in the final product never share an equitable space, and that the more power secondary sources have, the less genuine the original work is. The prefix "trans-" contains the idea that something is meant to be crossed, which works very well in studies focused on trans-Mediterranean passages and what happens during the crossings—but also works on the screen after editorial work has been performed. Indeed, that work-over (such as voice-over) is another crossing. Voice-over and other techniques are frequently used props in cinema. Subsequently, post-production may help create sense by making connections (e.g., linguistic through subtitles, narrative through assembling shots, etc.) But it can also provide an avenue for distortion, which shows that it has the potency to cross (border)lines. In this light, there are crossings of various kinds taking place when image and sound are being worked on or over in a studio. Therefore, the image should not be the only medium one examines to discuss manipulation, voice, positionality, agency, and intentionality.

Subtitles, which physically cross the screen, track what is going on in the narrative in both action and sound. They transpose dialogues: they place them somewhere (at the bottom of the screen) other than in the place of elocution (the mouth, or the body when body language is in play). Subtitles are signs that add a layer onto the screen. In doing so they transpose, indicating that the meaning is somewhere else: in the translated form. Indeed, the non-native spectator only makes sense of what is being said verbally through what he knows: his own tongue in printed form. As a result, his understanding of the film is enabled by a mediation in which meaning is possible only if translated, transmuted, or transferred. It is a negotiation between what is being said and how to say it. Transposition and positionality are two keywords in postcolonial films in that, for a portion of their public, these productions are understood only thanks to subtitles. The prefix in "subtitle" itself harkens back to the idea of positionality. Their placement and their status in the hierarchy of meaning is presented as being of lesser importance ("sub"). But do subtitles occupy a subjective, subjugated, or subjected position? Subtitles appear to be a deceptively low-profile crutch, due to their location on the screen, but for the foreign audience they constitute the main means of meaning and thus hold high status. Indeed, they are the fundamental resource in communicating the sonic components of a film in one or several foreign languages. These props translate/transcribe/ describe sounds of a linguistic, circumstantial, musical, or natural nature. It must be remarked that it is not the act of subtitling that is subordinated but the subtitled content, since it becomes mere ground for the message in the foreign tongue, which constitutes the only message that is taken into account by the extra-diegetic viewer not familiar with the original language(s), having no other way to verify the accuracy, completeness, or veracity of the final product. Despite consistently lacking in many regards (quality, transparency, versality, etc.), subtitles establish the principal source of knowledge for the viewer, risking depreciating aural messages highly valuable in a particular culture or society.

Non-speakers of the local language(s) have no choice but to rely on the subtitles, which become the ultimate authority and provide the biased basis for their "understanding." Hence, the viewer enters a fraught relationship in which monolingualism prevents him from extricating himself from the abuse of power made possible through inaccurate or incomplete mistranslations. Subtitles are a forceful occupying presence in that they erase the original language and replace it with another. They do so not by imposing it auditorily as is the case in dubbed films but by being written over sound, which is problematic when the aural— already weakened in standing in contrast to action—is a dialect, for instance.[6] A dialect suffers from less recognition than a language, which

---

6 Dubbing, which I do not have the space to tackle here, takes the potential, full or partial erasing process one step further by making it impossible for the spectator to ascertain that all original sounds—even if not necessarily understood in the foreign language—have been carried over.

is traditionally associated with a recognized alphabet in a given society. It is commonly displaced by more established and privileged forms of the written word, those sealed with official status. The choice of language threatens an additional form of domination if the language in which subtitles appear happens to be that of a colonizer or of a central government denying legitimacy to the dialect and stripping its right to exist or coexist.

Subtitling is a necessary method—one that has a multitude of benefits that it regularly performs efficiently. This being said, one must take a close look at the process and its implications. The fact that what is at stake in the diegesis is subtitled subjects it to the process of translation and transposition (read "posed somewhere else"), in this case, on a lower portion of the screen (at the periphery) where the non-central or marginal components of the visual landscape are relegated. Subsequently, subtitling equates to subjecting to a dominating or domineering force that regulates speech and relegates it to the category "object of discourse." This extreme act of coopting corrupts the original product. We shall see next that mistranslation—partaking in misinformation—is another common instance of coopting and corrupting, albeit not necessarily voluntary. The position of subtitles outside the focus of the action and place of elocution consequently forces the audience to make a concerted effort to reproduce through the gaze and the movements of their heads the act of transposition. With the visual and corporeal back-and-forth and up-and-down movements, the viewers impersonate the pattern, which consists of taking the spoken word above to the printed word below, out of the mouths of enunciators and into the hands of editors. The danger for the spectators is to miss information if they do not perform this demanding task steadily. Concurrently, by doing so, they irremediably miss corporeal movements, such as facial expressions and gestures, that go hand in hand with verbal interactions and therefore participate significantly in creating meaning in most cultures. Yet they do not make it into subtitles. Conversely, closed captioning does tend to account for nonverbal language, which adds a potent layer of meaning.

We know that the process of transposition (translation and transcription) creates a loss of meaning. In the case of translation, from the Latin verb *translatus*, which means "carried over," something is being migrated, thus uprooting it from its primary, essential, and defining setting. As for transcription, Ferdinand de Saussure and René Magritte maintained that the signifier is not the signified. Subtitles take this process of denaturalization further in that they routinely summarize a dialogue and rarely provide a full and accurate translation. Some come in the form of a loose and truncated rendering that irremediably leads to fabrication. Others simply mistranslate: "Elsewhere, the voice might undergo a rather different trajectory. It may end up censored, translated, or mistranslated by subtitles—or far more infrequently, left untranslated, and therefore unintelligible to a local audience" (Whittaker and Wright 2017, 3). Such is the case when the voice-over in Arabic in *Harragas* reveals that 3,000 harragas were in the detention center where Rachid was sent immediately after walking onto the beach in Spain. Yet the subtitles in French mention only 300. This particular case of written transposition is egregious in its error. It misleads the extra-diegetic viewer. While the voice-over was added to inform the audience in one language, the subtitles missed the mark and misinformed the foreign audience.

Tracks are pathways. Therefore, a *sound*track is a healthy pathway expected to deliver the impeccable goods promised by a rigorous transaction, namely, a flawless translation. Subtitles claim to provide this service along horizontal tracks that transform sound into print. Indeed, the lines that they draw across the screen are supposed to recreate the lines uttered by actors in which words form sentences, sentences create dialogues, and verbal interactions move the plotline along. Sometimes, they limit themselves to summaries. This is frequently the case for fast or long tirades and for song lyrics. Indeed, songs can be wrongly reckoned as simple entertainment or a whimsical addition, and therefore treated as not worthy or noteworthy—in short, inferior to other sources of sound. Thus, less space is granted to them and a minimalist approach is deemed sufficient. Often, songs are cultural commentaries. Summaries are formats that contain only what is deemed important, leaving details out. However, what makes a summary may not be important for the "original" culture although what is left aside is conceivably crucial to understand said culture.

Montage (French for "editing") encompasses the editorial work applied to both image and sound. Paradoxically, montage is what "builds" a film. However, overediting defeats the purpose. As the French term has it, a faulty process dangerously flirts with its opposite goal, namely, tearing down (*démontage*). Montage is a reformatting, which can be overdone, in which case excessive "mounting" is equivalent to starting from scratch by scratching the original message out of the picture. This is an act of subjugation to a narrative, not that of the film but that of established discourses in the industry, shaping practices that have the final say in how to format knowledge. These hegemonic forces may be diverse—ideological and political but also linguistic and cultural. For example, when a song is in a dialect, it could be regarded as not fully translatable because of the widespread assumption that a dialect ranks lower than a language. The positioning of songs and other sensory markers under the privileged status of the image and over the narrative leads to another set of questions that bring us back to the notion of authority (who gets to decide what may be inserted) and intentionality (what is meant to have been achieved and who gets to be content with the content). Sound editors will translate or transcribe ambient sound such as singing in the original language, while others will omit to make reference to it in the target language. The latter practice in which the local (voice) is not transmitted to the global (audience) even by way of notation, such as "native music playing" or "woman singing in Arabic/Tamazight/French/Spanish" is representative of resistance. Editors could rebuke the allegation of resistance arguing for practical economy by explaining that they do not wish to clutter the screen. But then, how can ignoring original sounds that plausibly contain crucial meaning for a viewer clutter a screen when subtitles are already a form of clutter?

Evidently, subtitles must be as concise as possible in order to avoid making them difficult or daunting to follow. Subtitles should indeed not take too much space while providing essential information in the most minimalistic fashion. The arduous search for balance triggers difficult editorial choices across languages that depend on many factors, such as density and complexity of dialogue, velocity of elocution, multiplicity of aural sources, and frequency of concomitant speech. Most decisions are justified but some cause pause, especially when what is silenced is the voice of characters because they happen to express a message that is deemed of lesser value in the enterprise of translation and/or not of interest to the extra-diegetic viewer. Consequently, to go as far as to eliminate original sound—or worse, omit to mention what it is or simply that it is taking place (as is commonplace in closed captioning) opens the door to biased selection, which is all the more problematic when undertaken by a different culture. The decision made on behalf of the audience is not only infantilizing, it also risks elitism and brainwashing. Since language is intimately tied to culture and carries a view of the world, to decide what to reproduce and what to leave behind in subtitles censors the worldview of the Other in part or in its entirety, voluntarily or not. Indeed, one must remember that subtitles seldom render everything. Even when they do an excellent job of translating language and transmitting meaning, they rarely render the cultural, social, spiritual, political, tribal, regional, or religious significance of certain moods, noises, sounds, etc. The translator makes an informed guess at determining what is important or unimportant, what is meaningful or meaningless, and what will resonate with viewers of a certain language or culture. This "choice" can take the form of a *parti-pris*, which in French translates into "to take a stance" or "to choose a side." The expression connotes that the side we take and the choices we make are ideological and political, such as when we support a party, "parti." Subtitles—those that are "under"—are actually "overtitles" because they inscribe a discourse that is entitled to be the most reliable source of information seeking to override the original, like a palimpsest. In addition, they often reveal an unequal relationship where the ultimate authority is the one that makes the final decision as to what is allowed to appear. Therefore, subtitles not only reimagine and reimage what the film is saying, what it means or should mean for a country or a region—they also carry out a screening and sieving process at the expense of countless constituents on both sides of the screen.

Music contains bridges—dramatic passages linking two different sections—and may itself also be a bridge. In the midst of what has been termed the "refugee crisis" and even earlier, numerous filmmakers indicated that their goal was to provide their own version of the story. Thus, in order to propose their visions, they employ the tools that allow them to reach their objectives. One of these is the soundtrack. For many of these *cinéastes*, the soundtrack is sound (it has a remedial property), in that in combination with the visual components of the work, the auditory (listening to characters' reasons for leaving, hearing their pleas, and witnessing their plights) helps decriminalize those they represent and debunk misconceptions about them. In this case, auditory tricks force themselves in for a good cause. As peaceful weapons, they launch pacifist invasions, to quote the title of yasser elhariry's book.[7] The soundtrack is an outlet to gauge and track the intention of the filmmaker. In the context of films recounting the passage of the Mediterranean Sea, music makes the corpses and memories travel to us even as the voices of the departed are stifled and their bodies stopped dead in their crossing. The soundtrack is a channel that the harragas' memories are invited to follow. It is the aural trace that continues when the harrag is

---

7 See yasser elhariry's *Pacifist Invasions: Arabic, Translation and the Postfrancophone Lyric* (2018).

out of our sight and reach. It partakes in the legacy that the film has to offer, and is perhaps one of the most memorable and effective mediums precisely because music speaks directly to our affect. This intangible memorial of sorts helps address (but not necessarily redress) a global lack of memorials. "Sound" tracks can be sound (i.e., healthy) amidst unwholesome discourses and attacks against harragas that cover and obfuscate, smear, and criminalize. Their *raison d'être* could precisely be just that—erecting a memorial in our minds and hearts for us to hold on to when we go back to our daily routines after the closing credits. The transposing nature of soundtracks is relevant in that it accompanies the trans-Mediterranean migration in all senses of the term.

Besides building smooth bridges, a soundtrack might insidiously, like a smuggler, lead us from one place to another, but not without imposing conditions. It has the potential to undertake a kind of traffic in a one-way agreement to move us, with others, via the melody toward a common outcome previously determined for us. Surely, it runs the risk of being blamed for manipulating our feelings, judgments, and positions, for channeling the sentiment of the viewer and dictating how the spectator is encouraged to "read" the soundtrack and listen to the film's message. The soundtrack can be viewed (or rather, heard) as ideologically charged. As I mentioned earlier, no decision is entirely impartial and even less so when it comes to the treatment of a tragic topic that has triggered diametrically-opposed, heated opinions.

In the opening lines of this chapter, I posed the question: "Does the addition of sound constitute an act of violence?" In light of the reflection above on what it entails to transpose sound onto image in a corpus examining narratives about deadly sea-crossings, it appears that certain measures taken to insert sounds in this repertoire could be a sign or product of violence. This is true whether it is intentional or circumstantial, foreseen, or after the fact. It is especially the case when external entities enforce the inclusion of certain material in order for the production to be released. When those sources are in the Global North and grant their financial resources only on the condition that their conditions are met, concerns are raised that neocolonialism is at play. And when conditions, originating in France for instance, or with a French-speaking authority in the industry, have to do with language, namely that French must be spoken by North African actors instead of Arabic, it is an act deemed even more violent in that a former colonial power is exerting a control reminiscent of imperialism. For many decades, Maghrebi thinkers and scholars have advocated for

Arabic to be a key language in Maghrebi fictional and non-fictional narratives. Others have advocated for the inclusion of Tamazight. The use of French actors, the French language, and French funding in films representing a North African country or any other that used to be a French colony, prompts critics' assumptions of neocolonial supremacy in cultural modes of expression. As for financing from France, they fear it might determine choices not only of language but also in casting, which is likely to undermine the goal of depicting a country or society though local eyes. They advocate for native talent expressing autochthonous realities through their vernacular for the sake of authenticity. In this light, the identity of the one who speaks the native tongue(s) and acts locally—as both a character (in fiction) and a person (in real life) consciously or unconsciously partakes in how, and how much, spectators are willing to hear or resist the message.

These considerations have been noted by scholars studying *Harragas*, the cinematic production of French Algerian Merzak Allouache that came out in 2009.[8] This feature-length film, which was awarded several international prizes, recounts the story of ten migrant-hopefuls, nine male and one female, who await the moment to embark on a motorized fishing boat on the beach of Mostaganem, Algeria, toward Spain. The passengers comprise individuals from various parts of the country and social strata. When they realize they are heading to France instead, the passengers panic. Besides the obvious fact that heading toward France is dreaded because this country is further away on the map and subsequently takes more time to reach, increasing the crew's risk of perishing, the film discusses the place of idioms, i.e., French, Arabic, Spanish, and the languages of hospitality and lack thereof, and of time (the past through leavism and the future through hope), which play a role in the life and death of those who can speak several of these languages, hear sounds, see signs, and seize tools that arm some of the harragas and dispossess others. The less educated passengers condemn their fellow citizens for resorting to the French language, which they do not speak. They find that move absurd and exclusionary in that the entire crew has Arabic in common and yet a portion of its members repeatedly employ French. Alternatively, those who repudiated French on the boat will utter Spanish words to beg for the assistance of a Spanish crew that meets their paths as they are stranded in the middle of the sea. The choice of keeping

8   For a variety of considerations pertaining to language in *Harragas* and for an analysis of the film, see Abderrezak 2016.

their distance from France and its language but welcoming Spain and making the effort to speak its vernacular has symbolic meanings—one of them is that nowadays, since the closing of the EU's external borders, France has turned its back on its former colonies. In this context, it has forced harragas to implore the nearest countries to allow them onto their shores and into their homes in spite of closed borders.

Tom Whittaker and Sarah Wright remind us that "the transmission of voices in film industries across the world can often serve to erect linguistic borders, thereby consolidating the formation of 'imagined communities' or 'discursive ghettoes'" (2017, 2). The criticism directed at Allouache for conforming to the demands of foreign film companies and especially for complying with the inclusion of a significant amount of French language, denaturalizing the auditory experience in order to provide ease for the French-speaking audience, recalls criticism made years earlier of Nadir Moknèche for filming his *Viva Laldjérie* (2004) exclusively in French, thus failing to provide an authentic vision of his society in his attempt to make it palatable to a foreign consumer. It must be noted that "Algerian" is the most Frenchified type of Arabic of all the varieties spoken in the Maghreb. Therefore, Algerian people speaking entire sentences in French is not anomalous. Granted, the bourgeoisie is more expected to employ French or Frenchified Arabic. The exclusive use of French by characters from all walks of life, as is the case in *Viva Laldjérie*, does sound awkward, hackneyed, and false. For that matter, one of the southern Algerian characters in *Harragas* exclaims in a fit of anger: "We don't understand a thing with your French. Speak a little bit in Arabic!"[9] This allows the man to voice a long-standing linguistic divide between the elite and the rest of the society that is a remnant of a colonial past and the expression of a neocolonial present (and most likely future). His interjection, however, is only a short-lived intervention, because the three educated characters go back to speaking French and end up jumping off the boat to reach the shore, leaving the southern Algerians, who do not know how to swim (symbolically, navigate unknown elements and territories) to their fate. Whether the language barrier is sustained because of the demands of French co-producers or to depict common Algerian linguistic modus operandi, *Harragas* crystallizes fundamental issues pertaining to language, class, race, gender, ethnicity, and religion. All of these explain why, what, when, where, and how harragas leave despite the many dangers ahead.

9   My translation.

The film contains a minimalistic soundtrack. This not only makes the French dialogues stand out even more, but also demonstrates that for the director, the tragic topic of "bare life"—to quote Giorgio Agamben—demands a bare minimum with regard to artificial sound, as if the intention were to convey the natural elements that the harragas have to face.[10] Indeed, from confinement back home in what I have called the *cementery*, to the *seametery*, the maritime mass grave, harragas move from being imprisoned in a suffocating society to a cell-like boat in an unfamiliar element that may engulf their boat-coffin and prove to be their final home.[11] Melodrama is by definition drama with music. Still, music—or any other type of sound, for that matter—is not necessary to dramatize the rising tension of harragas facing a treacherous sea, which threatens through its immensity but also through the ominous crashing of waves and the motor fighting to its last breath. Silence achieves this goal effectively as well, for silence is not the absence of sound. In fact, when the passengers of the *bote* become silent, sound becomes all the more moving, to the point of feeling intrusive. What one calls silence is when human voices are no longer heard, but are we in the presence of silence when all the sea sounds abound at the surface? The sound of water that was there when passengers were fighting suddenly takes center stage. It does so along with the other ambient sounds that, seconds ago, were less worthy of attention but now take a new dimension. In this film, Hakim and Mustapha die on camera. Their fellow passengers cry Hakim's name, and when it becomes evident that he has drowned, the absence of words and the heavy breathing of shocked fellow passengers render the noise of the natural elements, such as the clapping of the water, more powerful. When the camera scans the faces of the crew in "silence," it picks up everyone's thoughts and concerns, their unspoken words of sorrow, regret, worry, and anxiety. Silence thus carries heavy meaning. Should absence (death) be conveyed through minimal or no sound (track) at all? Is just silence, which is loaded with sounds echoing and at times magnifying inner thoughts and emotions, enough? Theoretically, silence speaks volumes and therefore ought to be rendered in subtitles rather than be treated to a systematic absence of indications. The fact that silences are rarely transliterated, transcribed, or translated—in

10 See Giorgio Agamben 1998.
11 A discussion of the *seametery* and *cementery* can be found in Abderrezak 2018.

a nutshell, transposed in one form or another—poses the question of what and how much is lost in the absence of translation.

Justin Horton coined the term "the voice-out" to examine "the circumstances in which characters are seen speaking but nonetheless go unheard partially or completely by audiences" (2013, 4). Horton's coinage can be applied to the act of drowning. Indeed, in his last moments Hakim is crying for help. Since water is filling his lungs, his words are indiscernible, although easily guessed to be imploring assistance from those standing on the *bote*. By the same token, his plea is made to the non-diegetic viewers as well as the international community, which are two of the intended audiences. In this instance, instead of asking, "What is a voice?" one ought to ask how to reproduce the voice of a voiceless character (the unwelcome harrag). How might the director give the voiceless a voice that could possibly be heard by those who did not listen to them when they were alive but out of sight? What happens on the screen when the voice is muffled by water in a scene of drowning? Is this precisely what makes the spectator become aware of the suppressed voice of marginalized beings? What happens when a voice-over is placed over the sound of drowning (which is the case in *Harragas*)? In such a scene, are we witnessing the silencing of a voice or its continuation? To complicate things further, we know that the drowning character is played by an actor and that the shortage of breath is likely part of the film's sound editing. Therefore, what is the ethical responsibility of the filmmaker who must resort to a double to imitate the death of a living actor? Of course, "to be out of breath" is *the* exaggeration, par excellence. Indeed, this expression is used loosely to connote shortness of breath: breathing made difficult for a short while. In films such as *Harragas* or *Retorno a Hansala*, the expression to be "out of breath" lives up to its meaning, since the act is taken to its extreme and its ending, the end of life. When the individual gasps for air, the trachea or "windpipe" fills with water.

Because transposition involves a movement from one point to another, and as each movement entails a mode and a route, transposing is synonymous with traversing, which simply means to cross over, and refers to what the ten passengers in *Harragas* are hoping to achieve. Some will and some will not. In nautical jargon, "traverse" refers to a zigzag movement that a ship, forced by contrary winds, draws as it tacks, which in the context of clandestinity recalls how ships carrying harragas must avoid a straight cruising line in order to outwit coastguards. In architecture, a traverse is a dispositive that cuts through to make connections. Nonetheless, in Allouache's film those who do complete the journey of traversing and set foot on European soil will soon be deported. Contrary to the French *traverser*, which unequivocally means to cross successfully, the Mediterranean Sea embodies ambivalence, for the water that carries harragas to another shore, country, and continent also threatens to end their lives. The double entendre of this term is also embodied in music, which is able to make us hear—literally—one thing and its opposite. Music helps to connect us with the narrative by affecting our emotions, but it also has the power to tease out or add a layer of meaning, especially when its function is to illustrate and educate, as is the case of lyrics. In the Arabic song of the closing credits in *Return to Hansala*, the music and song complement and supplement who and what is missing, namely, the anonymous dead, exploring how to represent the dying breath and body and the breathless body in death. Music is no stranger to ambiguity, duplicity, and duality. Indeed, if the spectator is not conversant in the language of a song's lyrics, the foreign words are experienced as a cacophony or, alternately—or simultaneously for that matter—the viewer appreciates the music for the beauty that it creates and can—in an instant release of his resistance—let himself be receptive and sensitive to (or captive of?) the feelings it seeks to awaken in him.

Conclusion

Despite its immensely important place and space in the film industry and in shaping our cultural knowledge and imagination, sound remains marginal in the study of some categories of cinema. Therefore, although the experience of film watching resides mainly in focusing on the image, sound partakes in the reception of the production, which calls for studies of the auditory backbone of films. Many have been published on topics other than clandestine migration, whose representation poses questions left for scholars to ponder, some of which I have posed here—yet more remain to be investigated. I conclude with a question posed earlier, framed here as what apparently sounds like a tautology, "is sound sound?" The multi-pronged act of transposing sound onto the image in films dealing with failed sea-crossings has enormous advantages. In this chapter, I scrutinized it mostly from the angle of its sinister and insidious forms to alert us to its actual and possible downsides. As the following lines demonstrate, both aspects are inherent to the process. Since cinema was able to incorporate sound, this component made it more enjoyable and easier for the spectator to follow the storyline. But whether it is intradiegetic or extra-diegetic, sound tells its own story. It may work hand in hand with the image or proceed along on its own track. It may have its "plotline," so to speak. Put differently, it has the potential to be both a prop and a prod. It could be utilized subliminally or not to plot a line of action to direct the audience's reception of and reaction to the work. The soundtrack can propel the narrative or serve an agenda or as propaganda.

Historically, tragic phenomena like wars have pushed individuals to risk their lives on unknown roads and seas and have been documented by professional filmmakers. During what has been termed "the refugee crisis," amateur harragas have filmed their own perils using cell phones, producing a body of documentaries that often lack the editorial work of feature films. The raw footage exposes the bare language of sound. It stresses distress, which music does not always dress up appropriately. Instead, not infrequently it covers a fundamental component of the lived experience of harragas, namely, the verbal and aural environments, such as the so-called absence of sound, which ignores the cries for help and the voice of rescuers nearby or on the phone, heavy breathing and suffocating, the ominous exhausted sound of the motor, the cracking of the hull, or of the sound of water filling the embarkation. The multiple Oscar-winning sound designer and re-recording mixer Gary Rydstrom noted, "It's long been said that you do a great job in sound when no one notices it" (Kushins 2016). To make sound go unnoticed is worthy of note, for it is a sign of successful editing. Nevertheless, it is also clear evidence of its power to manipulate. A vigilant approach to this matter is all the more urgent for films that represent an Other of a different status, for example in postcolonial cinema and more recently in films focused on harragas and clandestine crossings of borders and the Mediterranean Sea.

Works Cited

Abderrezak, Hakim. 2016. *Ex-Centric Migrations: Europe and the Maghreb in Mediterranean Cinema, Literature, and Music*. Bloomington: Indiana University Press.

——. 2018. "The Mediterranean Seametery and Cementery in Leïla Kilani's and Tariq Teguia's Filmic Works." In *Critically Mediterranean: Temporalities, Aesthetics, and Deployments of a Sea in Crisis*, edited by yasser elhariry and Edwige Tamalet Talbayev, 147–61. New York: Palgrave Macmillan.

Agamben, Giorgio. 1998. *Homo Sacer: Sovereign Power and Bare Life*. Translated by Daniel Heller-Roazen. Stanford: Stanford University Press.

Allouache, Merzak. *Harragas*. 2009. Librisfilms, Baya Films, France 2 Cinema et al.

Buhler, James, David Neumeyer, and Rob Deemer. 2018. *Hearing the Movies: Music and Sound in Film History*. New York: Oxford University Press.

Donnelly, Kevin J. 2014. *Occult Aesthetics: Synchronization in Sound Film*. New York: Oxford University Press.

elhariry, yasser. 2018. *Pacifist Invasions: Arabic, Translation and the Postfrancophone Lyric*. Liverpool: Liverpool University Press.

Higbee, Will. 2009. "Displaced audio: Exploring soundscapes in Maghrebi-French film-making." *Studies in French Cinema* 9 (3): 225–41.

Horton, Justin. 2013. "The Unheard Voice in the Sound Film." *Cinema Journal*, University of Texas Press, on behalf of the Society for *Cinema & Media Studies* 52 (4): 3–24.

Kushins, Jordan. 2016. "A Brief History of Sound in Cinema." *Popular Mechanics*. https://www.popularmechanics.com/culture/movies/a19566/a-brief-history-of-sound-in-cinema/. Accessed November 3, 2020.

Moknèche, Nadir. 2004. *Viva Laldjérie*. BL Prod., Gimages, et al.

Naficy, Hamid. 2001. *An Accented Cinema: Exilic and Diasporic Filmmaking*. Princeton: Princeton University Press.

Walker, Elsie M. 2015. *Understanding Sound Tracks through Film Theory*. New York: Oxford University Press.

Whittaker, Tom, and Sarah Wright. 2017. *Locating the Voice in Film: Critical Approaches and Global Practices*. New York: Oxford University Press.

CHAPTER ELEVEN

Black Transnationalism and Sketches of Mediterranean *Noir*

Edwin Hill

In 1886 the African American statesman Frederick
Douglass traveled to France for the first time. While
he admired Paris and enjoyed exploring the provinces,
Douglass was moved by his visit to Marseilles. For the
former slave, Marseilles represented France's window
on Africa; never in his life would he come closer to the
ancestral black motherland than while standing above
the docks of the Provençal port and gazing out across
the Mediterranean.

(Tyler Stovall, "The Fire This Time: Black American
Expatriates and the Algerian War")

Dream Liner Notes

1. It's as if Marcus Garvey's *Black Star Line* weren't the only dream
liner out there, the Atlantic not the only body of water worth crossing,
and Frederick Douglass and his generation not the only ones "touched
by the magic of the Mediterranean, sprayed by its foamy fascination"
(McKay 1957, 66). The transnational practices on record below simultaneously crisscross and decenter the black Atlantic, without ever losing
sight of it. Because, what if Europe isn't a site of arrival but a launching
point? Or a place one gets stuck on the way somewhere else? Or what
if it's not where we thought it was? Sometimes the fires that freedom
dreams ignite illuminate radical visions of the world that take us on a

path of self-discovery somewhere beyond the conventional coordinates of critical reflection. Black Atlantic scholarship, with its focus on European capitals Paris, London, and Berlin, at times can elide circuits of movement that, even if only dreamed of or briefly realized, disrupt or disorient modernity's north/south, east/west binary mappings of place and belonging. Consider the current introduction a set of "dream liner notes," our ticket for a sonic cruise guided by a constellation of port cities: Marseilles, Barcelona, Istanbul, and Tangier. And consider this chapter an album, black and *noir* on both sides. On the A-side, we hear the Miles Davis and Gil Evans recording *Sketches of Spain* (1960), an album composed of a range of musical transpositions that resonate with a broader set of transpositional practices constitutive of black transnationalism in the Mediterranean. On the B-side, we hear Jean-Claude Izzo's remix of Davis and Evans's now classic album in his Mediterranean *noir* trilogy: *Total Khéops* (1995), *Chourmo* (1996), and *Solea* (1998). Izzo marks each of the novels under the sign of music and musicians, like a set of sonic outposts in this path of (self/city-)discovery, culminating in *Solea*, a track from the *Sketches of Spain* recording.

2. My use of the term "transpositionality" in this discussion refers first to the practices of musical culture, understanding the latter as part of a set of black transnational cultural praxes at the intersections of critical thought and histories of diaspora and migration. These practices don't always involve trying to set up shop permanently, certainly not in Europe's capital cities. They navigate the politics of exile, but also live on intermittent *séjours* and short stays, friendly visits, and convenient stopovers. They emerge from the freedom dreams of black nomadism, but spring from state-sponsored trips and privately run tours. And they create burgeoning hubs and mobile networks of relation that may be transitory, but are no less impactful to projects of diaspora. Secondly, I will also consider transpositionality as a mode of being that involves simultaneously existing or making sense in and in-between the "here" and the "there"—of physically, socially, imaginatively, and even spiritually being in two places at once in a way that forces a reconsideration of local and global matrices of power and space. Imagine, like the Jamaican poet and black radical thinker Claude McKay, who split with the politics of Garveyism and spent years in the Mediterranean, digging "the warmth of Marseilles as a West Indian boy burrows into a heap of dried sugar cane after the liquor has been pressed out, and feels sweet and comfortable lying down deep in it" (2007, 216). Transpositional

practices often get pressed out and processed in the body and its relation to (trans)spatial sensibilities of being.

3. These ways of navigating, thinking, and creating within the transnational circuits of the Mediterranean, as McKay shows, amount to epistemological projects scratched into the counter grooves of modernity. Time in—and in-between—France, Spain, and Morocco in the interwar years was part and parcel of a process of political analysis and artistic imagination for McKay, who briefly visited the south of France first in 1924. After moving to Nice from Paris the following year, he settled in Marseilles in 1926. "It was a relief to get to Marseilles," he writes in his autobiography *A Long Way from Home*,

> to live in among a great gang of black and brown humanity. Negroids from the United States, the West Indies, North Africa, and West Africa, all herded together in a warm group. Negroid features and complexions, not exotic, creating curiosity and hostility, but unique and natural to a group [...] to feel the strength and distinction of a group and the assurance of belonging to it. (2007, 213)

McKay went to Antibes in 1927 where he finished *Home to Harlem*, then went back to Marseilles for a time before ending up in Barcelona. "I started off for Africa. But I lingered for a long time in Spain" (2007, 249). By 1931, McKay finally made his way to (Spanish) Morocco where again he found space to write, to study revolutionary politics, and to catch a feel for a different experience of blackness. "For the first time in my life I felt myself singularly free of color-consciousness," McKay writes of his experience in Morocco (2007, 230).

4. Practices of musical transposition animate McKay's landmark second novel, *Banjo: A Novel without a Plot*, a narrative inspired by his experiences in Marseilles and completed in Barcelona in 1929. The main protagonist, Banjo, having "hoboed" in America, intentionally gotten himself deported from Canada, and hitched rides to Genoa (twice) and Barcelona (once), dreams of forming a black music ensemble with a group of musically inclined black vagabonds and migrants that he encounters from around the world in the *Vieux Port* of Marseilles. Drawing on their own musical traditions, as well as the songs and styles they picked up on their travels, the group works out creative collaborations successful enough to keep food, wine, and new friends coming, at least for a time. They ground their musical practices in experience and experimentation, and design them to discover often unexpected

synergies in melody, harmony, rhythm, and lyrics as well as in energy, mood, and feeling. These practices involve creating arrangements and forms that accommodate the group but also allow for, even demand, individual expression. We have to insist on the "practices" when we imagine these musical transpositions; the process of creation matters as much as, in fact more than, the "objective" outcome of the musical work. These practices are richly transpositional in all the senses of the term sketched out above. (The novel's Haitian writer Ray muses: "You know when he was reading that paper [about the atrocities of French colonization,] it was just as if I was hearing about Texas and Georgia in French," 77). These cross-mappings lead to heated debates, and even a scuffle or two, among the group, but in the process, they open up space for thought about the black body in the world, about what blackness is, "ain't," and could be.[1] And as they search for the words to say it, music is at the center of it all, helping solidify, for a season, a sort of black fraternity assembled around dynamics of mobility, forms of hospitality, and dreams of freeness.

5. McKay's work itself amounts to a series of transpositions, akin to those adopted by the men he portrays, capable of transforming the place of Europe in projects of diaspora. "Travelling between mainland Europe and his home in Morocco, McKay understood Spain as a transitional site" (Reynolds 2000, 489). Like the men on whose lives the novel is based, *Banjo* works through the hybrid possibilities of narrative form, the breakdowns of language and difference, and the "cross-media impulses" that characterize jazz literature. Just as McKay sets up (Banjo) the musician and (Ray) the writer as mutually informing, McKay's *Banjo* is itself a sound-text, where clear-cut distinctions between media give way to their deep relation, and where the novel becomes an instrument for transposing musical expression. Below, we will listen to the way practices of transpositionality in late modernity continue to serve as a crucial mode of musico-thought that seeks out new ways of picking up and mixing up configurations of blackness. The A-side builds a critical apparatus from the blueprints that McKay has sketched out for us so we can hear *Sketches of Spain* as a major contribution to black Mediterranean thought. The B-side listens to how the Mediterranean *noir* writer Jean-Claude Izzo hears the album in his novel *Solea* (1998) as a signpost in his mythology of Massalia. Both works sound the

1   See Edwards 2003.

Mediterranean for a more capacious exploration of blackness, of *noir*, and of a sensibility for the world capable of affirming that "the history of tomorrow is 'not what we think.' Far from it" (Izzo 2013a, 35).

A-Side Expats: Sketches of Spain, Where Miles Sounds Out Postwar Black Transnationalism

1. In the postwar years, from the height of the Civil Rights movement to the rise of the Black Power movement, African American writers, musicians, thinkers, and militants continued to move in and through Mediterranean spaces as part of individual and collective projects of diaspora. Black Mediterranean transnationalism animated a range of cultural and intellectual efforts meant to connect and process black being in the world, and to fuel radical imaginings of worlds to come. James Baldwin played a central role in these transpositional practices— from his "Turkish decade," when regular trips to Istanbul in the 1960s served as "a kind of voluntary exile, a temporal and spatial process of artistic incubation and discovery that resulted in new ways of seeing and conceptualizing (African) Americanness" (Zaborowska 2009, 28), to his retirement in St Paul de Vance, a small village near Nice in the south of France in 1971, where Baldwin's villa served as a hub of the black transnational movement—as he hosted guests ranging from painter Beauford Delaney, to the writer Alex Haley, to jazz musician Don Cherry. Of course, Baldwin was not the only black writer who, fed up with the complications of post/colonial expatriate life in Paris, decided to position themselves differently in Europe. Chester Himes left Paris in the 1950s to spend many months in the south of France as well, renting "a flat in a villa in Vence with a view sweeping from the suburbs of Nice to the lighthouse at Antibes" (Sallis 2000, 279). In the 1960s Himes resettled on the Spanish Mediterranean coast between Alicante and Moraira, where he passed away in 1984. (Might we consider Chester Himes an author of Mediterranean noir fiction?) While anti/colonial warfare revealed "the strengths and weaknesses of [the black transnational] community [in France] and its ability to pose an internationalist response to racism" (Stovall 2000, 183), the practices discussed here decenter Paris, and disorient mappings of blackness rooted in black/white, north/south binaries. Here, Spain too becomes a transitional space for Mediterranean-afro-centric networks of relation and community building. Just as Claude McKay proclaims to have

"lingered long enough in Spain to become aware of the strong African streak in its character" (2007, 228), black Atlantic interest in Spain was also routed through sensibility to alternate paths of diasporic history and contemporary relations. Thus, *Pagan Spain*, Richard Wright's ethnographic, hybrid account of Spanish culture appears as the last of three non-fictional studies on the global politics of blackness and black nationalism in the 1950s. (*Pagan Spain* was preceded by *Black Power* in 1954, based on his travels in the colonial Gold Coast in 1953, and *The Color Curtain* in 1956, his report on the Bandung Conference in 1955.) If, "[l]ike many African American intellectuals and artists, including Langston Hughes, Richard Wright, Ralph Ellison, and Romare Bearden, Miles found himself drawn to Spain and Spanish culture" (Griffin and Washington 2008, 242), I suggest that the latter's importance came from its transpositional location in projects of diaspora rather than its geopolitical situation as part of Western Europe.

2. The move across the Mediterranean corresponds to a movement in jazz from Paris to the South of France. Many musicians began making regular trips to the south of France to play at jazz festivals from 1948 for what was touted as the first ever jazz festival in the world, held in Nice, and followed by the Cannes Jazz Festival in 1958, and finally, in 1960, the Juan-les-Pins jazz festival in Antibes. In addition, many musicians traveled the Mediterranean region for the first time in the context of the US State Department jazz tours, beginning in 1956 with Dizzy Gillespie. The latter's 1940s jazz standard "A Night in Tunisia" was not created with Tunisia in mind—Gillespie always simply called it "Interlude" until, he explains in his autobiography, "[s]ome genius decided to call it 'Night in Tunisia'" (Gillespie 2009, 172)—it can be thought as having "expanded on the idea of a north–south cultural dialogue in Afro-modernist jazz by musically commenting on the [African diasporic] past [African diasporic] futures of the musical style" (Ramsey 2004, 98). While so-called jazz ambassadors faced the paradox of representing American goodwill abroad while facing segregation and racial terror at home, the tours paved the road to Afro-modernist futures by affording an opportunity to travel and perform in places like Beirut, Istanbul, Cairo, and Athens that "would simply not have been possible—not commercially viable, or politically or logistically negotiable—without government sponsorship" (Von Eschen 2004, 37). For the purposes of the current discussion, the jazz pianist Randy Weston's participation in the program exemplifies the

minor transnational connections being made through these tours. With State Department sponsorship, Weston and his group toured in West Africa and North Africa along with dates in the Middle East. "Coming from a family with a strong Pan-Africanist bent, he […] saw the tours as fostering ties between African and black American musicians" (Von Eschen 2004, 170). Weston tapped into

> [t]he diasporic ties encouraged by the tour […] evident in North Africa as well as West Africa. In April, as the tour neared its end with concerts in three Algerian cities, the paper *El Moudjahid* ran an article entitled "Randy Weston in Algiers" that clearly showed an identification with black Americans. (Von Eschen 2004, 172)

In the summer of 1967, Weston moved to Tangier for a period of seven years.

3. Weston's father was Jamaican-born. Weston describes his father as a Garveyite who immigrated to the United States by way of Panama, then Cuba. His mother had moved to New York from Virginia, part of the Great Migration. "Culturally, Randy enjoyed the best of two worlds: his mother exposed him to the rollicking, soulful music of the black church with its Deep South roots; his father surrounded him with the cultures of the British and Spanish Caribbean" (Kelley 2012, 43). Weston's background helped him foster a beautifully ambitious dream of creating clubs, cultural centers, and festivals in Africa that would bring people across the diaspora together through music. Once in Tangier, he set about successfully realizing this dream, opening the African Rhythms Club above a movie theater in the center of Tangier, and organizing an international festival in fall 1972 that featured heavyweight black artists like the folksinger Odetta and the trumpeter Cecil Bridgewater but also local musicians, specifically members of the Gnawa black brotherhoods in Morocco. Weston's most commercially successful album, *Blue Moses* (1972), released just before the festival, features four original compositions and arrangements marked by Gnawa spiritual and musical practices he learned about and experienced first-hand during his time in Tangier. As he explains in his autobiography, the album can be heard as a series of transpositional reflections on blackness:

> "Blue Moses" was simply the translation of Sidi Musa. Musa was Moses for the Gnawa people; for them the color representing Moses is the color of the sea, the blue of the sky. When I attended a Gnawa ceremony in 1969 in Tangier it was my first of several Lilas with the powerful Gnawa

elders. As I said earlier, I was in a trance for a couple of weeks after this ceremony, it was so powerful, and this one particular melody stayed with me. So instead of Sidi Musa I called it "Blue Moses," based on traditional Gnawa music that I adapted and rearranged. When I first wrote this piece the Gnawa elders forbade me to play it in public; but after about a year they finally relented after I pleaded with them that people needed to hear this melody. (2010, 204)

Weston's transpositional practices tap into forms of black mysticism that speak to the centuries-old history of trans-Saharan slavery and the enslaved black populations it brought to North Africa. Gnawa musical culture carries animated spiritual practices whose genealogy can be traced to West Africa. Ethnomusicologists locate the dance and musical practices of Gnawa religious ceremonies as "more reminiscent of the rites of West African hunting societies, or even of Haitian *Vodun*, than of the rites of more orthodox Muslim brotherhoods in North Africa" (Schuyler 1981, 5). All this to say that Mediterranean transpositionality and cross-media practices formed something of a critical praxis for black Atlantic writers, artists, and musicians. It worked through local and global politics of anti-black racism, and the constraints of citizenship and state sponsorship, by being in more than one place at once. It built more capacious ideas about blackness by forging minor transnational connections, often centered quite literally on musical transpositions but extended to all kinds of creative and cross-media exchanges, intellectual debates, and jam sessions, all grounded in forms of hospitality.

4. *Sketches of Spain* merits being heard as a major contribution to this Mediterranean nexus of black transnationalism in the postwar years. While Davis didn't settle in the Mediterranean like Baldwin, Himes, and Weston, and he was far too controversial to be selected officially for a State Department tour, he did move through these same transnational circuits physically, socially, intellectually, and artistically. Davis frequently traveled to the south of France for the jazz festivals, and was good friends with James Baldwin, whom he "first met in the early 1960s," Davis's biographer Ian Carr explains,

when Miles had already read some of Baldwin's books, and the latter had a good knowledge of Davis's music, so that the respect and admiration were mutual. Every time Miles went to the south of France to play at the Antibes festival, he would try to spend a day or two at Baldwin's villa in St Paul de Vence, relaxing, swapping stories, and in Davis's phrase, "lying our asses off." (Carr 1998)

Davis first traveled to Paris in 1949 for a jazz festival that was broadcast live on national radio. The experience was transformative for him:

> This was my first trip out of the country [he writes in his autobiography], and it changed the way I looked at things forever. [...] That's where I met Jean-Paul Sartre and Pablo Picasso and Juliette Greco. I have never felt like that in my life since. The only other times that I felt that good was when I first heard Bird and Diz in B's band and that time in Dizzy's big band up in the Bronx. But that was about just music. This was different. This was about living. (Davis and Troupe 1989, 125–26)

By 1957, "Miles was busy consolidating his status as an artist of major significance and as an icon of cosmopolitan black masculinity" (Griffin and Washington 2008, 169). Perhaps his composition and performance of the soundtrack for Louis Malle's *Ascenseur pour l'échafaud* [Elevator to the Gallows] (1957) played a crucial role in that consolidation, while also setting up an important association between Davis, French *noir*, and "cosmopolitan black masculinity" that still resonates today (as we will see on the B-side).

5. *Sketches of Spain* was the last of a trio of projects, preceded by *Miles Ahead* (1957) and *Porgy and Bess* (1959), that Miles Davis recorded in collaboration with composer/arranger Gil Evans in the 1950s. Side one features a (black transnational) transposition of the adagio movement of "Concierto de Aranjuez" (16'19"), originally composed for Spanish guitar by the Spanish-born–French-trained composer Joaquin Rodrigo in 1939 and premiered in Barcelona in 1940; and "Will o' the Wisp" (3'47"), originally composed by Spanish composer Manuel de Falla for his 1915 ballet *El Amor Brujo*. On side two are "The Pan Piper" (3'52"), "Saeta" (5'06"), and "Solea" (12'15"). Evans is credited with the composition of the latter two tracks, while "The Pan Piper" transposes a melody entitled "Alborada de Vigo" [Vigo Daybreak], originally played on panpipe by José Maria Rodriguez, an itinerant pig castrator in Galicia. In his biography, Davis explains that the album project was inspired by a recording he heard when he went to visit

> Joe [Mondragon], a great studio bass player, who lived in the San Fernando Valley. Joe was a Spanish Indian from Mexico, a very handsome guy. When I got to his house, he played this recording of *Concierto de Aranjuez* by this Spanish composer, Joaquin Rodrigo, and said, "Miles, listen to this; you can do this!" [...] I knew right there that I had to record it [...]. When I got back to New York, I called up Gil and discussed it with him and gave him a copy of the record. (Davis and Troupe 1989, 241)

Columbia Records was at the center of a web of recording and distribution that made what seems like completely by chance encounters with a set of recordings much more likely. The album Davis heard of Rodrigo's guitar concerto was most likely the one that featured Catalan guitarist Renata Tarragó and the Madrid Concerto Orchestra conducted by Odon Alonso, originally recorded in 1958 on the Spanish label Hispavox, and later released again on Columbia Records in 1959. After Evans transcribed the music from the recording, he worked out an arrangement of the Adagio movement to which he added original material. "By the time we did that," Evans explains, "we began to listen to other folk music, music played in clubs in Spain, where you could hear the glasses crashing and the guitars playing along, not paying any attention to all the racket. So we learned a lot from that" (Crease 2002, 206). The music Evans refers to came from Alan Lomax's field recordings of Spanish folk music from regions including Andalusia, Catalonia, Mallorca, and Ibiza in 1952/53, also released by Columbia Records for its World Library of Folk and Primitive Music series in 1955. At a basic level, Davis and Evans's musical practices of transposition involve directly transcribing recordings gathered from the increasingly international archives of Columbia Records, creating new material inspired by recordings and personal experiences, and transforming it all through experiments in timbers and sound textures created by surprising voice and instrumental combinations.

6. But there is more to these transpositional practices than the technical transference of notes recomposed with creative arrangements. I want to train our ear to that voice in "Saeta" and "Solea"—the two tracks that Jean-Claude Izzo's protagonist Fabio Montale can't get out of his head, as we will hear on the B-side—because it's about how people hear it, not what it (always already) is. Our hearing cannot, and even must not, separate itself from tropes of sound in the context of black vernacular culture. Farah Jasmin Griffin's notes on the original stories of authentic sound in the black jazz tradition help here. Like many jazz *men*, Miles Davis locates his sound in the trope of the "singing New World black woman whose voice, linked to nature, inspires cultural memory in the hearer and sets him on his own path of creative discovery" (Griffin 2004, 113). For Griffin, it typifies the ways in which this cultural work comes at the expense of a displacement, and disembodiment, of the black woman's voice, and its replacement with mythical figures of (jazz) patriarchy. Griffin opens up room for a complex consideration of the

lively diasporic gender dynamics functioning at the core of the transpositional practices under study in the current discussion. "Saeta," Davis
explains, enacts

> [a] street procession, and the singer, a woman, stands on a balcony
> grasping the iron railing overlooking the procession, which stops beneath
> her balcony while she sings this song. I was supposed to be her voice on
> trumpet. [...] Now, that was the hardest thing for me to do on *Sketches
> of Spain*, to play the parts on the trumpet where someone was supposed
> to be singing, especially when it was ad-libbed, like most of the time.
> (1989, 242)

Not unlike the black woman's voice he heard as a young man in the
woods of Arkansas at night, the "new sound" of blackness that Davis
had been hearing in his head and searching for is mediated by the Lomax
recordings, made space for through the arrangements of Gil Evans, but
rooted in his imagination of this affectively gendered voice. "My voice
had to be both joyous and sad in this song" (1989, 242) Miles explains;
"you've got all those Arabic musical scales up in there, black African
scales that you can hear. And they modulate and bend and twist and
snake and move around. It's like being in Morocco" (1989, 242). Miles
insists on the pre-modern black African trajectory of *Sketches*. "The
black moors were over there in Spain," he writes,

> because Africans had conquered Spain a long time ago. In the Andalusian
> area you have a lot of African influence in the music, architecture, and in
> the whole culture, and a lot of African blood in the people. So you had
> a black African thing up in the feeling of the music, in the bag pipes and
> trumpets and drums. The "Saeta" was an Andalusian song known as the
> arrow of song, and it was one of the oldest religious types of music in
> Andalusia. (1989, 241)

Miles Davis was not alone in hearing the (real) African history and
the (imagined) blackness of the Andalusian voice: "This quality of 'vocal
darkness' usually comes from cultures where the pitch of the speaking
voice is lower. [...] Both Ralph Ellison and Nathaniel Mackey have
drawn links between these dark or Moorish sounds, flamenco, and black
American blues" (Griffin 2004, 108).

7. On "Solea," the title-track of Izzo's novel, we again hear that cry that
opens this movement of solitude:

> There was a little bit of the same thing, the same kind of voice, that
> I played on trumpet in "Solea." "Solea" is a basic form of flamenco.

It's a song about loneliness, about longing and lament. It's close to the American black feeling in the blues. It comes from Andalusia, so it's African-based. (Davis and Troupe 1989, 242)

Unlike the lugubrious drone of "Saeta" that provides that dark curtain at the back of this sound stage, in "Solea" Miles cries out against a shimmering and scintillating backdrop of harp, woodwinds, French horn, and tambourine shakes. Suddenly, some 67" into it, Evans's arrangement hits us with the dazzling power of the brass sun, which will recede almost as suddenly as it appeared, leaving room for another ostinato vamp, reminiscent in many respects of Maurice Ravel's experiments with Spanish musical colors and timbres. But then, here comes Miles, blue as a motherfucker. And black as the Mediterranean Sea. The sea and its many shades of blue, the Mediterranean sun, and the blinding white *calanques*; the smells of the ocean and of food, but also the smell of death, and the climate of fear. Miles blows all these crucial elements, lays bare weathered skin. When we hear Davis's cry in "Saeta" and "Solea," "it is crucial to appreciate the extraordinary lengths to which Davis goes to make playing the trumpet even more difficult and risky than it already is, and to understand the musical results of his doing so" (Walser 1993, 353). The black scream comes through in this play of half-valves, loose embouchure, slurred tones, slid, bent, and cracked notes. The breathiness of Miles Davis's performative style gives off the texture of his lips, his lungs, it all positions Miles's body as the crux of this transpositionality. By 4' in, what had been a pure straight ostinato pattern in 6/4 is transformed with a walking bass line. It's not quite swinging, but it's not *not* swinging either, suspended between two worlds somehow. We get carried away in the wake of the cross-currents of changing meters and rhythmic feel. By 8' in, things sputter and anticipation again swells, and 60" later Miles rises again from the depths to let loose a full wail, before gently falling back down to earth. But now he's done messing around, he's swinging, jabbing, pivoting on a dime, rising up, pulling back, sassing us, testing us, reaching down low, talking shit, feeling all the way through us, and before we know it, he's gone. Player.

8. *Sketches of Spain* builds from and contributes to a project of diaspora that involves black transnational critical praxes of creativity and thought. This is not "third stream." Maybe some will say that Rodrigo and Falla remain composers of the Western tradition, and thus the third-stream label still makes sense. But Miles and Evans

found the blackness in the Western tradition; the diasporic and black transnational practices provide a more compelling framework for this album's meaning-making. As Robert Walser has argued, when we hear Miles Davis through the framework of Western aesthetics, we can only fail in trying to account for how he touches us. As Walser contends, analysis of Miles's solo voice must "confront the challenges of signifyin', the real-life dialogic flux of meaning, never groundable in a foundationalist epistemology, but always grounded in a web of social practices, histories and desires" (1993, 360). In this transpositional system of sounding and hearing, rather than a move toward a musical "third stream"—defined by Gunther Schuller and others as a fusion of contemporary Western art music and jazz—*Sketches* resonates with songs like Weston's "Blue Moses," offering a much more radical experiment in reconfigurations of blackness beyond the hegemonic, linguistic, and vibrational boundaries of the West than concepts like "third stream" and "world music" can contain. Like "A Night in Tunisia," *Sketches of Spain* must be heard as a project in Afro-modernism, where musical transpositions perform diasporic work and imagine more capacious futures and histories for blackness. *Sketches* heard this way becomes understood as a knowledge project where Miles Davis's probing solos (re)search out new ways of orienting the affective terrains of race and place.

B-Side Blues: Jean-Claude Izzo's *Solea*, Where Audiotopias Are Not Without Dissonance

1. They say home is where the record player is, especially if you're an analog man like Fabio Montale, the (former) detective of Jean-Claude Izzo's crime trilogy. Play me your record collection, and perhaps, along with the music, I will hear *you*: your personality (I listen for patterns and surprises), your sensibilities (I hear what you hear as beautiful there), your history (I listen for traces of that which and those who passed through your life), and perhaps even who you'd like to be (how you imagine yourself as a listener of music, how and what you think you are through this playing of sound). What do Montale's musical practices allow him to do, to feel, and to know? How does Izzo's way of playing (on) *Sketches of Spain*, and African American musical forms more generally, relate to his sense and sensibility of home, of history, of Marseilles, and of the world? Thumbing through his stacks we find:

a) African American jazz artists: Thelonious Monk, Dizzy Gillespie, Art Pepper, Sonny Rollins, Billie Holiday, Anita O'Day, and Miles Davis, but also Belgian-born Romani jazz guitarist Django Reinhardt, contemporary French jazz pianist Michel Petrucciani, and the South African jazz artist Abdullah Ibrahim;

b) Afro-Cuban musicians, especially Mongo Santamaria and Rubén González, but also the Panamanian salsero Rubén Blades, the Puerto Rican American conguero Ray Barretto, the Argentine tangueros Edmundo Rivero, Carlos Gardel, and Astor Piazzolla, as well as the Spanish rumba flamenco group Los Chinguitos;

c) Classic blues musicians and singers, including Pinetop Perkins, Lightnin' Hopkins, Buddy Guy, Ray Charles, and Calvin Russell;

d) Popular singers and singer-songwriters including the Algerian-born, Paris-based Lili Boniche, known especially for his interpretations of an Arab Andalusian genre called Haouzi; the Italian guitarist Gianmaria Testa who sang in Italian and French; and Léo Ferré, one of the so-called "holy trinity" of French *chanson* (along with Jacques Brel and George Brassens);

d) Marseilles 1990s rap groups IAM and Fonky Family;

e) One-offs including Bob Marley and ZZ Top (!), this mix reminds us of the influence of the blues tradition on the latter group's sound.[2]

On the A-side of the current chapter, I put Miles Davis in the mix with a range of black transnational cultural practitioners, focusing especially Randy Weston. On this B-side mix, Izzo has Fabio Montale hearing *Sketches of Spain* in the company of a cross-section of artists and styles rooted in jazz, rumba, and the blues but extending to Argentine, Italian, French, and Algerian popular music and song traditions. This carefully curated playlist constitutes a collection of memories. It tells the story of a lifetime, a family with Italian roots and French and Argentine branches, a dreamer and romantic whose sentimental education assumes the posture of yearning (for love, for change), an appreciation and ethics of national and regional languages and styles of speech. This collection is 1950–1970 heavy, the collection of someone maybe kind of stuck on the past, but like the way you get stuck on a sweetheart. It's definitely the expressive listening of someone connected to the (French) postwar generation, someone who came of age in the context of May '68, and

---

2   See "Fabio Montale's Music" in Izzo 2013c.

it makes salient how the revolutionary imagination of that generation was sonically and affectively plugged into African American freedom dreams in a certain kind of way. It's also the collection of someone who would like to connect with today's youth, but doesn't quite know how. Importantly, this collection includes dance music, it interpellates the body and the body's imagination of itself, the image of one's own body and the body of others. This record collection is not without nostalgia, but these records still hold up today. They're still relevant. These records still speak to us and for us. They still make us feel. In Fabio Montale's hands, this collection is for listening, thinking, dancing, and singing along with—or at least watching others do so—for driving (that's when a more rockin' blues sound often comes in) or just falling asleep (read: passing out). But I want to tune in to how these records, and especially *Sketches*, are for dreaming and for mourning.

2. Izzo's soundtrack reminds us how sound, vibration, and rhythm impact modes of narration and identification in *noir*. While the predominant take insists that "[i]ssues of point of view are, of course, preeminent in the detective novel, a genre whose obsession with ways of seeing and ways of knowing constitutes its specificity" (Ross 2010, 100) I suggest that the cross-media impulses in *noir* make seeing and hearing constitutive of one another. From opening chapters of the trilogy, Izzo capitalizes these cross-media impulses to establish musical and vernacular culture as key to catching a feel for Marseilles and for Montale. Both involve a sensibility to the world fueled by histories of diaspora and migration as well as by dreams of elsewhere and other times (past, present, and future). The trilogy goes far beyond the mix above, connecting sounds to several key characters and moments. We encounter the *canzone napoletana* made famous by Marino Marini and Renato Caresone and that his family would listen to and sing along with, after consuming copious Italian dishes with family and friends when Fabio was a child. Music does not just represent this history, it was part of a family tradition, a ritual way of being together, that keeps alive their connection with Italy, connecting Fabio's hometown, Marseilles, to his parents' hometown, Naples. They didn't have much, but they had the music, each other, and a modest two-room cabin by the sea in Les Goudes, just outside of Marseilles proper, their only possession. That was when Fabio was a child, before his mother's death, after which his father cannot bear to go there anymore. We learn in *Total Khéops* how it later became a hangout for Fabio and his close teenage friends

Ugo (whose family also immigrated from Italy) and Manu (whose family immigrated from Spain).

> Nous n'y emmenions jamais les filles. C'était à nous. Notre repaire. Nous ramenions au cabanon tous nos trésors. Des livres, des disques. Nous inventions le monde. À notre mesure, et à notre image. [...] Les livres, c'est Antonin, un vieux bouquiniste [...] qui nous donna le goût. On taillait la classe pour aller le voir. Il nous racontait des histoires d'aventuriers, de pirates. La mer des Caraïbes. La mer Rouge. Les mers du sud. [...] C'est là aussi qu'on écouta Ray Charles pour la première fois. Sur le vieux Teppaz de Gélou. C'était le 45 tours du concert de Newport. *What' Id' Say* [sic] et *I Got a Woman*. Dément. Nous n'arrêtions pas de tourner et de retourner le disque. Plein volume. Honorine craqua. (Izzo 1995, 52–53)

Chez Izzo, cassettes and records, and even record players (his cousin's old Teppaz) are more than just a means of hearing the music; they are a kind of material evidence, sonic remains that viscerally stimulate a rememoration of the past, and an elusive dream for new futures. But it also puts our protagonist and (former) detective into an embodied place and space of reflection that is needed to work his cases in the present. In addition to being the master thinker of "golden age" crime fiction, the detective of *noir* must be a master listener. Rhythm, sound, and vibration saturate meaning (un)making processes, and locate feeling as the foundation for "ways of knowing." (Face to face with Cûc, the Vietnamese *femme fatale* in *Chourmo*, always "prête à tout. Même à me tomber dans les bras," Montale can't hold back: "Vous avez de superbes oreilles, m'entendis-je murmurer": Izzo 1996). This world requires a fleshy ear as much as a "mind like a steel trap." Practices of listening and listening in, overhearing, and sounding out, help catch a vibe for the scene in a way that goes beyond establishing a mood, although it's important it do that too. In other words, this *noir* soundtrack provides more than just atmosphere, and atmosphere provides more than "just atmosphere" in *noir*. It's a way of listening and looking for. It puts the detective, and the reader, on the path to certain dark illuminations.

3. With musical culture as our guide, Izzo soundtracks us through Marseilles's underserved neighborhoods from le Panier to Canebière, le Vieux Port to Les Goudes, where we discover rich pockets of social life and intimacy under the threat of erasure. Izzo's approach to soundtracking *noir* life and death in Marseilles attends to modes of

sociality he finds capable of serving as a bulwark against the toxic forces mentioned above. Music makes this possible by sounding out Marseilles' "'audiotopias,' small, momentary, lived utopias built, imagined, and sustained through sound, noise, and music" (Kun 2005, 21). In Izzo's imagination, the possibilities of Marseilles through its musical culture exemplify the notion of the audiotopia as a musical space of difference, where contradictions and conflicts do not cancel each other out but coexist and live through each other. Thus, in a sense, audiotopias can also be understood as identificatory "contact zones," in that they are both sonic and social spaces where disparate identity formations, cultures, *and* geographies, historically kept and mapped separately, are allowed to interact with each other as well as enter into relationships whose consequences for cultural identification are never predetermined (Kun 2005, 23).

In the end, we hear much more than just Fabio's music; we also hear and overhear the musical scenes, voices, and dancing of others, music in homes on record players, in live group settings, in bars and *boîtes*, on jukeboxes and car radios, on cassette and on 45s. The broad corpus of musical genres and styles and artifacts document the ongoing "changing same" (Baraka) of a struggle against forces of oppression and alienation. In this model, Marseilles becomes a patchwork, if not a complete *métissage*, of social vibrations that break up the traditional mapping of sound, sight, and site:

> Chez Hassan, Bar des Maraîchers à la Plaine, ni raï, ni reggae, ni rock. De la chanson française, et presque toujours Brel, Brassens et Ferré. L'Arabe, il se faisait plaisir en prenant les clients à contre-pied. —Salut, Étrangers, dit-il en nous voyant entrer. Ici, on était tous l'ami étranger. Quelle que soit la couleur de la peau, des cheveux ou des yeux. (Izzo 1995, 287)

These diverse and hybrid social (and linguistic) practices encountered in the music and its spaces of resonance make the audiotopic possibilities of the city felt. It's here that Marseilles assumes its true identity, and plays its rightful role as a *terre d'accueil*—a territory that is welcoming and open to the world

> C'était ça, l'histoire de Marseille. Son éternité. Une utopie. L'unique utopie du monde. Un lieu où n'importe qui, de n'importe quelle couleur, pouvait descendre d'un bateau, ou d'un train, sa valise en main, sans un sou en poche, et se fonder dans le flot des autres hommes. Une ville où, à peine le pied posé sur le sol, cet homme pouvait dire "C'est ici. Je suis chez moi." (Izzo 1995, 287)

Izzo's audiotopias build on the mythological story of the city circa 600 BC when, according to legend, the princess Gyptis chose the Proteus, the stranger from other shores, to be her love, and the Greek colony of Massalia was founded. As scholars have noted, this mythology, which Izzo emphasizes throughout his trilogy and his essays, resonates with a broader move in political discourse in the 1990s that cites Marseilles as a French model of multiculturalism, one distinct from "the Anglo-Saxon model." Several scholars have noted the pitfalls facing this origin myth and its Mediterranean imagination.[3] Less attention has been paid to the ways in which the audiotopic figures in this mythology, and also opens an entry way for its critique.

4. While Miles Davis appears throughout the trilogy, references become especially anchored to *Sketches of Spain* in the second novel, *Chourmo*. Late, after long days and nights of work, he plays it:

> Habituellement, à cette heure, c'est ce que je faisais, assis sur la terrasse, face à la mer. Je buvais, avec autant de plaisir que d'application. En écoutant du jazz. Coltrane ou Miles Davis, ces derniers temps. Je redécouvrais. J'avais exhumé le vieux *Sketches of Spain* et, les soirs où l'absence de Lole me pesait trop, je passais et repassais Saeta et Solea. La musique portait mon regard jusqu'à Seville. J'y serais bien allé, à Séville, là, maintenant, tout de suite. Mais j'étais trop fier pour faire ça. Lole était partie. Elle reviendrait. Elle était libre, et je n'avais pas à lui courir après. C'était un raisonnement à la con, et je le savais. (1996, 77–78)

Fabio had rediscovered the album recently among his jazz records in the cabin, and "exhumed it" (translated as "dug out" in the English edition). The record has been unearthed—not unlike the ancient remains threatened by real estate deals but uncovered by an Algerian archeologist and historian in the novel in a key narrative line in *Chourmo*. The record serves as a sonic artifact that triggers his mind's eye ("portait mon regard jusqu'à Seville," given in English as "made me think of Seville") onto a geography of loss. *Sketches of Spain* makes him think about and feel his lost love, but it also the threatened the loss of Mediterranean "treasures" and values. The point is that Izzo's Marseilles is a combustible site of contestation where French white nationalism, islamophobic anti-black racism, institutional corruption and organized crime, and diverse local and transnational groups and communities struggle over space, resources, respect, money, and power. As Susan Ireland notes, "the attack on

3 See Wesley 2014; Head 2015.

multicultural Marseilles in many respects constitutes the main "crime" portrayed in the novels" (Ireland 2004, 23). Montale's record collecting and listening practices take hold of music, especially black musical forms and practices, as a lifeline of aspiration, but also as a ritual of mourning for navigating a physical and socio-political environment contaminated by toxic forces. The record's transpositional sound practices provide a diasporic "articulation" (Hall quoted in Grossberg 1986), resourcing a poetics of feeling capable of linking and thus amplifying black Atlantic and Mediterranean histories of dispersion and loss. We heard it in Miles already, on the A-side, this cry that sounds the Mediterranean "in the wake" (Sharpe 2016, 14) of modernity's originary histories of passage, a Mediterranean "occupy[ing] and [...] occupied by the continuous and changing present of slavery's as yet unresolved unfolding" (Sharpe 2016, 14). That unfolding, like the plot of the novel, is a *noir* affair, its resolution far from clear. Musical practices in this way perform ritual "wake work" (Sharpe 2016, 14) in Izzo's *noir* sensibility, creating space and enacting self-fashioned practices of mourning and critical reflection, as well as ways of being with and caring for.

5. Lole seems to dwell on Latin music and musical scenes in the trilogy. She puts on salsa, like the record *Pura Salsa* (1974) by Panamanian singer Azuquita. And she works at a club whose orchestra features tangos, boleros, mambos, and cha-chas. It's Lole who explains the B-side ("Saeta" and "Solea") of *Sketches* to Montale. In *Solea*, now that Lole has left him—not just for Spain, but to be with a Spanish guitar player—Fabio increasingly finds himself at Hassan's bar. Sensing Fabio's mood, Hassan, who usually plays French *chansons*, switches things up:

> Il m'avait fait un clin d'œil. Complice, jusqu'au bout. Et Miles Davis avait attaqué *Solea*. Un morceau que j'adorais. Que j'écoutais sans cesse, la nuit, depuis que Lole m'avait quitté.
> —La *solea*, m'avait-elle expliqué un soir, c'est la colonne vertébrale du chant flamenco.
> —Pourquoi tu ne chantes pas, toi? Du flamenco, du jazz ...
> Elle avait une voix superbe, je le savais. [...] Mais Lole s'était toujours refusée à chanter en dehors des réunions familiales.
> —Ce que je cherche, je ne l'ai pas encore trouvé, m'avait-elle répondu, après un long silence.
> Ce silence, justement, qu'il faut savoir trouver au plus fort de la tension de la *solea*.
> —Tu ne comprends rien, Fabio. (Izzo 1998, 29)

Sketches becomes a refrain in the trilogy for silence as much as sound. It crystallizes an intensely felt silence. In Hassan's hands, it becomes a way of looking after Montale, giving him what he needs. Fabio has learned that Lole does sing now, with *him*. She has even recorded with her new Spanish musical lover. Deeply connected with his sadness, and with his drinking, Fabio hears the album like a Mediterranean blues record. Not completely unlike the imagined female voice at the heart of the origin myth of his musical voice (Thompson), the *noir* performance of white French masculinity here finds itself tethered to a spectrics of sound rooted in the moving body and voice of an absent (post/colonially) othered woman. Black musical culture and cultural practices facilitate Montale's working through an existential crisis, but also remain "the exclusive domain of blackness" (Higginson 2017, 84). Put differently, if black musical culture crystallizes crises in French white masculinity, contributing to the dark tone of French *noir*, it seems French white men collect and play that music in order negotiate uneasy relationships with their privilege. Izzo's use of *Sketches of Spain* resonates with a history of French literature and thought whereby "black music in general, and jazz in particular, remains a vital, unselfconscious origin out of which, for better or worse, the white subject emerges" or fails to do so (64). Like the (sonic) cabin hideout, this fraternity of sound tends to be inherited from the father and strictly appropriated for (white French) men.

6. Izzo sonically maps the Mediterranean in relation to black Atlantic (musical) culture, history, and thought—Edmund Smyth even reports that Izzo "wrote an agit-prop play calling for the liberation of Angela Davis" in 1971 (Smyth 2007 [1971], 112)—but if we're being honest, we must admit that Izzo's "racial scores" (Higginson) script black life in a way that recalls the stereotypical casting and sounding practices of French cinema, *noir* or not: the only black character to play any kind of important role in this scenario is the young French West Indian prostitute, Marie-Lou:

> Elle avait débarqué dans le quartier il y a trois mois. Elle était superbe. Genre Diana Ross, à vingt-deux piges. [...] Rien n'était vulgaire en elle, même pas sa manière d'être assise. Elle était presque hautaine. [...]. On aimait bien se retrouver. Pour elle, j'étais un client idéal. Pour moi, c'était plus simple que d'aimer. Et ça m'allait bien pour le moment. (Izzo 1995, 100)

It seems that for Marie-Lou, *noire est son métier*;[4] her blackness and femininity directly correlate to her sexual (permanent) availability, her role in the narrative, and ultimately her substitutability. For the context of the current discussion, black static in Izzo's *noir* audiotopia comes from its disconnections at the intersections of gender and race. What interests us here is Montale's description of Marie-Lou as a "22-year-old Diana Ross," a sonic and visual icon whose brand of black femininity was a carefully crafted performance. Once famously described (by Jamaica Kincaid no less) as the "last of the black white girls,"[5] Diana Ross carefully worked with her stylists and producers to create an image that would have strong crossover appeal:

> The making of Diana Ross as a black celebrity icon in the late 1960s/ early 1970s, as she transitioned from being a member of the Supremes, is a fascinating case study in how the artist and her producers were able to incorporate certain racial markers of difference into her image and persona while simultaneously cultivating her as an exemplar of cultural assimilation, luxury capitalism, and mainstream acceptability. (Fleetwood 2015, 57)

Marie-Lou also plays this role for Montale and the (assumed) reader, building especially on post/colonial *doudouiste* tropes of French West Indian sexual/musicality. Transposing Diana Ross's voice and music onto Marie-Lou's body sets her up for what will be her lot in the novel: to serve as a surrogate ("at the moment") for (endless post/colonial) others. The passage reminds us that much hardboiled sensibility is anchored in performances of (French) white masculinity simultaneously in crisis and in affirmation, where the former mode provides an alibi of sorts for the latter one.

7. After meeting up with Marie-Lou, they decide to bar hop, and she takes him to the latest underground spots for music:

> L'ancien arsenal des galères s'ouvrait sur un couloir d'écrans télé. Au bout, sous les voûtes, des salles rap, techno, rock, reggae. Tequila pour commencer, et reggae pour la soif. Depuis quand n'avais-je plus dansé? Un siècle. Mille ans. On changea de lieu, de bar. D'heure en heure. Le Passeport, Le Maybe blues, le Pêle-Mêle. Aller voir ailleurs, toujours, comme en Espagne. Nous avions atterri au Pourquoi, rue Fortia. Une boîte antillaise. [...] Tequila. Et salsa! Nos corps trouvèrent très vite leur

---

4   See *Noire n'est pas mon métier*, by Aïssa Maïga (2018).
5   *Village Voice* article (1976) quoted in Kooijman 2017, 106.

accord. Collé-serré. [...] Dans mes bras, Marie-Lou était de plus en plus légère. Sa transpiration libérait les épices de son corps. Musc, cannelle, poivre. Basilic aussi, comme Lole. J'aimais les corps épicés. (1995, 108)

Although Izzo's cast of women share certain characteristics with classic *femmes fatales*, they tend rather toward tropes of colonial love based on myths of reciprocity that seek to elide the ways in which power foundationally structures the entire relationship. This is where they meet up with the Gyptis and Protis myth of Massalia. In casting Marie-Lou as this intoxicating, yet highly replaceable, musically black being, Izzo produces a racialized and gendered scripting of blackness that finds its antecedents in the ways in which Western thought's philosophical "authorities have over time 'scripted' musical performance as a specifically racial phenomenon; [...] race itself emerges from this process as (newly or further) essentialized" (Higginson 2017, 4). Gender dynamics are key in Izzo's audiotopic transpositions. Like Fabio and his boys, contemporary French noir fiction seems to love hanging out on the trail and the (crime) scene of African American jazz greats. Check out Michel Boujut's *Souffler n'est pas jouer* on Sydney Bechet (2000) and *La vie de Marie-Thérèse qui bifurqua quand sa passion pour le jazz prit une forme excessive* centering on bluesman Big Bill Broonzy (2008). Or read Maurice Dantec's *Comme le fantôme d'un jazzman dans la station Mir en déroute* where free jazz artist Albert Ayler serves as the protagonist's guardian angel. Or, for example, *Les Treize morts d'Albert Ayler*,[6] where a collection of French *noir* fiction writers were invited to write short story variations on Albert Ayler's (semi-) mysterious death in 1970.[7] Izzo's trilogy can be likened to *noir* novels, and jazz fiction, where

musical creation is a form of absolute self-alienation [...] [where] references to black sexual energy, playfulness, childishness, and general lack of inhibition are now replaced by names that begin to represent the racial score [i.e., the inscription of sonic blackness] metonymically: (famous tenor saxophonist) John Coltrane, (famous altoist) Charlie Parker, (famous trumpet player) Miles Davis. (Higginson 2017, 84)

6   See Anquetil et al. 1996.

7   Although he left it for other forms of expression, Ayler reformed a free jazz group and toured in France less the five months before his death, including at the Maeght Foundation museum of modern art on the Colline des Gardettes overlooking Saint-Paul de Vence in the south of France. See the recording *Nuits de La Fondation Maeght* (Albert Ayler), released in 1971 by the French record label Shandar Records.

Miles Davis serves as a global figure of black American masculinity, amplified in France by the popularity of the *Ascenseur pour l'échafaud* soundtrack, supplemented by photo spreads of him and Jeanne Moreau, and feature appearances on French TV. Izzo borrows this blackness, and brandishes sonically and materially it in the performance of (black) French and Mediterranean *noir* masculinity. In the process, metonymical and metaphorical slippage (dis)locates black American jazz artists at the center of a disappearance that presages, results in, and looks back on their loss. Izzo's black Atlantic sound dreams are haunted by forms of post/coloniality whose poetics of exoticism and primitivism (which we can liken to Georges Saint Pierre or Victor Segalen) tend to ghost black life.

8. Ultimately, Izzo's mythic notion of Marseilles and of the Mediterranean—an audiotopia that echoes the black Atlantic and projects across the violence of European border controls, the restrictions of and restricted access to citizenship, and the racial and gender dynamics that structure the possibilities of claiming home, feeling home, or being dispossessed of home—"generally requires a delicate ideological balancing act," as Moulakis shows. While they "represent a reaffirmation of the distinctiveness of the Provençal south vis-à-vis the national center" (Moulakis 2005, 30), and while they expand the transnational geography of the Mediterranean to the black Atlantic, they still produce gendered and raced vantage points that distort the transmission of ideal sonic futures. The blackness of *noir* pulls from the blackness of the black Atlantic, and the *noirceur* of black life. To hear the *noir* and black on both sides of the current record, we need "big ears," fleshy ears, attuned to the ways in which histories of post/colonial desire, fueled by the voice of women in mythic landscapes, animate the sonics of this *vivre ensemble*.[8] We have to listen to the intense silence as much as the black scream. Still, this "listening to the sea" has no meaning "unless it becomes a project," Izzo contends:

> Marseilles proudly proclaims its experience of the world. We might add: its Mediterranean experience. Because we have no other. But could we ever have any other? That's the question I ask, as a bastard from Marseilles, a half-bred product of Italian, Spanish and Arab cultures. And although I may be a French citizen today, the sea—this Mediterranean of ours, on which my eyes, my heart and my thoughts are focused—remains the only

8   See Rustin-Paschal and Tucker 2008.

place where I feel that I exist. Where I can envisage a future for myself. In spite of everything. [...] Yes, I believe, as I look at the sea, that there is a future for Europe, and a beauty in that future. It lies in what Edouard Glissant calls "Mediterranean Creoleness." (Izzo 2013b, 33)

Izzo's Mediterranean *noir* calls for "the blue against the black." In his essay "The Blue and the Black," Izzo holds up the Bible as the first *noir* narrative: Cain and Abel. The struggle against hate, jealously, envy, the struggle to love one's brother, is as old as the story of humanity itself, it is part of the human condition. The Mediterranean isn't a utopia, it's a stage where that drama has been played out since ancient times, and where it continues to be played out, for better and worse, today. Mediterranean history is as much a story of darkness as it is of light. The question is whether we can get through it, live together, and love one another enough to survive it all. *Spoiler alert!* Fabio doesn't. He can't quite make it through. He gets sucked into the wake, into the waves ... By the story's end he returns to the water, to the deepest depths of the blue, the bluest depths of the *noir*.

Works Cited

Anquetil, Gilles, Patrick Bard, et al. 1996. *Les Treize morts d'Albert Ayler*. Paris: Gallimard. Série noire.

Carr, Ian. 1998. *Miles Davis: The Definitive Biography*. Philadelphia: Da Capo Press. Kindle.

Crease, Stephanie Stein. 2002. *Gil Evans Out of the Cool: His Life and Music*. Chicago: A Capella Books.

Davis, Miles, and Quincy Troupe. 1989. *Miles: The Autobiography of Miles Davis*. New York: Simon and Schuster.

Edwards, Brent Hayes. 2003. *The Practice of Diaspora: Literature, Translation, and the Rise of Black Internationalism*. Cambridge: Harvard University Press.

——. 2017. *Epistrophies*. Cambridge: Harvard University Press.

Fleetwood, Nicole. 2015. *On Racial Icons: Blackness and the Public Imagination*. New Brunswick: Rutgers University Press.

Gillespie, Dizzy. 2009 [1979]. *To Be ... Or Not to Bop*. Minneapolis: University of Minnesota Press.

Griffin, Farah Jasmine. 2004. "When Malindy Sings: A Meditation on Black Women's Vocality." In *Uptown Conversation: The New Jazz Studies*, edited by Robert G. O'Meally et al., 102–25. New York: Columbia University Press.

Griffin, Farah Jasmine, and Salim Washington. 2008. *Clawing at the Limits of Cool: Miles Davis, John Coltrane, and the Greatest Jazz Collaboration Ever.* New York: St. Martin's Press.

Grossberg, Lawrence. 1986. "On Postmodernism and Articulation: An Interview with Stuart Hall." *Journal of Communication Inquiry* 10 (2): 45–60.

Head, Gretchen. 2015. "'The Sea Spits Out Corpses': Peripherality, Genre and Affect in the Cosmopolitan Mediterranean." *The Global South* 9 (2) (Fall): 38–59.

Higginson, Pim. 2017. *Scoring Race: Jazz Fiction and Francophone Africa.* Rochester: James Currey.

Ireland, Susan. 2004. "Representations of the *Banlieues* in the Contemporary Marseillais Polar." *Contemporary French and Francophone Studies* 8 (1): 21–29.

Izzo, Jean-Claude. 1995. *Total Khéops.* Paris: Editions Gallimard.

——. 1996. *Chourmo.* Paris: Editions Gallimard.

——. 1998. *Solea.* Paris: Editions Gallimard.

——. 2005. *Total Chaos.* Translated by Howard Curtis. New York: Europa Editions.

——. 2006. *Chourmo.* Translated by Howard Curtis. New York: Europa Editions.

——. 2007. *Solea.* Translated by Howard Curtis. New York: Europa Editions.

——. 2013a. "The Blue and the Black." In *Garlic, Mint & Sweet Basil: Essays on Marseilles, Mediterranean Cuisine, and Noir Fiction.* Translated by Howard Curtis. New York: Europa Editions.

——. 2013b. "Listening to the Sea." In *Garlic, Mint & Sweet Basil: Essays on Marseilles, Mediterranean Cuisine, and Noir Fiction.* Translated by Howard Curtis. New York: Europa Editions.

——. 2013c. *Garlic, Mint & Sweet Basil: Essays on Marseilles, Mediterranean Cuisine, and Noir Fiction.* Translated by Howard Curtis. New York: Europa Editions.

Kelley, Robin. 2012. *Africa Speaks, America Answers: Modern Jazz in Revolutionary Times.* Cambridge: Harvard University Press.

Kooijman, Jaap. 2017. "Whitewashing the Dreamgirls: Beyoncé, Diana Ross and the Commodification of Blackness." In *Revisiting Star Studies: Cultures, Themes, and Methods,* edited by Sabrina Qiong Yu and Guy Austin. Edinburgh: Edinburgh University Press.

Kun, Josh. 2005. *Audiotopia: Music, Race, and America.* Berkeley: University of California Press.

Maïga, Aïssa. 2018. *Noire n'est pas mon métier.* Paris: Editions du Seuil.

McKay, Claude. 1957 [1929]. *Banjo: A Novel without a Plot.* Orlando: Hope McKay Virtue.

——. 2007 [1937]. *A Long Way from Home*. Piscataway: Rutgers University Press.

Moulakis, Athanasios. 2005. "The Mediterranean Region: Reality, Delusion, or Euro-Mediterranean Project?" *Mediterranean Quarterly* 16 (2): 11–38.

Ramsey, Guthrie. 2004. *Race Music: Black Cultures from Bebop to Hip-Hop*. Berkeley: University of California Press.

Reynolds, Guy. 2000. "'Sketches of Spain'": Richard Wright's *Pagan Spain* and African-American Representations of the Hispanic." *Journal of American Studies* 34 (3): 487–502.

Ross, Kristin. 2010. "Parisian Noir." *New Literary History* 41: 95–109.

Rustin-Paschal, Nichole, and Sherrie Tucker. 2008. *Big Ears: Listening for Gender in Jazz Studies*. Durham: Duke University Press.

Sallis, James. 2000. *Chester Himes: A Life*. New York: Walker Publishing.

Schuyler, Phillip. 1981. "Music and Meaning among the Gnawa Religious Brotherhood of Morocco." *The World of Music* 23 (1): 3–13.

Sharpe, Christina. 2016. *In the Wake: On Blackness and Being*. Durham: Duke University Press.

Smyth, Edmund. 2007 [1971]. "Marseille *Noir*: Jean-Claude Izzo and the Mediterranean Detective." *Romance Studies* 25 (2): 111–21.

Stovall, Tyler. 2000. "The Fire This Time: Black American Expatriates and the Algerian War." *Yale French Studies* 98: 182–200.

Von Eschen, Penny. 2004. *Satchmo Blows Up the World: Jazz Ambassadors Play the Cold War*. Cambridge: Harvard University Press.

Walser, Robert. 1993. "Out of Notes: Signification, Interpretation, and the Problem of Miles Davis." *The Musical Quarterly* 77 (2): 343–65.

Wesley, Bernabé. 2014. "La nostalgie d'un autre present." *Études littéraires* 45 (2) (Summer): 121–34.

Weston, Randy, and Willard Jenkins. 2010. *African Rhythms: The Autobiography of Randy Weston*. Durham: Duke University Press.

Zaborowska, Magdalena. 2009. *James Baldwin's Turkish Decade: Erotics of Exile*. Durham: Duke University Press.

Discography

Davis, Miles. 1960. *Sketches of Spain*. Columbia Records.
Weston, Randy. 1972. *Blue Moses*. CTI Records.

CHAPTER TWELVE

Transposed Modes

Musical Mapping and Literary Lapping in Current Francophone Migratory Texts

Alison Rice

> Sur quoi se fondent les élans migratoires? Bien sûr : la guerre, la terreur, la peur, la souffrance économique, les désordres du climat ... Mais aussi: sur l'*appel secret de ce qui existe autrement.*
>
> (Patrick Chamoiseau, *Frères migrants*)

> On part au nord comment ça se fait
> Que c'est là que vivent les contes de fees
>
> (Magyd Cherfi, "On part")

> Il progressait. Et chacun de ses pas le ramenait à son passé, à sa vie de cavales.
>
> (Fabienne Kanor, *Faire l'aventure*)

Authors of current francophone migratory texts find themselves at once following in the wake of a long literary tradition and on the verge of making waves by writing in new ways. A plethora of precedents exist in a variety of languages for the contemplations of exile and singularity that are necessarily part of the voyages of such iconic characters as Ulysses. There are not as many examples for literary depictions of contemporary figures whose names and stories have so often been obscured by what Alexis Nouss refers to as "le phénomène migratoire" (Nouss 2018, 162). As a result of an "effet de masse" that renders them "indistincts et menaçants," migrants from a variety of locations who attempt to reach Europe in this century are often stripped of "toute subjectivité et toute individualité" (Nouss 2018, 161). What is needed to counteract the tendency among Europeans to overlook the complicated predicaments of migrants today is a textual creativity that renders in writing "la densité de l'expérience éprouvée en son corps et en son âme par chaque migrant," and thereby inspires readers to "porter un autre regard sur ceux-là qui apparaissent dans les jungles, les villes, les camps ou les écrans de télévision" (Nouss 2018, 161). In his praise for the potential of literature to relate in intimate, intricate terms the singular struggles of migrants, Nouss mentions a recent text that meets this challenge: Nathacha Appanah's *Tropique de la violence* (2016). This novel tells the tales of individuals affected by migration with an urgency and an audacity that artfully reflect the text's eponymous violence as well as the upheaval that so often accompanies displacement across national borders. Nouss is right to cite Appanah's publication, for it is part of what I discern to be a new movement of fresh, brazen portrayals of migration.[1] Indeed, recent works are propelled by a necessity to accomplish in the specific context of the present what Nouss extols literature for more generally: "La littérature nomme le visage des sans-visages" (Nouss 2018, 162). Appanah's *Tropique de la violence* is an exemplary novel that I propose to examine alongside the revelations and intimations in Fatou Diome's *Celles qui attendent* (2010) and Fabienne Kanor's *Faire l'aventure* (2014), two works of fiction that also depict migrant experiences from unprecedented angles.[2] In each of these three

---

1   A number of relatively recent publications in French focus on migration, exploring the phenomenon at its different stages in an attempt to reveal the realities of this increasingly common experience. A few prominent examples include the following: Tahar Ben Jelloun, *Partir* (Gallimard, 2006); Ananda Devi, *Ceux du large* (Bruno Doucey, 2017); Laurent Gaudé, *Eldorado* (Actes Sud, 2007); Marie NDiaye, *Trois femmes puissantes* (Gallimard, 2009); Boualem Sansal, *Harraga* (Gallimard, 2007).

2   Alexis Nouss contemplates the difficulty of determining exactly what works can be attributed to the category "littérature migrante" in France today. He outlines the confusion that abounds concerning whether "migrant literature" must depict "les thèmes de la migration" or whether it must be written by an author who can be considered to be a migrant: "La notion de littérature migrante est floue et hésite à qualifier les auteurs ou les œuvres" (Nouss 2018, 162). I have opted for the expression "migratory texts" to refer to written works that engage with migration, rather than get caught up in loaded questions of nomenclature and categorization in a literary conversation that is already rather saturated with predisposed possibilities ranging from "littérature immigrée" to "littérature frontalière" (Nouss 2018, 163).

literary creations, the author steps outside of herself and ventures beyond her personal path to explore with profound empathy the varied itineraries of others.[3] Taken together, these three novels can be seen as illustrative of an important burgeoning current of literary works composed in what I call "transposed modes." These texts are inventively plurilingual and musical, displaying forms of expression that often defy translation in an effort to represent the complexity of contemporary migration with appropriate emphasis and emotion.[4]

Overture

"It was, it *is* a journey," are words that author Fabienne Kanor pronounces[5] to describe the endeavor that became *Faire l'aventure*, her 2014 novel. This picaresque text spans six eventful years in the life of a young Senegalese man whose eyes are fixated from the outset on a particular horizon that he intends to reach no matter the cost. The composition of the book was inspired by the writer's own desire to experience transcontinental movement in its many forms. Kanor, whose professional activities include journalism and documentary filmmaking, wasn't content to study the plight of migrants from afar. The above-quoted words evoking a trip pertain to her own undertaking, as she devoted herself to meeting with migrants of all sorts, some of whom were seeking better lives in preferable

---

3   It may be that their different familial backgrounds and various journeys have inspired them to be especially attentive to the diversity of others' experiences. Nathacha Appanah was brought up on the island of Mauritius—where her ancestors had come from India—before moving to France, and she has taken a number of long trips for her work as a journalist. Fatou Diome spent her childhood and adolescence in her native Senegal before relocating to France. Fabienne Kanor was born in France to parents from the French overseas department of Martinique, and she spent significant time in the island home of her parents as well as in Senegal.

4   It is noteworthy that a number of recent French-language publications on migration are collective volumes that unite a variety of authors—and often artists— in a gesture of activist solidarity that seeks to represent migration with renewed purpose. Two prominent examples include the following: Patrick Chamoiseau and Michel Le Bris, eds., *Osons la fraternité!: Les écrivains aux côtés des migrants* (Philippe Rey, 2018); Béatrice Vallaeys, ed., *Ce qu'ils font est juste: Ils mettent la solidarité et l'hospitalité à l'honneur* (Don Quichotte éditions, 2017).

5   Personal telephone conversation with Fabienne Kanor, April 7, 2018.

climes, while others were simply hoping to survive. The journey was necessarily involved, entailing stops at a variety of locations the author lists as follows in a reflective moment: "Je suis allée à Lampedouze [*sic*], Ténérifé [*sic*], Bamako, Nouadhibou, Nador, Ouarzazate, Madrid, Almeria, Rome, Mbour, Dakar" (Kanor 2016, 408). It is significant that Kanor does not provide the names of these places in any obvious order. Her apparently disorganized enumeration disrupts a sense of progression from one country to the next, from one locality to another. What she iterates instead is quite possibly a spontaneous evocation of spots as they come to mind, a stream-of-consciousness accounting that veers away from any clear itinerary. Rather than conveying a hierarchy ascending toward European cities, the desirable destinations that so often constitute the unwavering goals of these movements north, Kanor takes advantage of this naming to point to other places, beginning with islands on the outskirts of the continent, precariously perched places that are officially a part of Europe but that are undeniably on the edges. These are the locations that have increasingly taken on clandestine individuals in recent years; they are places that are often inhabited only temporarily, as migrants seek to move on. Kanor's insightful novel is appropriately concerned with islands and outskirts and caught up with movements toward the mainland.

Kanor's *Faire l'aventure* is a work that acknowledges that migration across vast expanses of water is not a new phenomenon. Indeed, a human smuggler is quick to assert that the Mediterranean Sea has always been a place of passage: "Depuis toujours, ça passe et ça défile. C'est pas pour rien qu'on l'appelle la mer du milieu" (Kanor 2014, 291). But it has arguably never been the location of such large-scale movement undergone by so many, as the principal protagonist later observes: "Au temps du prophète, les hommes ne s'absentaient pas de chez eux aussi longtemps et aussi loin" (Kanor 2014, 320). In like manner, philosopher Achille Mbembe asserts that we are living in a "nouvel âge de dispersion et de circulation," a period marked by "l'intensification des migrations" (Mbembe 2016, 226). Most migrants are motivated by more than simplified facts, as Patrick Chamoiseau contends in the epigraph to this chapter. A large percentage find the impetus to board boats and traverse borders not solely because of ecological or economic hardship or political or religious persecution, but also because something has spoken to their imaginary so powerfully that they cannot be dissuaded from pursuing their geographical goal. Even when they come up against *repeated setbacks* and are *repeatedly sent back* to their native countries, they are nonetheless prone to keep trying, to continue circling back again toward Europe. This tendency to remain focused on a desired destination— even when it means completely starting over after each new arrest and expulsion—is exemplified in the plight of Biram from *Faire l'aventure*. But it is significant that this protagonist finally exhibits a change of heart at the close of the novel and opts to embrace a permanent return to his native Senegal after a storied itinerary. In the end, he comes to terms with his imperfect homeland as a viable alternative to the tumults of the sea and the torments of the clandestine lifestyle.

Plurilingual Trappings

The movement that is caught up in migration necessitates new forms of textual representation that are pushing francophone works in new directions. Admittedly, francophone studies have perhaps always been concerned, at least in some ways, with foregrounding "the interaction of cultures," "plural notions of identity," and "the presence of the French language across borders and frontiers," as Brian Nelson explains in *The Cambridge Introduction to French Literature* (Nelson 2015, 238). But the role of the French language is changing in recent texts as other tongues are integrated into the writing in wide-ranging ways, expanding the vocabularies of many readers in a carefully conceived apprenticeship that immerses them in new settings and instructs them in other idioms. The inclusion of a variety of languages in the French-language text destabilizes the tongue that might otherwise be perceived to be dominant. This gesture appears to place French on a level playing field with a multitude of forms of expression that are at times vying for attention, but that in most circumstances coexist in a plurilingual situation.[6] The work of fiction appears to reflect a semantic reality that

6   I employ the adjective "plurilingual" in light of the observations of Geneviève Brisson, for whom "the lens of plurilingualism entails a dynamic view of linguistic and cultural repertoires and allows for the inclusion of different levels of competence in many languages" (Brisson 2018, 77). The insertion of words and phrases from various other languages into the literary work contributes, in my view, to a textual creation that bears witness to the "repertoire of more than two linguistic and cultural resources" that "plurilingual transnational" individuals often acquire out of necessity. Competence in more than one language is something they gain from their migratory movements and an accompanying requirement to engage in "a negotiation of subject positions" (Brisson 2018, 78).

has been occasioned by vast movements of people from different native tongues who find themselves in the same space. When Kanor cites the cities on her research itinerary for her novel on migration, it is not anecdotal that she neglects to mention a single French location. France is far from the sole imagined destination of many migrants from a variety of countries. In fact, the Hexagon is often deliberately eschewed by a number of aspiring foreigners who would prefer to end up in neighboring European countries, such as Spain and Italy, where they believe they can benefit from more abundant opportunities.[7]

Fabienne Kanor's novel contains a plethora of plurilingual moments, featuring words from Arabic and Wolof that are known to her Senegalese protagonists as well as other terms that come from Spanish and Italian, and many words from English. The latter erupts in a significant scene on a beach on the Spanish island of Tenerife, where Biram has taken up temporary residence on his way from Senegal to the European mainland. He is selling trinkets to tourists on vacation when a pirogue overfilled with migrants arrives on the shore and is immediately greeted by two forces: the Red Cross and the police. The wealthy visitors to the island gather and gape at these sudden intruders, commenting on the spectacle before them: "*Unbelievable*, ils répétaient que c'était dingue, autant de jeunes dans un bateau. C'était dingue, *really*, c'était dingue, de quitter un pays quand il y avait tout à construire : routes, hôpitaux, hôtels, écoles" (Kanor 2014, 207). The use of these two English words in italics provides a particular rhythm to these insensitive comments,

7   A variety of francophone texts depict other locations in Europe as alternative destinations to France. This focus on other European nations in French-language literary works reveals that France is not the only country that has caught the attention of those who aspire to move to more prosperous places. Indeed, not only have recent migrants focused on reaching different European spaces, but places other than France have long spoken to the imaginations of those in colonial—and postcolonial—francophone countries. In Tahar Ben Jelloun's aforementioned novel *Partir*, it is significant that the clandestine characters are clustered in Spain, not France. In a brief text coauthored by Alain Mabanckou and Christophe Merlin, *L'Europe depuis l'Afrique* (2009), the narrative voice enumerates a list of European cities that capture the fancy of children educated in francophone Africa, and it is significant that not one of these urban centers is located on French soil: "Plusieurs noms de villes européennes allaient revenir pendant le cours d'histoire de Madame Paraiso, noms qui allaient être graves dans nos mémoires: Berlin, Helsinki, Dantzig, Varsovie, Nuremberg, Sarajevo, Vienne, etc." (Mabanckou and Merlin 2009, 14).

adding to the impact of the opinions they frame and accentuating the thrice repeated judgment that this occurrence is "crazy." It is impressive how the precise points of insertion of the English terms into these phrases serve to emphasize their own ludicrousness, and undermine what otherwise might constitute valid assertions. Their inclusion also hints that the supercilious individuals uttering them are monolingual, failing to grasp the subtleties not only of other languages, but also of other ways of life. This passage does not contain any translations or indications to non-English speakers of what these words mean, in line with a choice throughout the text to include terms from different languages without explanation.[8] Such a choice would presumably render reading slightly less fluid for some, but slowing down those who are comfortable in a single tongue might be part of the purpose. Putting the monolingual French reader in contact with another form of expression accentuates that reader's lack of familiarity with other tongues, creating a sense of linguistic precariousness that approximates the multiple vulnerabilities—linguistic and otherwise—known to many migrants as they move from one location to another. In general, such plurilingual moments count less on communicating an exact message than on conveying a mood or intimating an experience, and this is where the literary work succeeds most saliently. Indeed, the layers of the text come through with particular strength as Kanor smoothly moves between expressions without explanations, footnotes, or a glossary.

In contrast to Kanor's sparse linguistic commentary in *Faire l'aventure*, Appanah's novel set on the French island of Mayotte features a glossary on its final page with 11 Maore Comorian words and their meanings

---

8   An exception exists in the final chapter of *Faire l'aventure*, wherein the principal protagonist Biram grabs the hand of his beloved Marème and implores her with a question that figures in italics, "*Li lan la?*," and is translated in the only footnote of the novel: "1. Qu'est-ce qui se passe? (wolof)" (Kanor 2014, 332). It appears meaningful that this deeply emotional moment includes a footnote, a textual insertion that provides readers with a precise rendering of this query in French. This annotation stands out in contrast to so many other plurilingual passages that remain approximative for many readers who are left to guess the exact translation of diverse terms. It may be, in this instance, that the words themselves are not as significant as the pause that is created in the reading experience by the glance at the bottom of the page to ascertain the meaning of this heartfelt question. This textual device makes readers aware of language in a jolt, removing them from the apparent seamlessness that marks the plurilingual strategies that are present throughout the novel.

(Appanah 2016, 177). The author has incorporated these terms into the text in roman font, with an asterisk signaling the word on its first appearance. Ranging from "kofia," the word for an embroidered Comorian bonnet (Appanah 2016, 86) to "mourengué," the expression for an ancestral barehanded combat (Appanah 2016, 102), these specially selected terms contribute to the telling of the unfortunate tale of an adolescent driven to murder on this island in the Indian Ocean where his migrant mother landed one night when he was just a babe in arms. Taken in immediately thereafter by a Frenchwoman who had moved from the Hexagon to this far-off place for love but whose amorous relationship had ended, Moïse could reconcile neither his dark skin with his adopted mother's lighter pigmentation nor his different origin with his French upbringing. This central character feels as if he doesn't belong, but a similar sense of disillusionment clearly haunts all of the six narrators who express themselves alternately in the pages of this novel. The polyvocal portrayal highlights an overwhelming situation in this French enclave in the Comoros archipelago: a large number of undocumented children are left entirely alone following the deportation of their parents, and these youngsters are forced to fend for themselves in a society plagued by severe destitution and searing violence.

Mayotte may be a French overseas department, a status it has held since 2011, but it bears little resemblance to France in the experience of Stéphane, one of the narrators who express themselves in the eponymous chapters of Appanah's *Tropique de la violence*. A volunteer from France who works with youth on the island, Stéphane discovers soon after his arrival that Mayotte is very different from his homeland. Indeed, there are tremendous tensions between those who are from this location and those who have arrived illegally, and this has led to a potentially explosive situation:

> On te dit que si ça continue, si l'État français ne fait rien, ce sont les Mahorais eux-mêmes qui prendront leur destin en main et ficheront tous les clandestins et les délinquants dehors. Tu as alors l'image de centaines de Noirs descendant dans la rue avec des machettes et tu ne sais plus si c'est une image du Rwanda ou du Zimbabwe ou du Congo et tu dis *Ça n'arrivera jamais dans un département français.* (Appanah 2016, 138–39)

Not only is he a foreigner to the codes of understanding and the ways of life that are rendered fragile by an abundance of new arrivals on this densely populated island, but Stéphane is also initially unfamiliar with the language that is spoken around him: "J'étais content, j'avais appris quelques mots en mahorais : *kwezi, wawe ouhiriori bani, jeje bweni, marahaba, ewa,* 'bonjour, comment t'appelles-tu, bonjour madame, merci, oui,' et mon accent les faisait rire mais jamais ils ne discutaient avec moi" (Appanah 2016, 114). Interestingly enough, these commonly employed words are not present in the glossary, and this sentence that emphasizes the narrator's ostracization thereby also gives the reader of French a vocabulary lesson.

It becomes clear in *Tropique de la violence* that the inhabitants of Mayotte for whom French is not a mother tongue consider language and race to be inextricably intertwined. Indeed, when Moïse's adopted mother passes away and he is left to his own devices at the age of 15, it is his command of French that subjects him to the scrutiny of the most powerful figure of the ghetto, Bruce. This terrifying teenager chastises Moïse for speaking French too well, and he frames his critique in racial terms: "Y a que toi qui parles et tu parles bien ah ça oui tu mets des mots bien propres, bien ordonnés, des mots bien français, bien blancs" (Appanah 2016, 64). The same character reformulates this accusation later in the text, underscoring through his condemnation the perceived treachery that is bound up in a fluent command of French and its implications for identity in this setting: "Je devais changer les règles, je devais montrer que les gens comme toi, qui ont la peau aussi noire que moi mais dont les paroles sont blanches et fades comme celles des muzungus, je devais montrer que je savais régler leur compte à ces gens-là" (Appanah 2016, 97). The indication of the speaker's domination in this sentence is inseparable from his wielding of the term "muzungu," the word for "foreigner" on an island where those from elsewhere are looked down upon. Unitalicized and integrated into the text in a variety of passages, muzungu is one of the well-chosen words from this language of Mayotte that Appanah has woven seamlessly into her French writing.

In Fatou Diome's 2010 novel focusing on the excruciating experiences of a number of Senegalese women who are left behind while their husbands and sons attempt to make it to—and in—Spain, italicized terms from a variety of tongues provide rhythm to a text that depicts the doldrums of waiting day after day for any news of those who have departed. Expressions from Arabic occasionally enhance greetings, such as "Moi, ça va. *Alhamdoulilahi!*" (Diome 2010, 33), and intensify exclamations, as in "*Wallahi*, j'avais oublié" (Diome 2010, 102). While these italicized terms may not be well-known to many readers familiar with French, other Arabic words like "*Mektoub!*" (Diome 2010, 69) are more readily recognizable. Words from Wolof also frequently

enter the text, ranging from everyday expressions for popular games—
"awalé"—to oft-prepared dishes—"yassa"—that are neither italicized
nor accompanied by descriptions, but that readers can generally figure
out thanks to context clues (Diome 2010, 121). In some circumstances,
an explanation is included, such as in the phrase that follows the
mention of instruments called "pélinguères" that provide beats that
inspire great movement: "ces tam-tams taquins qui éperonnent la
fougue des danseurs" (Diome 2010, 281). Wolof sometimes slips into
the French-language text without a French-speaking reader's awareness
when it is translated into French, as in this saying: "La réussite d'un fils,
c'est à cela qu'on reconnaît une bonne mère" (Diome 2010, 51). A fourth
tongue makes its way into this work that is set not only in Senegal but
also in a distant Spain, where the men play a delicate game with local
women:

> Parce qu'ils pensaient encore à leur chère mère, à leur tendre épouse, à leur
> beau pays, Issa et Lamine se méfiaient des lassos qui menaçaient de les
> enserrer, surtout lorsqu'ils sortaient avec des femmes encore jeunes. *Mi
> amor, te quiero*: ils gloussaient, posaient leurs valises pour un moment.
> *Te quiero, quiero un niño*: là, ils prenaient la poudre d'escampette, sans
> trop s'expliquer. (Diome 2010, 207)

These simple, significant phrases in Spanish confer a certain movement
to this passage, plunging the reader into the linguistic setting that
requires the right reaction if a man hopes to maintain a love life
without becoming trapped in a country that he intends to inhabit only
temporarily.[9] This is an effective plurilingual textual technique by which
the language of the book is continually affected by the tonalities and
vocabularies of various tongues.

Diome's most unusual stylistic development, a signature of sorts that
runs throughout her oeuvre, comprises repetitive insertions of words or
phrases, often from Wolof. A brief example can be found in a child's
triumphant announcement, sung out in *Celles qui attendent* when his
relative has finally returned after a long absence: "*Fapa La-mine a*

---

9   The Spanish tongue enters Kanor's text in much the same way it is inserted
into Diome's novel, reinforcing the portrayal of women from the Canary Islands as
formidable foes to the unsuspecting foreigner: "Si tu les maries, elles te prennent
ton argent et si tu les emmerdes, on t'enferme, tu vas direct en *cárcel. Aquí, la
mujer manda*" (Kanor 2014, 126). In this work that thrusts the reader into a
location where plurilingual forms of expression are the norm and the necessity, no
translation is provided.

gata! *Fapa La-mine a gata*! Tonton Lamine est arrivé! Tonton Lamine est arrivé!" (Diome 2010, 265). The repetition here reinforces the sense of joy that flows from the exuberant boy, and the phrase in Wolof adds to the impression of authenticity and spontaneity that marks the celebratory moment. In another striking example from this novel, an alliterative expression that recurs at various points in is transported from the streets of Senegal to the page. This important exclamation has been repeated by many aspiring migrants who swear that their fate is focused on one of only two options, that they will either reach Spain or die: "'Barcelone ou Barsakh!' répètent hardiment les malheureux, prêts à jouer leur vie à la roulette russe" (Diome 2010, 201). This is one of several sayings that serve as refrains giving the literary text the feeling of an oral document, of a notated song, of a chorus that repeatedly emphasizes certain ideas until they enter indelibly into the mind of the reader, until they hit home.

Unlike Diome, Kanor is not originally from Senegal, but she has engaged in travels that have familiarized her with a similar soundscape, on which she draws to enhance her textual evocations of migration. Kanor comments on the expression that inflects Diome's novel when she explains the realities that influenced her own novel depicting migration: "Barça ou la mort ... C'est ce que disent les Sénégalais qui tentent de se rendre en Espagne par n'importe quel moyen, à n'importe quel prix" (Kanor 2016, 408). This mindset is present in the very title of *Faire l'aventure*, a term that is not of the author's own invention, but is instead a common expression in several West African countries to refer to this desire to migrate against all odds: "Aventurier parce que, on le sait, c'est toute une aventure, une folie, d'aller aujourd'hui en Europe sans papiers" (Kanor 2016, 408). The inspiration that the author has found in her own interactions with migrants at various locations in their itineraries, familiarizing herself with the places she lists in the quotation above, comes through in the very language of this novel, which records speech as it is evolving in transit. Her research into the lived experiences of migrants involved transcribing the voices of protagonists whose stories so often go unheard, as Kanor explains: "On les connaît ces images et aussi les chiffres qui vont avec, et aussi les lieux où ces tragédies modernes se déroulent. Ce qu'on sait moins, c'est la parole du dedans, ce que l'aventurier au jour le jour vit et ressent" (Kanor 2016, 408). In order to truly tell of these trials, of the cycles of suffering that are borne of migration, literary innovation is required. This is why from the title page, *Faire l'aventure* grasps the French language and transposes it, making it foreign for all readers, no matter their relationship to this tongue, revealing exigencies that have emerged from the myriad movements that its characters undertake between Africa and Europe. If the need to navigate a variety of spaces leads to a polyglot text, the resulting written work isn't merely decorated with fancy foreign terms. Instead, its plurilingual trappings are essential to the ripples of meaning that are made throughout the movements of current francophone fiction.

Musical Mappings

In his poetic treatise on the topic, Martinican writer Patrick Chamoiseau homes in on the strikingly marginalized status of migrants in the contemporary world: "des migrants restent échoués en marge de toutes les marges" (Chamoiseau 2017, 14). Throughout *Frères migrants*, Chamoiseau eloquently articulates a poetic opposition to this systemic ostracism. He lauds instead the possibility of an "écosystème relationnel" that would transform the current "mobilités du monde" from their exclusive orientations toward the dominant, the wealthy, the peaceful, and the abundant. The author envisions instead the emergence of movements that are less single-minded and that lead to "une cartographie de désirs erratiques" attracted to the unknown, the foreign (Chamoiseau 2017, 103). It is important that this theoretician should propose the possibility of interactions governed by different forces than those that determine today's well-worn migrant paths. Indeed, Chamoiseau's formulation recalls that of Charles Forsdick, whose focus on "literature of mobility" or "travel literature" led him to articulate a vision for French Studies that was open to "modes of mobility and contact" (Forsdick 2011, 97). These modes are continually transposed, changing their orientations and emphases in relation to varying forms of contact.

   If any locations are predisposed to allowing for such modes, it is the oft-adopted stops on the routes of migration such as those that figure in Kanor's list above. These are places that Chamoiseau identifies as particularly fruitful for all kinds of encounters:

> Les camps migratoires sont des lieux où quelque chose de nous s'étiole, où autre chose de nous s'ébranle vers autre chose. Nous y avons une faiblesse et une force Faiblesse immense, force balbutiante. En avoir conscience, considérer cette force et cette faiblesse ensemble, les associer comme une

grâce, les transmuter en Relation. Nul n'avait tiré leçon relationnelle de la Traite des nègres; la porte se vit ainsi ouverte aux génocides des Héréros et des Namas, aux camps nazis, aux goulags, aux carnages coloniaux, aux exécutions d'anticolonialistes. (Chamoiseau 2017, 122–23)[10]

When one individual comes up against another in a migratory camp far from their respective hometowns, the two are transformed by the meeting, leaving each of them a little less like the person they were beforehand. This is one more moment in a journey that has shaped each of these migrants, perhaps in deeply different ways, but that has also undoubtedly created resemblances among them due to the general experience of a similar plight. The language that communicates the strength of this encounter is paradoxically characterized by a form of "stuttering" that comes through in this passage's curtailed poetic line, by uncertain linguistic strides that reveal immense vulnerability, a weakened state wherein lies the opportunity for change. Chamoiseau asserts that it is impossible for migrants to remain entirely faithful to the perceived markers of identity that defined their person at the outset of the trip: "Aucun migrant ne transporte un pays, une culture, un absolu de langue, une religion complète. Uniquement les combinaisons utiles à sa survie" (Chamoiseau 2017, 98–99).

It isn't surprising that a reference to speech slips into Chamoiseau's evocation of the migratory camp, for learning to stammer in a foreign tongue is often a part of the transformation that individuals undergo when they change location. This is the case for Biram, the principal protagonist in *Faire l'aventure*, who can presumably get by with his knowledge of French in certain situations, but who is compelled to learn some Spanish in Spain and Italian in Italy, and who often also finds himself obliged to speak in English in various locations. He even gains a certain command of Russian in order to cater to some visitors to Tenerife, a competency which prompts an interlocutor to put his identity in question: "Depuis quand tu baragouines leur langue? T'es plus un Africain, toi. T'es un citoyen du monde" (Kanor 2014, 173–74). The Senegalese-born migrant whose story is related in a text divided into four parts bearing the titles of cities and islands—"Mbour," "Tenerife," "Lampédouse," "Rome"—laments that his identity is indeed less clear

---

10   In an interview, Chamoiseau comments on the particular style of this poetic text in terms that highlight its musicality: "The language in *Frères migrants* has a particular sound because it is meant to be read, sung, recited in all possible places" (Verstraet 2018, 128).

cut than it once was, as he moves consistently further from his homeland, his native tongue, and his Muslim faith.[11] This man, whose sights remain set on Europe despite countless setbacks, realizes in a contemplative moment that he really has become a different person, and it isn't just the languages he has taken on, but also the itineraries that necessitated such linguistic apprenticeships, that have combined to shape him:

> Il avait marché comme un fou entre Inhalid et Tamanrasset. Il avait eu chaud et soif dans le désert de Libye. Il avait pris des mers, tourné dans des villes, traversé des gares et des frontières. Il était monté dans des camions. Il avait roulé dans des cars rapides, voyagé dans des rafiots minus et des bateaux de prince. Ce n'était plus jamais Mbour qui revenait lorsque son esprit vaguait. Ses histoires se déroulaient désormais à Tenerife, Kita, Bamako, Naples, Almería, Madrid, Tripoli, Gao, Djamet, Kidal, Niamey, Tinzaouatine. (Kanor 2014, 283–84)

This vertiginous revisiting of places on his personal path in a listing that provides neither description nor explanation participates in a complicated method of mapping that, reminiscent of that spelled out by Kanor in the essay quoted above, doesn't privilege one location over another. Instead, this sequence of sites points toward what Iain Chambers terms "fluid cartography," a way of perceiving space that is promoted by "the sea itself" (Chambers 2008, 24). If it is true that, as Chamoiseau suggests, it is easy for migrants to be so marginalized that they fail to figure on many radars, it is now more important than ever to put them on the map.[12]

---

11   The character Biram struggles immensely in Fabienne Kanor's *Faire l'aventure* with questions of identity and integrity, and the text features frequent interrogations such as this one: "Qu'étaient devenues sa culture, sa mentalité, sa moralité?" (Kanor 2014, 145). Madeleine Dobie's understanding of the potential of "francophone Mediterraneanism" is pertinent to the personal predicaments this protagonist faces, for this approach "generally reflects a critical stance toward one-dimensional or exclusive models of identity, e.g., certain forms of postcolonial nationalism or linguistic or confessional identitarianism" (Dobie 2014, 401). The ability of "francophone Mediterraneanism" to "represent identity in relational and pluralistic terms" allows for a more complex formulation of characteristics that may combine in unusual ways in the context of migration (Dobie 2014, 401).

12   The maps in question, both literal and metaphorical, may bear little resemblance to the cartographic creations to which many have grown accustomed. Conceptions of space evolve with migratory movements, and notions of place benefit from a newfound fluidity, in Patrick Chamoiseau's estimation: "'Place' is multi-trans-cultural; multi-trans-linguistic" thanks to the fact that "it is nourished

In Appanah's *Tropique de la violence*, the first voice to find expression is that of Marie, a woman who recounts her personal story in the present tense, providing an overview of her life in a movement that spans a number of years in the space of a few pages. In what amounts to a fast-paced sequence, the narrator nonetheless pauses to recall the ritual that she inherited from her mother, a happy habit that the Frenchwoman from France and her adopted son Moïse regularly indulge in when she puts on a well-known musical recording and they sing along:

> C'est étrange comme ça vous rattrape ces choses-là. Quand vient *L'aigle noir*, nous attendons la partie que nous préférons de cette chanson et là, en chœur, moi dans la cuisine, lui dans le salon, nous entonnons à voix haute *Dis l'oiseau, oh dis, emmène-moi. Retournons au pays d'autrefois, comme avant, dans mes rêves d'enfant, pour cueillir en tremblant des étoiles, des étoiles. Comme avant, dans mes rêves d'enfant, comme avant, sur un nuage blanc, comme avant, allumer le soleil, être faiseur de pluies et faire des merveilles.* (Appanah 2016, 28)

The impact of this tradition in his early home life had on Moïse comes through when he revisits these shared instances in the aftermath of his mother's death:

> J'ai repensé aux soirées à la maison quand Marie mettait son disque de Barbara. La nuit restait dehors, à cette époque-là, la nuit était pour les chiens les roussettes les voleurs. J'ai formé les mots du bout de mes lèvres *Dis l'oiseau, oh dis, emmène-moi. Retournons au pays d'autrefois, comme avant, dans mes rêves d'enfant* … J'ai recommencé encore et encore jusqu'à ce que le sommeil me prenne. (Appanah 2016, 42)

There is no question that the experience of singing together, of producing sound simultaneously in a movement of enjoyable solidarity, is part of what makes these moments so memorable for both mother and son. But the words that they are singing are not anecdotal in this case, for they represent a possible return to another land, to a beautiful place far from their present reality. This song, written in French and made famous by a French singer, undoubtedly evokes the hexagonal space of France for Marie, whose current abode is far from the places of her past. For Moïse, who longs to know the story of his own past, the idea of return that the words of this song convey is shrouded in a mystery that he would love to uncover, but that his mother does not divulge. When Marie passes away,

---

through experiences in the world from those who have become very mobile," and who have benefited from "interactive multiplicity" (Verstraet 2018, 126).

this song takes on a new layer of meaning, as formulating these lyrics allows her child to reconnect with a time of safety and security, when he was loved and protected by a devoted maternal figure. The fact that both of these narrators recall with such intensity and accuracy the words they intoned in unison points toward the power of music to enter minds, affect emotions, and reinforce memories.

The idyllic words from Barbara's best-selling song of 1970, repeated at considerable length in these early pages, do not recur later in Appanah's novel. Perhaps the fact that they hark back to an idealized past begins to seem nonsensical to Moïse in the larger context of Comoros, where many migrants look longingly at birds not as a connection to a former life but as a promise of a more perfect future: "L'histoire d'un pays qui brille de mille feux et que tout le monde veut rejoindre. Il y a des mots pour ça : eldorado, mirage, paradis, chimère, utopie" (Appanah 2016, 53). Local music comes to take on more significance for this protagonist, as he witnesses its power to spur a friend to dance with spastic jerks. But these sounds quickly fade away and become a seemingly distant memory when a more powerful leader imposes his own musical preferences: "Après, ils ont mis du rap américain avec beaucoup de mots comme *nigga*, *fuck*, *ghetto*. Bruce aimait bien ces mots-là" (Appanah 2016, 76). Moïse becomes completely caught up in this music, even if it is incomprehensible to him, and he engages in replicating its terms and dancing to its beat: "Je suis debout et je chante avec des mots que je ne comprends pas. *Nigga nigga nigga nananana fuck fuck fuck nananana*" (Appanah 2016, 78). His absorption in this form of escape is so complete that he has the impression that he is no longer situated in a particular place and time: "Et moi, Moïse, j'ai quatorze ans, je fume, je bois, je chante et je danse avec les copains, je n'ai pas de passé, pas d'avenir, je suis heureux" (Appanah 2016, 78). He has internalized the rhythms and appropriated the English words that have made their way to this location to such an extent that his very being has been emptied. It is significant that Moïse makes this declaration just after engaging in a recitation from a French text that is upended by a rap:

> Je suis debout et je récite. "Quand j'étais tout enfant, nous habitions la campagne. La maison qui nous abritait n'était qu'une petite métairie isolée au milieu des champs. Là nous vivions en paix. Mes parents gardaient avec eux une grand-tante paternelle, Tante Martine." Bruce se met à rire quand il entend "Tante Martine" et je chante *Tante Martine fuck Tante Martine Tante Martine iz a nigga*, et je rappe comme si j'étais

le plus grand rappeur de tous les temps. Mo Tupac Mo Jay Z Mo Dr Dre.
Et Bruce rit tellement qu'il pleure. (Appanah 2016, 77–78)

The words Moïse rehearses here come from *L'enfant et la rivière* by
Henri Bosco (1945), a work of fiction that he has read over and over
and that he adores. But on this evening the quotation is ridiculed by the
chief of the ghetto called Gaza, and the text suddenly loses its resonance
for Moïse. These teenage boys, who are entirely on their own, with no
familial support or home to turn to, find this literary evocation out of
sync with their current surroundings. As a result, Moïse improvises,
taking the words "Tante Martine" and turning them around in a
cadence that isn't governed by understanding, but that instead allows
him to take pleasure in reworking the original for rhythmic effect.
Moïse places his own curtailed name into his rap, a name that in a single
syllable is no longer French, but sounds much more universal, and his
references become much more universal as well. He places himself not
in a literary lineage, but surrounds himself instead by names from the
contemporary music world. Mo thereby responds to the French culture
that has been inculcated in him not by writing back, but by rapping
back, in a spirit of raucous fun. This passage is a presage of the violence
to come, for Moïse's move to desacralize a written work at this moment
of musical madness portends how the beats that his companion Bruce
idolizes will imminently serve as the soundtrack for the slum he rules,
and will quite literally blow up in Moïse's face: "Écoute le bruit de mon
pays qui gronde, écoute la colère de Gaza, écoute comment elle rampe
et rappe jusqu'à nous, tu entends cette musique nigga, tu sens la braise
contre ton visage balafré" (Appanah 2016, 164). This is music that is tied
to the terrestrial, far from the soaring air Moïse once harmonized with
his mother.

Just as Moïse finds solace in a sensation from his past when he sings a
particular tune, so Biram from *Faire l'aventure* discovers that his current
challenges disappear for a moment when he is transported by a melody
from his own history:

il se mit alors à chanter *Bitim Rew, Bitim rew … bitim rew … bitim
rew*. Il était gosse lorsque Moktar, le mari de sa tante Maguette, lui avait
fait découvrir cette chanson de Youssou N'Dour. Il avait vingt-quatre
ans aujourd'hui et la voix du ntama, le tambour d'aisselles en peau
de chèvre, l'obsédait encore, l'hypnotisait. *Bitim Rew, Bitim Rew …*
Biram ne marchait plus, il planait. Il quittait les Canaries, l'Europe, et
enjambait les mers. Maintenant, il survolait Dakar, Dieuppeul-Derklé,

Yoff, Grand Yoff, Médina, Pattes d'Oie, Sicap Liberté. Il distinguait les minarets, des gueules d'arbre, des carreaux de champs, le va-et-vient des hommes qui vus d'en haut étaient à peine plus balèzes que les petits pois secs du marché. La cité s'effaça. Il vira vers Mbour, Thiès, Ndar. Il volait au-dessus des plantations de cannes vert treillis du gouverneur Richard Toll. Comme il en grouillait, des tiges! On les réduisait en carreaux de sucres que des employés payés à quelques jetons jour enveloppaient dans du papier fin qui casse. Des paquets de canne à sucre. Et puis, tout de bon, au cœur des flèches : la demeure du gouverneur, pas bien grandiose au bout du compte, mais qui l'avait été deux siècles plus tôt, au temps où les nègres marchaient à la cravache. (Kanor 2014, 204–05)

What begins as a flight portrayed in potentially positive terms quickly takes a turn for the worse as Biram soars over a sugar plantation that is laden with years of exploitation. The relationship between the slave trade and other historical atrocities that Chamoiseau underscores in a passage cited above from *Frères migrants* comes to the fore in this musical interlude that slips from a seemingly joyful lift to plunge into the dumps of a past that has unfortunately fashioned the present. This point comes through with special strength, thanks to the fact that this musical accompaniment will hum in the heads of most readers who are familiar with this overwhelmingly popular award-winning song by Youssou N'Dour. Indeed, this was the track that thrust the celebrated Senegalese singer into the international limelight in 1984. Even if the words do not strike a particular chord with all readers because they are not translated in the text, the widespread knowledge that this musical creation is about immigration will undoubtedly influence readers' perusal of this passage. The musical mapping of this work bespeaks global interconnectedness that stretches back over centuries of domination and holds hope for future itineraries marked by greater compassion and understanding, in line with Chamoiseau's exclamation: "une autre cartographie de nos humanités!" (Chamoiseau 2017, 59).

Literary Lappings

The lapping of water on the shore is a calming sound and a gentle movement that the works of Nathacha Appanah, Fatou Diome, and Fabienne Kanor evoke in common. At various textual moments, the peaceful beauty of the beach comes into play in written works that are otherwise plumbing harsh migratory pain. In *Tropique de la violence*, the aforementioned volunteer named Stéphane, who has come to Mayotte to work with youth, expresses how much he is mesmerized by his gorgeous surroundings on this island: "Chaque matin, mes yeux plongeaient dans le vert des arbres, le roux des cases et enfin le bleu du lagon. Je serpentais en esprit dans les S des passes et je nageais avec les dauphins" (Appanah 2016, 111). Stéphane goes on, however, to indicate that while this natural splendor helps him to forget it, there is a rough reality underlying this paradisiacal setting: "Chaque matin, ce paysage magnifique et irréel sur la baie de Mamoudzou suffisait pour me donner de l'énergie, et j'oubliais la lie, j'oubliais la violence, j'oubliais la fange" (Appanah 2016, 111). On a day that is particularly difficult, however, he views the sea entirely differently: "je ne vois que la mer violée par les morts et le sang" (Appanah 2016, 111). The sea in question here is not the Mediterranean, but it has some similar characteristics to the sea that has become the very emblem of migration in general, and of migrant suffering in particular, in recent times. This body of water off the eastern coast of Africa is often treacherous, and yet those who are desperate to reach the European shore of Mayotte embark upon it with little hesitation, overfilling boats called kwassas kwassas (Appanah 2016, 15), and risking everything for a better life.

The Mediterranean is filled with contradictions such as those that figure in the observations narrated by Stéphane above. Recognizing these discrepancies and properly taking into account the resulting intricacies is important to the development of what Iain Chambers identifies as "a diverse cartography in which both the resonance and dissonance disseminated in the Mediterranean can be recorded in the interleaving of historical, cultural, and ecological complexities" (2008, 24). Chambers later repeats the sonorous terms "resonance and dissonance" in an exploration of how this space shapes thought:

> It is in this arduous combination of communication and difference, of shared encounters and marked distinctions, of resonance and dissonance, that the Mediterranean proposes a multiplicity that simultaneously interrupts and interrogates the facile evaluations of a simple mapping disciplined by the landlocked desires of a narrow-minded progress and a homogeneous modernity. (Chambers 2008, 25)

It is significant that Chambers identifies such concepts as progress and modernity as "landlocked" in this provocative passage, for a shift in focus to the fluidity of the vast waters that also make up our planet promises to yield a decidedly different worldview. Françoise Vergès concurs that our concentration has far too often been on events that transpire on land, to the detriment of a more complete and comprehensive understanding of global affairs: "Notre tendance à considérer la terre comme seul lieu des échanges, conflits, tensions, nous fait oublier l'importance des mers et des océans, enjeux environnementaux, économiques, militaires, scientifiques, culturels" (Vergès 2017, 56). If the reasons that occasioned the creation of what Vergès terms "alternative cartographies" were lamentable, what has emerged is praiseworthy: "Si de la mer, terrain de la conquête, sont arrivés les bateaux négriers, les armes, les idéologies raciales dans les marges, les interstices, des rencontres échappent à l'hégémonie, traçant des cartographies alternatives, semant les graines des résistances" (Vergès 2017, 56). Even if resistance has begun to take shape, it is certain that many of the forms of thinking and speaking that emerged on the margins of movements on the waters have not made it to the page, either in books or on maps. As Vergès has expressed the phenomenon elsewhere, "behind the scenes of official history and geography stood a series of hidden, marginalized, and forgotten narratives and maps of precarious, disposable lives" (Vergès 2015, 22).

The choice to focus in works of fiction on characters whose lives would certainly be interpreted by many to be both "precarious" and "disposable" is a literary gesture with the potential to change this perception. Devoting hundreds of pages to the fates of protagonists who have rarely made the "scenes of official history and geography" is an action that holds the promise that their stories will emerge from obscurity, cease to be "marginalized," and ultimately become not only more widely known, but also understood with greater nuance and sensitivity. When I interviewed Fatou Diome in 2005, her best-selling novel *Le ventre de l'Atlantique* (2003) was still featured in the windows of many bookstores throughout France, and she explained that this positive attention to her text was bringing about much-needed transformations in attitudes toward those anonymous individuals who had traversed many miles to finally find themselves in their streets and squares:

> En France, quand le livre venait de sortir, j'ai surtout reçu des lettres d'Européens, peut-être parce qu'ils découvraient une autre façon de regarder les immigrés. Ils les voyaient juste là, sans savoir ce qu'ils avaient laissé derrière eux : Quel était leur rapport à la famille restée au pays? Qu'est-ce qu'ils portaient en eux? Ils voyaient juste un Noir qui passe. Mais c'est qui ce Noir? Pourquoi est-il là? Qu'est-ce qu'il a laissé derrière lui? Qu'est-ce qu'il cherche? C'est quoi, sa mélancolie? Sa joie? Donc, ils ont peut-être essayé de le regarder autrement. (Rice 2005)

Olivier, a policeman in Mayotte, explains his dismay in *Tropique de la violence* that so few people seem to be truly aware of the havoc the migrant situation has wreaked on the island. He admits that he became optimistic that things might turn around at a particular point in time: "Il m'est arrivé d'espérer quand il y a eu le petit Syrien échoué sur une plage turque. Je me suis dit que quelqu'un, quelque part, se souviendrait de cette île française et dirait qu'ici aussi les enfants meurent sur les plages" (Appanah 2016, 52). But he reveals his deep disappointment with an assertion that nothing ever changes, that even when a powerfully provocative image makes headlines around the world, nothing that happens in his forsaken island ever seems to cross the ocean to reach anyone else: "Nous sommes seuls" (Appanah 2016, 53).

If the articles and media coverage that evoke the risky aspects of migration today do not modify mindsets or move people to action, there may be hope that literary composition can touch people differently, if it does what Fatou Diome's first novel did so well and effectively employs "[m]usic, sounds, and silence" in creative manners that "announce refusals to adopt a readily recognized representation or to settle within the boundaries of preexisting meaning," in the words of Iain Chambers (2008, 21). He extols the capacity of written works to express "the nontranslatable," communicate "the excess of language that refuses to mean," and employ repetition to renew language "in a reply to power" (Chambers 2008, 21). In these comments, Chambers points to the capacity of literature to come back to earlier historical episodes that have been elided or dismissed and demonstrate their pertinence to the present, as Kanor does in her textual depiction of a flight that heads back toward a plantation. In line with this awareness of the past, Chamoiseau decries a personified Europe's fallacious belief that she owes nothing to anyone, that she is a self-made entity: "L'Europe, amputée de sa propre mémoire, se voyant née d'elle-même, se nourrissant d'elle-même, achevée en elle-même sans besoin de l'Humain ..." (Chamoiseau 2017, 42). Biram of *Faire l'aventure* denounces this forgetfulness as well: "Votre richesse à vous, les gens d'Europe, elle s'est pas bâtie toute seule mais sur le dos de nos ancêtres" (Kanor 2014, 198). In Chamoiseau's estimation, all humans are in this together: "Ce que vivent les migrants relève d'une seule aventure, très ancienne, qui continue encore : notre aventure humaine" (Chamoiseau 2017, 118). No one will get ahead if we forget that this race is a relay, not a solo display of prowess. This interpretation resonates with Diome's declaration on the French television show *Ce soir (ou jamais)* on April 24, 2015, that "On sera riche ensemble ou on va se noyer tous ensemble!" Believing that what happens to a migrant from elsewhere has nothing to do with oneself, when one is European, is a stance that is profoundly erroneous. Fortunately, it isn't unanimous.

Chamoiseau's *Frères migrants* is upbeat in its praise for those Europeans who have dared to go against the law that prohibits them from helping foreigners who are deemed illegal, the standouts who have braved scorn in societies that discourage them from showing concern and care for the many in their midst who are homeless and destitute after reaching this promised land at long last. What is remarkable is that the hospitality these exceptional individuals have incarnated cannot be dissociated from song and dance, indeed from music, as it is the very essence of this opening up and including others, and it allows them to communicate beyond the boundaries of languages: "*Casa nostra, casa vostra!* Chants, danses, musiques, petites choses petits gestes petits mots qui recèlent sans doute l'éclat ténu d'un autre monde : une intuition qui désavoue des vérités ténébreuses et puissantes. *Casa nostra, casa vostra!*" (Chamoiseau 2017, 43). When literature combines with song and dance, when it speaks through aesthetic means to the reader's soul, it becomes profoundly powerful as it disproves the misunderstandings that have widely been accepted as givens and unveils truths that have long been unknown:

> C'est cela la force d'une donnée esthétique. Il faut conter, il faut chanter, il faut danser, fréquenter les feux de la couleur, les opéras de la lumière, faire musique, écrire dans des langages inouïs, aller au numérique, s'en remettre aux gestes et aux mimiques, voir et faire voir, répéter, répéter, et répéter encore, en espérant chaque fois les fulgurances hélas imprédictibles de la beauté. (Chamoiseau 2017, 107)

This moving quotation is compelling in its incitation to create and perform both music and dance, as well as to tell stories, and to write in renewed languages, in tongues that have never before been heard. It significantly enacts its own emphasis on repeating, again and again, as essential to seeing and showing effectively. In all of these elements, this passage sings the praises of a creative process that results in "transposed modes," leading to the possibility of unforeseen textual developments in new keys that are apt to relate evolving patterns of communication that are attuned to the movements of migration.

Prior to embarking on his adventure, Biram was not attracted to difficult texts in French when an erudite autodidact introduced him to them in his native Senegal: "ce français plus que parfait que son idole

Sony et le poète-politique Césaire lui avait légué" (Kanor 2014, 17). Rather than finding inspiration in these forebears, the young protagonist asked himself about the usefulness of studying these written works: "À quoi bon se remplir des idées et des mots des autres?" (Kanor 2014, 18). Maybe, in order to reach reluctant readers who might bear some resemblance to this character, it is necessary to create new works of francophone literature. It is possible that recent texts like these three novels by Appanah, Diome, and Kanor employ linguistic ingenuity and vibrant musicality in a manner that effectively reflects the rhythms of migratory realities that are so pressing at present. These publications *at once* draw from *and* diverge from textual precedents in order to exemplify a more fluid language with different points of departure and arrival, not to mention multiple returns and repeats, and make up written creations that communicate new combinations and constitute renewed compositions.

If the word "lapping" can refer to the soothing sound of the sea, it can also indicate the completion of a turn, such as that run by an athlete on a track. In his ode to those who have sheltered and assisted migrants, Chamoiseau employs an expression from Guadeloupean Creole to depict the perseverance of these individuals who have shown hospitality even when faced with police persecution: "elle renaît quand même, désapparaît pour resurgir encore, ni à la même place ni au même endroit mais toujours dans l'ici, ou encore, comme on dit en créole: *an mitan isiya! ...*" (Chamoiseau 2017, 46). The circling kindness he celebrates in this passage demonstrates a persistence akin to that of the migrant who doesn't let go of the desired destination, who heads tirelessly toward the "lieu d'une arrivée, qu'ils ont choisi ou qu'a choisi pour eux leur perception du monde," in Chamoiseau's astute analysis of why one particular place is proposed as paradise and dominates the vision of a given traveler (Chamoiseau 2017, 67). Biram's efforts to reach the continent are filled with ups and downs, and that's the paradoxical nature of the migratory endeavor, according to the narrative voice:

> Car c'était cela, après tout, faire l'aventure : perdre son argent et en gagner d'un coup, vouloir La Mecque et délaisser l'Éternel, nettoyer la merde des autres et s'acheter des complets étincelants, respirer l'air des princes et zoner en chien, ne plus jamais revoir sa mère et croiser son premier amour par hasard. (Kanor 2014, 347)

It is crucial to note that the highs and lows of this adventure do not cease once the migrant has made it within the borders of Europe's "forteresse"

(Kanor 2014, 209). The longing to assert, indeed to insert, himself abides even when Biram is in Rome, and an act of lovemaking with the woman he has desired since before he left Senegal cannot be dissociated from the ongoing symbolic strength of the sea that persistently served as a barrier to his dreams: "Il désirait forcer cette Méditerranée, plissée comme une robe de bourgeoise, pénétrer avec Marème Doriane Fall dans cette mer en strass dont les jeunes de là-bas persistaient à rêver" (Kanor 2014, 356). When it becomes clear that this longtime object of his affection does not want to leave her Italian husband to be with him, Biram heads back to Senegal on his own, renouncing once and for all the adventure that has tossed him about for so many years.

In a similar move, the aforementioned Lamine in *Celles qui attendent*, decides to leave Spain for good and return to his native Senegal. It is almost as if this husband and son had listened to the melancholic Serer lullaby that Fatou Diome has chosen to include in the original tongue in italics and then translate in its entirety into French. This tune evokes in exclamatory rhythms the hope of all those who are left behind that their loved ones who have attempted to migrate will one day come back. The first two lines of this version of the song are strong: "Ayo, ayo, Lamine Yandé! Écoutez l'oiseau chanter à l'entrée de la maison!" (Diome 2010, 247). The lyrics are repeated, again both in the original and in translation, in the epilogue of the book, returning in a reinforcing textual passage. Lamine may have obtained the proper papers to remain in Spain, but he had grown thoroughly disillusioned with Europe, and wished to share with his compatriots in Senegal the truth about what he had endured as a migrant: "l'Europe! La faim, le froid, le racisme, la solitude, les petits boulots, l'esclavage économique!" (Diome 2010, 276). He knows that his warnings are in vain, as the pirogues along the shore are weighed down with hopeful individuals who can't wait to head out to sea. But his own definitive homecoming makes an undeniable statement. In a significant final scene, the droning of the boats whose motors create a constant soundscape in this coastal location are drowned out by a different soundtrack, by a sounder track. The festivities that characterize a ceremony with Lamine's family and friends are filled with music and celebration that indicate a thorough embrace of the instruments and the dances of their heritage, and a focus on home rather than on movements abroad.

Diome's *Celles qui attendent* closes with the possibility of return, and even suggests that coming back to the place of departure can constitute a happy ending. In like manner, the central character of Kanor's *Faire l'aventure* completed a large lap through the Mediterranean and much of Southern Europe before effecting a definitive return to *La Signare*, a slave boat dating back three centuries that has been transformed into a beach bar, the very spot whence he departed with his gaze focused on a far-off northern horizon. And the final paragraphs of Appanah's *Tropique de la violence* also enact a return of sorts: "je cours vers la mer qui m'a amené ici" (Appanah 2016, 175). The misunderstood Moïse plunges headlong into the waters that brought him to the island of Mayotte as an infant, regaining the ocean in a movement that liberates him from a vengeful crowd intoning his curtailed name as one, "MO!" (Appanah 2016, 174). What these three current francophone migratory texts accomplish with conviction is the disruption of a linear sense of progression, whether geographical or temporal. By engaging in plurilingual writing that employs music to punctuate and pinpoint the written work, these authors have composed narratives that sing human stories in deeply moving tones. They have succeeded in creating cartographies that bring to light heretofore overlooked itineraries that reveal the extent to which so many migrants are denied the possibility of reaching fruition at the finish line of their dreams and are often condemned to circle back, again and again, until the place where the race began becomes the final note.

Works Cited

Appanah, Nathacha. 2016. *Tropique de la violence*. Paris: Gallimard.

Bosco, Henri. 1945. *L'enfant et la rivière*. Paris: Gallimard.

Brisson, Geneviève. 2018. "Plurilingualism and Transnational Identities in a Francophone Minority Classroom." *Jeunesse: Young People, Texts, Cultures* 10 (2): 73–99.

Chambers, Iain. 2008. *Mediterranean Crossings: The Politics of an Interrupted Modernity*. Durham, NC: Duke University Press.

Chamoiseau, Patrick. 2017. *Frères migrants*. Paris: Seuil.

Cherfi, Magyd. 2018. "On part." *Au Coeur de l'errance: Étoiles d'encre* (73–74): 93–95.

Diome, Fatou. 2003. *Le ventre de l'Atlantique*. Paris: Anne Carrière.

———. 2013 [2010]. *Celles qui attendent*. Paris: Flammarion.

Dobie, Madeleine. 2014. "For and against the Mediterranean: Francophone Perspectives." *Comparative Studies of South Asia, Africa and the Middle East* 34 (2): 389–404.

Forsdick, Charles. 2011. "Mobilising French Studies." *Australian Journal of French Studies* 48 (1): 88–103.

Kanor, Fabienne. 2014. *Faire l'aventure*. Paris: J.C. Lattès.

———. 2016. "Là d'où je viens." *Contemporary French and Francophone Studies* 20 (3): 404–10.

Mabanckou, Alain, and Christophe Merlin. 2009. *L'Europe depuis l'Afrique*. Paris: Naïve.

Mbembe, Achille. 2016. *Politiques de l'inimitié*. Paris: La Découverte.

Nelson, Brian. 2015. *The Cambridge Introduction to French Literature*. Cambridge: Cambridge University Press.

Nouss, Alexis. 2018. "Littérature, exil et migration." *Hommes & Migrations* 1320 (1): 161–64.

Rice, Alison. 2005. Unpublished interview with Fatou Diome. Villa Mont Noir, France.

Vergès, Françoise. 2015. "A Cartography of Invisible Lives." *eTropic* 14 (2): 22–29.

———. 2017. "Afriques océaniques, Afriques liquides." In *Penser et écrire l'Afrique aujourd'hui*, edited by Alain Mabanckou, 50–59. Paris: Seuil.

Verstraet, Charly. 2018. "Poetics of humanity, politics of migration: A conversation with Patrick Chamoiseau." *Francosphères* 7 (1): 121–37.

Index